INVESTING in the DREAM

INVESTING
in the DREAM

Personal Wealth-Building Strategies
for African Americans in Search of
Financial Freedom

Jesse B. Brown

With an Introduction by
Congressman Jesse L. Jackson, Jr.

NEW YORK

This book is designed to provide information with regard to the subject matter covered. It is sold with the understanding that the publisher and author are not engaged in rendering legal, accounting, or other professional services. If legal or other expert assistance is required, the services of a competent professional should be sought.

It is not the purpose of this book to reprint all the information that is otherwise available to the author and/or publisher, but to complement, amplify, and supplement other texts. You are urged to read all the available material, learn as much as possible about investing and to tailor the information to your individual needs. For more information, see the many references in the library.

Investing in the Dream is not a get-rich-quick scheme. Anyone who decides to invest must expect to invest a lot of time and effort. For many people investing is more lucrative than other ways of making retirement income.

Every effort has been made to make this book as complete and as accurate as possible. However, there may be mistakes both typographical and in content. Therefore, this text should be used only as a general guide and not as a source of specific investing advice. Furthermore, this book contains information on investing only up to the date of printing and predicts nothing for the future and only talks about past performance.

Since the cover of this book includes testimonials regarding the quality of Mr. Brown's investment advice, please be advised that the testimonials may not be representative of the experience of other clients. The testimonials are not indicative of future performance or success and no fees or other considerations were paid for these testimonials and all testimonials concerning a technical aspect of investing were made by persons with knowledge and experience to form valid opinions. Some names have been changed in the book at the request of the client for personal reasons unrelated to stock, bond, or mutual fund transactions.

Mr. Brown is a registered representative and general principal of the NASD firm NPC Securities, Inc./ Wall Street Electronica.

The purpose of this book is to educate and entertain. The author and publisher shall have neither liability nor responsibility to any person or entity with respect to any loss or damage caused, or alleged to be caused, directly or indirectly, by the information contained in this book.

Library of Congress Cataloging-in-Publication Data
Brown, Jesse B.
    Investing in the dream : personal wealth-building strategies for
African Americans in search of financial freedom / by Jesse B.
Brown. — 1st ed.
        p.   cm.
    ISBN 0-7868-6462-1
    1. Afro-Americans—Finance, Personal.   2. Investments.
3. Finance, Personal.   I. Title.
HG179.B74646   2000
332.024'0396073—dc21   99–22119
                                                         CIP

Designed by Adam Chasan

FIRST EDITION

10   9   8   7   6   5   4   3   2   1

To the memory of my mother and father,
both of whom lovingly taught me the true value of a dollar.
Along with my Aunt Sister and Uncle George,
who gave me my first silver dollar, they were the first
to tell me to invest in my dreams.

Acknowledgments

I have a number of people I'd like to thank for investing in the dream of this book. My literary agent Jan Miller turned my idea into gold; my collaborator Wes Smith turned my thoughts into prose; and my editor at Hyperion, Maureen O'Brien, turned my manuscript into a real book. Thank you all for what you put into this project.

I am also thankful for the support and encouragement I received from my wife, Delores Brown, and my daughter, as well as those friends and clients who graciously allowed me to tell their stories in this book.

Contents

Section IV

Smart Money Moves

Foreword

I have watched with bittersweet emotions in recent years as many Americans have benefited from one of the most extended booms in the history of the U.S. economy. While it is true that millions of hardworking men and women have been able to build wealth during this extended bull run in the stock market—thanks largely to the explosion in tax-deferred retirement plans and IRAs—far too many of my constituents on the South Side of Chicago and in its south suburban area have not shared in the financial rewards.

African Americans, in particular, have arrived late at this party, if they've come at all. Studies show that blacks simply have been reluctant to embrace the stock market as a method for building wealth. Part of it is cultural. Most African Americans have had limited or no exposure to this type of investment. Some believe it takes large sums of money to buy in. Others are uncomfortable with the risks involved. Many are interested but have not had access to information on how to do it.

This book by my friend Jesse B. Brown is intended to open the doors to one and all. As a stockbroker and financial advisor to hundreds of black men and women on all economic levels, Jesse Brown champions wealth-building in our community and for all underinvested Americans. Like me, he understands that the stock market boom has had little impact for those who need it most. These are the same people with skills but no decent-paying jobs, with children but no child care, and with health concerns yet no health care coverage. Too many of my constituents—and too many African Americans around the country—have been locked out of the American dream.

In this book, they will learn how to buy their way in, even if they have to do it week by week, $10 at a time. Jesse Brown and I share the belief that the last leg of the civil rights movement begun by my father's generation remains to be traveled. The final freedom is economic freedom. The last step is to invest in the dream with the goal of building lasting wealth.

While many more affluent Americans may fret over their investments with each dip of the stock market, the angst and insecurity of those who have not invested in the dream is constant and debilitating. That is why I applaud Jesse Brown. I embrace his cause and I enthusiastically endorse this book. I have known him for some time now and I have watched him work assiduously to educate and encourage thousands of underinvested Americans to build lasting wealth through wise investment practices.

Jesse Brown goes where very few financial advisors have gone before. He speaks the parlance and teaches the principles of Wall Street to Main Street so that more of us can share the wealth. He preaches the gospel of financial freedom to my constituents in civic halls, church meetings and community forums. He offers investment advice, encouragement and hope for a secure future to those who most need to hear it. He assures them that prosperity is our birthright, and that financial freedom is the ultimate goal in the great and continuing march for our full share of America's promise.

Mr. Brown knows that while many African Americans have moved into the middle and upper classes, there remain those who are still struggling. He sees that many still dream of owning their own homes. He knows also that many stretch their incomes to the point of breaking in order to provide college educations for their eager children. He sees first-hand that the social fabric of many loving black families is torn by the costs of child care on one hand and senior care on the other. And he has consoled those who fear that they will retire at a time when both Social Security and Medicare programs are failing.

In response to these concerns and quandaries, Mr. Brown offers solid financial advice. Save as much as you can on a regular basis and use the system to your advantage. Capitalize on the proven benefits of dollar cost averaging, compounded interest and the steady growth of the American economy. Take your savings out from under the mattress and low-interest savings accounts and put them to work building wealth in mutual funds, stocks or bonds. I encourage you to heed his message and buy into it for your future profit. It doesn't matter that you don't have a lot to invest in the beginning. What matters is that you begin investing now. Short-term sacrifices will yield long-term security. Get in the game.

I have heard the financial gospel according to Jesse Brown, and I have seen my constituents and friends benefit. Their nest eggs are growing and their lives are more secure for it. The future is far less daunting and the present much more enjoyable when you own shares in the strongest companies in the greatest nation in the world. On behalf of my constituents and African Americans across the country, I commend Mr. Brown for his contributions and I encourage you to heed his message. Not for my benefit. Not for his benefit. But for yours.

Build wealth. Invest in the dream. And reap the rewards for the rest of your lifetime.

— *The Hon. Jesse L. Jackson, Jr.,*
U.S. Representative from the State of Illinois

Section I   Taking Control of Your Finances

> *We refuse to believe that there are insufficient funds in the great vaults of opportunity of this nation. So we have come to cash this check—a check that will give us upon demand the riches of freedom and the security of justice.*

The Rev. Martin Luther King, Jr.
Washington, D.C.
August 28, 1963

No Longer Invisible, but Still Underinvested

1

Jackie Joseph is a hardworking, intelligent and resourceful young woman who is representative of many African Americans in her attitudes about saving and investing. Jackie is a union electrician in Chicago who has proven herself in a field dominated by men—generally white men at that.

I admire Jackie. But I worry about her.

You see, Jackie pays out money to just about everybody but herself.

When her paycheck arrives every two weeks, she hands out money to her elderly father, who is ill. Then she hands more out to her teenage son. And finally, she helps out her best friend, who is going through rough times.

I know all this because Jackie told me. When I asked her if she was ready to sign up for a retirement investment plan that I manage for her union, she explained her situation. I told her she could get started in the plan by putting as little as $10 or $25 into it with every paycheck—a relatively painless way to save for the future. But Jackie just looked at me sadly and said it wasn't possible. Not yet, anyway.

"I just don't have any money right now," she told me.

I know a lot of black folks like Jackie Joseph. In fact, I'd be willing to bet that a high percentage of African Americans who don't have a lot of extra money have reached down deep at one time or another to help out family members, friends, loved ones and coworkers. It is who we are.

When you have known hard times yourself, it makes you far more willing to help others. It is part of the best of us.

I am concerned, however, that far too many African Americans plan on starting their own investment savings plans *tomorrow*. It reminds me of a sign I once saw in a neighborhood bar: Free Beer! TOMORROW! Of course, the free beer never flows because tomorrow never comes. Far too often, people never get around to starting a long-term savings and investment plan. For many, procrastination is the easiest response to the challenge of putting their financial affairs in order. But putting off doesn't pay off.

It's funny how tomorrow never comes but old age sneaks up on you. I know because hardly a day goes by when I don't hear from a client thanking me because I cajoled and prodded him or her to get a nest egg growing. Sometimes people resent that at first, but down the road they bless me. I admire the generosity and caring nature of my fellow African Americans. But I worry about the future of those who have not made their own financial security a priority. As my friend the great motivational speaker Les Brown says, "If you keep on doing what you're doing you're going to keep on getting what you've been getting. So if you don't like what you've been getting, you should change what you've been doing. Prosperity is your birthright!"

By investing wisely, you can turn your savings, however modest, into long-term wealth, just as Jesus turned water into wine. Minister and author Catherine Ponder of the Unity Church Worldwide in Palm Desert, CA, has written that prosperity has a spiritual basis. Just as prosperity is your birthright and your divine right, it is also your responsibility. You are responsible for your own financial health, just as you are responsible for your own physical well-being. Having a dollar and a dream is not enough. You must invest in that dream in order to build lasting wealth.

I was nearly driven to madness when I read recently that the residents in just one predominately black ward of Chicago had spent $70 *million* on lottery tickets. I guarantee that if you drive through that neighborhood you will not find a single millionaire. What if those people had invested that money wisely instead? What if they had bought Microsoft or Wal-Mart stock? What if they'd bought a mutual fund returning 16 percent a year? Then they could have built *long-term* wealth that could be built upon and passed from generation to generation. Instead, they bought lottery tickets and threw their hard-earned money out the window.

"History has proven that through hard economic times and boom years, bull markets and bear markets, a disciplined, long-term strategy of saving and investing is the best way to accumulate wealth, and more importantly, *pass it on*," notes Earl Graves, publisher of *Black Enterprise* magazine.

If you don't feel prosperous, it may be that you have not yet committed yourself to prosperity by setting goals and developing and sticking with an investment plan. We deserve security and peace of mind in retirement. But in general, we have poor saving and investing habits—not just blacks, but *all* Americans. Compared to every other industrialized nation in the world, the United States of America is a nation of savings slackers. We may be the richest nation in the world but we also lead the globe in bankruptcies. According to one poll, one fourth of all adults between ages 35 and 54 have not yet begun to save for retirement. While the US stock market went on an unprecedented bull run in the 1990s, nearly 60 percent of employed Americans missed out because they didn't own stock or an equity mutual fund either on their own or through their employer. "The fact that less than half of the nation's households are participating in this unprecedented creation of stock market wealth is exacerbating the gap between rich and poor that widened in the 1980s and 90s," wrote a *Chicago Tribune* financial reporter.

BRIDGING THE WEALTH GAP

When anyone starts talking or writing about the rich and the poor, you and I know who stands where. African Americans are among the least aggressive people in the nation when it comes to using our money to create greater wealth through investment. As a result, we get poorer while the rich get richer. "The reality is, no matter how great incomes become for individual blacks, our wealth is not sustained because we have very few assets that can be passed on from generation to generation," noted Hugh Price, president of the National Urban League, in his introduction to a 1998 study of the state of black America's wealth. "Individual self-sufficiency, as important as that is, cannot be the ultimate goal. Black folks must push past that and go for economic power."

Citing the tremendous gap between blacks and whites in the accumulation of wealth, Price said, "It undermines your ability to achieve financial stability, it undermines your ability to carry the tuition load when children reach college age and it affects your ability to carry out your old age in a comfortable style."

The unequal distribution of wealth, power and resources has stagnated growth in black communities, according to the president of the Coalition of Black Investors (COBI), based in Winston-Salem, NC, who believes that in order to build wealth, African Americans must get into the habit of saving and investing, and do so at a higher rate.

In 1952, a great writer named Ralph Ellison eloquently expressed his anger at racism in this country with a novel entitled *Invisible Man.* This classic story explored the sense of racial alienation experienced by blacks, who were treated as though they were "invisible" by the white majority.

Nearly fifty years later, the thirty-three million African Americans in this country are anything but invisible thanks to many hard-won victories over racial discrimination. Since the Civil Rights era, we have made our presence known in politics, in business and in the marketplace. But we still have one major battle to undertake: The fight for economic independence.

"GOD WANTS US TO PROSPER"

Middle-class African Americans have been blessed with jobs and wealth—we must not bury our gifts or talents. We must multiply them by practicing financial responsibility and investing wisely. As a spiritual people, we must understand that "God wants us to prosper," as my minister the Rev. Dr. Johnnie Colemon is fond of saying. My goal with this book is to inspire and motivate you to join that battle for economic equality, and to help you arm yourself for it. All men and women may be considered equal under the law in this country, but believe me, when it comes right down to it, your net worth is what counts. It determines where you live, where your children are educated and the quality of your life in your retirement years.

Yet, in a household survey conducted by researchers at the University of Michigan in 1998, only 4 percent of African Americans had a net worth of $170,000 or more compared to 25 percent of all others. Half of black families polled in the survey had a net worth below $8,400, while the median for other families was above $63,000.

What do those statistics *really* mean to African Americans? They mean that while most whites have enough money in the bank to purchase a new car with cash, far too many blacks have difficulty coming up with the full payment for a decent *used* car. It means that the majority of blacks are far less likely than whites to have the money for a down payment on a first home, or enough money put away for emergencies like a quick flight to visit a loved one in need or even to pay for the funeral of a family member who dies unexpectedly.

Surely there are more prosperous African Americans today than ever before. The growing affluence among black professionals is undeniable. Yet, far too many hardworking African Americans still live paycheck to paycheck and never build lasting wealth—even as whites at the same income levels are putting money into retirement plans, investment clubs and individual retirement accounts (IRAs). There are African Americans capitalizing on the historically high rate of return for the stock and bond markets. There are black men and women whose investments are paying for their children's college educations, for starting new small businesses and for comfortable retirements. But there are not enough of them.

Too many of us are still missing out on the opportunity to turn our water into wine, our tens and twenties into hundreds and thousands, our thousands into tens of thousands and even hundreds of thousands. Some are missing out because like Jackie, they take care of everyone but themselves. Others have missed out because they are afraid *to use the money they have as leverage to create the wealth they deserve.*

Too often, African Americans regard money as something magical, mysterious or sacred when it is really nothing more than a tool—a very useful and powerful tool that you should learn to use to your greatest advantage. Many blacks I know have stories about an uncle, aunt, parent or cousin who has a life's savings stashed in a shoe box or sock drawer. The only thing that money will grow is mildew. Your savings should not be locked away, buried in the backyard or put in a treasure chest. Nor should your money be wasted on things you don't really need or can't afford to pay for outright. You work hard for your money, and you should make certain that at least some of it is put to work for you and your loved ones.

The secret is to put your money where it will do you the most good; for the last fifty years or so—with a few short-term exceptions—that place has been in the stock and bond markets. The same African Americans who bury their savings in the backyard will have nothing to do with stocks or bonds that have made millions for white investors. Why? Blacks simply have had less access to information about stocks and bonds, and, like all people, they don't trust what they don't know.

I'll let you in on a trade secret: Investing in the stock market really is not very complicated at all. Many times stockbrokers try to make it seem that way so they can impress you, but it really boils down to some pretty simple mathematics and common sense. Many people tell me that they have not taken advantage of stocks, bonds and mutual funds because they feel those forms of investment are beyond their understanding. Believe me, if you can balance a checkbook or put together a household budget, you can learn to understand those investment vehicles and cash in on one of this nation's best methods for building personal wealth.

I am going to teach you many things about investing and building wealth in this book. Some of it may seem complicated at first, but none of it is out of your reach. It is important to understand that if you buy shares of good companies, even just a few shares, your investment will grow substantially over time. That is how wealth is created.

I have written this book because I am concerned that African Americans generally have not worked at building wealth. I hope to inspire, motivate and teach you the basics of wise financial investing and planning so that you and the people you care about can enjoy life without constantly worrying about your finances. I am confident that I can help you because I have already made believers, and investors, of hundreds of black clients across a wide range of incomes.

I am not a miracle worker. I will not promise you instant wealth or surefire investment techniques. But I *will* teach you the same basic principles that have given hundreds of my clients financial security for the first time in their lives. These working class and professional men and women now have tens of thousands of dollars—in some cases far more. They have a peace of mind they've never known. But *I* won't have peace of mind until I've spread the word to many, many more!

THE NEXT BATTLE IS FOR ECONOMIC FREEDOM

The African American community is not invisible, but its investment earnings are barely discernible. Blacks in this country are seriously underinvested in the American economy, specifically in that great creator of wealth, the stock market. I understand that in the past you may have been reluctant to invest in stocks, bonds or mutual funds because you didn't think you knew enough about how they worked or what the risks were. Maybe you even had the sense that those investment opportunities simply weren't available to you. I'm here to tell you that they most definitely are open to you and that you should take advantage of them. Don't let lingering racial insecurities or fear of discrimination keep you from participating in the dynamic American economy. It is your right. You owe it to yourself and to your loved ones. And you deserve it.

Whether you're talking about George Washington Carver, Cotton Mather, the Rev. Martin Luther King, Jr., Louis Armstrong, Oprah Winfrey, the Rev. Jesse Jackson, Sr., or his son, Congressman Jesse Jackson, Jr., African Americans have played a major role in making the United States the dominant social and economic force on the globe. Our sweat, our brains, our hearts, are heavily invested in this country. It is time we invested money in the economy that we helped create, and it is time we cashed in on this nation's success.

We marched courageously and successfully in Selma, Little Rock, Montgomery and Washington, DC. Now we must march on Wall Street. We aggressively claimed our civil rights in this country, but we have been far too passive in pursuing our rightful share of this nation's wealth. We need to be as aggressive about our personal finances as we have been about our individual freedoms.

Survey after survey reports that African Americans in general tend to place their hard-earned money into low-return savings and money market accounts rather than in high-return investments. When most blacks invest, we too often place our money in "safe" things like certificates of deposit or real estate.

Because of our conservative approach to finances, we are not fully sharing in the economic fruits of this great nation. In the middle of one of the longest and biggest buying runs in stock market history, far too many of us have been sitting on the sidelines.

- Only 22 percent of us have invested in mutual funds, compared to 35 percent of white Americans, according to a 1997 study of African American saving and investment habits conducted by Roper Starch Worldwide on behalf of Ariel Capital Management in Chicago.
- Only 27 percent of us have invested in stocks and bonds, compared to 38 percent of the white population, according to the Roper Starch study.

Because we tend to invest more conservatively than whites, we end up with less retirement savings than they have. Nearly twice as many blacks as whites are counting on Social Security to make up at least half of their retirement income, even though more than a third of both blacks and whites believe Social Security will no longer exist by the time they retire.

Analysts who track wealth and income distribution in the United States are concerned that less than half of the nation's households are participating in the stock market. Why? Because those who are invested in it are pulling farther and farther ahead, leaving those who are not farther and farther behind.

FINANCIAL KNOWLEDGE PAYS DIVIDENDS

In general, African Americans don't know enough about investment strategies, and as a result many are afraid to invest in mutual funds and stocks. Blacks of all ages are less likely than whites to describe themselves as "knowledgeable" investors. In fact, 38 percent of African Americans (compared to only 21 percent of whites) say lack of knowledge was a major reason for not investing more of their income.

This is alarming, but I certainly understand why it has happened. I know I certainly didn't hear anything about the stock market when I was growing up. The Dow Jones industrial average (the Dow) was not a topic of discussion at my family's dinner table, nor was our phone ringing off the hook with calls from stockbrokers. The same national brokerage firms that enthusiastically chase white professionals have been notoriously slow to recognize the potential of the African American investor. It could be that those investment firms simply don't know where to look. After all, blacks make up only 2 percent of those selling stocks, bonds, mutual funds and other securities in this country, according to Equal Employment Opportunity Commission (EEOC).

Since there are so few of us working in the industry, most brokerage firms don't have a clue about marketing to the African American community. Not surprisingly, stockbrokers traditionally have done their prospecting for clients in white neighborhoods, white corporations and white country clubs. They have done very little to seek out middle-class investors of any other race. Instead, they have focused on the "status" professions, such as doctors, lawyers and corporate executives.

With far too many black investors ignoring the stock market and investment professionals shunning the African American market, both have missed out. A great many blacks have not benefited as investors, and stockbrokers have failed to take advantage of a huge market. But believe me, it's hurt us more than it's hurt them. The investment brokers have neglected to develop inroads into the most dynamic consumer group in the world, but in the meantime many middle-class African Americans have missed opportunities to greatly enhance their savings during one of the longest and most lucrative bull markets in stock market history.

MY MISSION IS TO TEACH YOU HOW TO INCREASE YOUR WEALTH

I first began to see the disparity between black and white investors while I was working as a researcher and analyst for the Senate Finance Committee, and later for the U.S. Department of the Treasury (the Treasury). Now, as a private investment advisor to hundreds of African Americans of all income levels, it is not only my business but my passion and my mission to assist underinvested minorities in overcoming this one great remaining obstacle to the only true form of freedom in a capitalistic society—financial independence.

For nearly ten years, I quietly went about my mission by working my own turf in Chicago. I met clients in churches, employee cafeterias, construction sites, weddings, funerals and minority-owned businesses. I convinced scores of African Americans to build their savings bigger and faster by investing in the stock market. I don't mind telling you, I made a lot of people a lot richer, or at least a lot more financially secure than they'd ever dreamed.

I went about my mission quietly until the fall of 1997, when a *Wall Street Journal* reporter spent several weeks interviewing me and accompanying me on my visits to clients in the Chicago area. Why me? Because I was one of the very few financial advisors he'd found who actually sought out minority clients and enjoyed working with them. He spent weeks checking my credentials because he couldn't believe I was for real: a broker who actually cared about the little guy.

"Mr. Brown is a rarity in a field that hasn't done well gathering assets from minorities. About half of his $133 million portfolio belongs to black investors, he says, much of it coaxed from people who had never read a stock table before they met him," reporter James S. Hirsch wrote on the front page of the *Wall Street Journal* on September 17, 1997.

In truth, I find it disturbing that a national newspaper would consider a professional investment advisor seeking out minority clients to be front-page news. It should disturb every African American that we have been so neglected and so underinvested that it ranks up there with the most significant news of the day. I know it bothered me that blacks were ignored by financial advisors when I first joined a national investment firm's Chicago office as a stockbroker. I had moved from working for the

Treasury and the Senate Finance Committee into a major bond firm. After a while, I grew restless because I wanted to be more involved with clients, so I became a stockbroker.

I was in that position only a short time when I noticed that none of my coworkers—all of whom were white—had any black clients. It was apparent that most of them had little or no previous contact with *any* African Americans because they often treated me as if I were their inter-preter to some alien population. They'd ask me questions about famous black athletes or celebrities as if all blacks know each other. Most of them had grown up in all-white neighborhoods and gone to all-white schools, and had never had any dealings with African Americans of any social or economic class. They had no concept of the black community as a diverse and vibrant part of the country's population.

They were stunned to discover that not all of us were poor, Democrat, athletic or musically inclined. Yes, I told them, blacks come in a wide variety of shapes, sizes, abilities, intellects and political inclinations. And believe it or not, the majority of us have regular jobs that allow us to put money away for savings and investment.

In many ways, I was shocked by the ignorance of my white colleagues when it came to the African American community. It is hard to believe that blacks and whites can live so close to each other, but remain so far apart. I did come to be grateful that the white stockbrokers had failed to recognize the great hunger among African Americans for investment ad-vice. They had no idea how much money blacks had to invest.

But I did.

My introduction to saving and investing as a child was probably sim-ilar to that of most African Americans. What I learned came from those close to me. When I was twelve years old, my Uncle George gave me a silver dollar and said, "Little buddy, as long as you keep this, you'll never be broke."

Looking back now, I realize that maybe Uncle George was saying that as long as I kept that silver dollar at least I'd have *one* dollar to my name, but at the time it seemed to me he was telling me to save whatever money came my way. I loved my Uncle George. He was a retired master sergeant who lived to be ninety-two years old. To this day when I go back home to San Antonio, I run into men who remember him as the Worshipful Master of his Masonic lodge and others who fondly remember his work as a church trustee. He first instilled within me the basic concept of saving for the future. It was a simple lesson, but a vital one.

Shortly after Uncle George gave me my first silver dollar, my first dollar of any kind at all, my mother took me to the Alamo Savings and Loan and got me a dime card. Do you remember those? They were cards with slots in them to hold dimes. When you filled one up, you had enough money to purchase a $10 savings bond. I filled a few of those cards up and bought savings bonds as a boy. That was the extent of my exposure to savings and investment until much later in life.

Like most of my peers, I grew up in a very nurturing environment where hard work and saving one's money were emphasized. But there was never any discussion of stocks, bonds, mutual funds or any other way of savings besides the typical bank account. I had to learn that for myself, and so have most other African Americans. Nobody was knocking down our doors to teach us the importance or the value of investing in the stock market.

When I first became a stockbroker in 1988, I tried to play the game the same way my white coworkers played it. I struggled in my first few months as I followed the traditional approach of "cold-calling" white professionals and trying to solicit their business over the telephone. That was what I was trained to do, but it didn't work very well for me. Even when I did manage to sign clients, I found that I was spending so much time trying to sell them stocks, bonds and mutual funds—because that was how I earned my commissions—that I really wasn't doing what I wanted to do, which was to manage clients' portfolios to fit their specific needs, interests and goals.

One day, after several months of struggling and feeling discouraged,

I asked the advice of a successful senior stockbroker at the firm. He seemed to have a lot of clients, and he appeared to be making a lot of money simply by talking to them on the telephone all day.

I told him that I'd been working harder than I ever had in my life, coming into the office at 7:00 A.M. and calling hundreds of potential clients but having limited success. "All the while, I've been watching you too," I told him. "You seem so relaxed. You come in later in the morning, sip coffee and chat on the phone to clients who seem to throw money at you all day long. How do you do it?"

He told me that the secret to being a successful broker is to identify a niche market and develop long-term trusting relationships with it. Interestingly, his niche market was built around his love for seventeenth-century classical music by composers like Johann Sebastian Bach. He was president of the Baroque Society in Chicago, and most of his clients were music lovers whom he met through their shared interest.

I will resist all temptation to make a pun about his amazing ability to sell stocks and bonds to a bunch of "baroque" clients, but it did dawn on me that if he could build a lucrative client base based on his relationships with fellow music lovers, I could do the same thing by developing business relationships among people with whom I shared experiences and interests.

I only had to look at all the white faces in my office to determine where my unique niche should be. There I was, a black stockbroker in Chicago, home of some of the most successful and affluent African Americans in the world, not to mention a thriving black middle class. Once I identified my niche market, I only had to go out and talk to people. I didn't even have to wander off my normal path. I found them in my neighborhood, at my church, at gatherings for my college fraternity, in my grocery store and at social functions. It's amazing how easy invisible people are to find!

In this book, I'll be telling you about many of my clients and their success stories. At this point I want to introduce you to one of my favorites. His name is Charlie Jones. I love this guy, and his story is typical of the people with whom I deal.

Charlie is a maintenance supervisor and union steward at the huge McCormick Place convention hall on the shore of Lake Michigan in Chicago. For many years my company had a contract to manage the retirement plan for Charlie and the other employees of the Metropolitan Pier and Exhibition Authority, which operates McCormick Place. I helped invest their savings in mutual funds so that they would have enough money to be comfortable in their retirement years. There are 526 Metro Pier employees and I helped more than 450 of them enroll in one mutual fund plan or another. Now, I did earn commissions from those enrollments. But believe me, if I were in this purely to make money for myself, I probably would be hanging out with all those white stockbrokers, hustling for clients at their country clubs. I get much more satisfaction in helping people like Charlie.

I met Charlie one day while visiting with clients at McCormick Place. I would check in on them frequently to make sure things were going all right and to see if anyone had questions. Charlie was sweeping the floor when I walked in and we struck up a conversation. I asked him if he was enrolled in the deferred compensation retirement plan that I manage for his employer. "No, I live paycheck to paycheck like most people I know," he said.

Later in the book, I will describe these plans in detail to you, but for now, you should understand that they are perhaps the greatest thing that has ever happened for working men and women in this country. By having a small portion of each paycheck automatically taken out and put into stocks, bonds and mutual funds each pay period, millions and millions of Americans have been able to save more for their retirement than they had ever dreamed possible.

Like far too many people, though, Charlie had not enrolled in his company's retirement plan because he felt he didn't know enough about how it worked. Looking back, he remembers having a sense of helplessness when it came to investing. "In the black community, most people know next to nothing about investing their money," Charlie said. "I didn't understand stocks. I didn't know that you didn't have to be a millionaire to invest in stocks or bonds or commodities. I was frustrated because when Jesse started talking about it to me, it wasn't something I could relate to at all. Like most people, I thought putting twenty dollars a week in the bank was saving, but he showed me how to put it into the stock market so it would grow into something."

In talking to Charlie that first day, I learned that he was divorced and that he had custody of a young son. I asked Charlie if he was setting aside any money for his son's future, or in case something happened to him before the boy reached adulthood. Charlie said that he hadn't been able to save much. He also said that he dreamed of his son going to college one day so that he could have a better job and maybe an easier life than he'd had.

It bothers me to think that men and women who work that hard easily might end up one day with no place to live, or no one to care for them in their later years. I know it doesn't have to be that way. Even people who don't make $40,000 or $50,000 a year can save a little at a time and then take advantage of investment opportunities that can provide them with security for the rest of their lives.

Charlie makes $35,000 a year, which would put him solidly in the middle class of this country—a group that does not include nearly enough people who look like me and Charlie. Out of the 33 million African Americans in this country, about 12.5 million of them have middle-class incomes. With his income, Charlie should be doing better. I'm not saying that he will ever be able to retire to a condominium in Florida, but there is no reason that he should ever have to go hungry or go without a place to live even after he retires, if he saves and invests wisely.

After talking with him on several occasions, I got Charlie to enroll in the retirement plan. He started investing just $20 a week and within a relatively short time, he had $5,000 saved up. Sadly, it turned out that

Charlie needed that money long before he was ready to retire because his mother died unexpectedly. She had no money, and no one else in the family could pay for a funeral. Charlie had to go into his retirement savings and take out $2,000 to bury his mother properly. I don't advocate taking money out of retirement savings because there is generally a big tax penalty, but sometimes you don't have any choice. Charlie was grateful that I had talked him into joining the retirement plan, because otherwise he wouldn't have had the needed money and his mother would not have had a proper burial.

"When I told Jesse about the situation with my mother's funeral, he helped me take care of it, and it was like having a great burden lifted off my shoulders when I realized that I could use my savings from the retirement account. Instead of being dejected, I was proud that I was able to take care of her funeral," Charlie said.

A well-conceived investment plan is a form of *life assurance*; if you stick with it, the wealth you build will provide you with the assurance that you will have what you need, when you need it the most. It takes a little money to get started with this plan, but it takes even more of an investment in the truth. You have to accept the truth that saving money is vital to your future happiness and security.

Now, let me show you how to do it.

When I first asked Denise Yelvington if she was investing her money wisely, she was only nineteen years old. She had just dropped out of college, even though she'd had a full scholarship, a move she came to regret. Back then, Denise was working as an administrative assistant. It was a temp job that became a permanent position. She was making less than $18,000 a year and had saved "only pennies." Denise told me that she didn't have enough extra money to invest in her company's retirement plan, but I talked her into putting $50 a month into it by having the money taken directly out of her paycheck so that she never got her hands on the cash. Denise's pennies have turned into thousands. She is now twenty-four, paying her own way through community college *and* boasting more than $8,000 in her retirement account—thanks to that $50 a month and the wonders of a disciplined investment program.

Two of the most difficult things to get going in this life are a diet and an investment plan. In fact, when I preach the value of investing in the stock market to some folks, I often feel like a doctor advising patients to lose weight by eating right. I'm sure the diet doctors and I hear the same sort of response—one that usually begins, "Yeah, I know I should do it but . . ." Then I generally hear at least one of the excuses from my

Ten Standard Reasons Given by African Americans
Who Don't Invest in Stocks, Bonds or Mutual Funds

1. I don't make enough money to invest.
2. It's something rich people do.
3. I don't know how to invest.
4. I don't trust the stock market.
5. I'm too young.
6. I have a bank savings account/money market fund/certificate of deposit (CD).
7. The Lord and Social Security will take care of me.
8. Having a lot of money is not one of my goals.
9. I'm going to hit it big on Powerball.
10. I put my money in safe things like real estate.

I particularly like that last item. A 1998 survey of the investment habits of 1,232 black and white households with annual incomes of $50,000 or higher found that many African Americans consider real estate to be the best overall investment. Whites chose stocks. Other studies of investment habits have shown that real estate, life insurance, annuities and bank savings accounts are most favored among blacks looking to save for the future. The truth is that none of these forms of investment offers the rewards of the stock market. I can tell you from my own experience that investing in real estate other than your own home can be like walking in a minefield.

GETTING REAL ABOUT REAL ESTATE
AS AN INVESTMENT

If you are one of those people who thinks real estate is the best way to invest your savings, I have a house I want to sell you. No, really, I do. It is a four-bedroom, single-family house. Two stories with a porch, full basement and eat-in kitchen located on Seventh Street in Maywood, a western suburb of Chicago. It's a nice place.

Please buy it. *Please.*

If nothing else, this may be the first book you've ever read in which the author begs you to buy his house. There is a reason for that, of course. You see, like many people, I once thought investing in real estate made sense. I now believe that it makes sense only in very special cases, and generally only if the real estate you are investing in is the real estate you are going to live in.

I bought the house in 1987 after watching one of those late-night infomercials on the wonders of real estate as an investment. I must have been sleepwalking. Brain-dead, maybe. I followed the advice of the guy in the infomercial and bought the house in a government foreclosure sale because the owner had defaulted on a Veterans Administration loan. The plan was that by buying the house at an auction, I would get an especially good deal. It *was* a pretty good price: $25,000. Of course, the owner who had failed to make his payments to the bank hadn't been much on taking care of his property either. So, I had to put another $25,000 into fixing up the place.

In a perfect world, I would have earned back my investment from rent payments. I would've made enough from the rent to pay all of the expenses of owning the property. In the meantime, the value of the home would have increased every year so that, eventually, I could have sold it for a handsome profit.

According to the property tax appraiser, my real-estate investment is now worth $80,000. I wish he'd write me a check right now, since he seems to be the only one who thinks the house is worth that much. I followed every bit of advice given by that infomercial guy. I bought a decent house at a great price and I put some money into fixing it up. But Mr. Infomercial was mistaken. I have not made my money back.

Maywood has some very nice homes at reasonable prices. Unfortunately, it also began having crime problems. Because of this, I have not been able to sell the property for what I need to get out of it. I've even had difficulty renting it for a decent return. So now I'm paying a mortgage and nearly $4,000 a year just for insurance and taxes. Because the rent is so low, it seems like we're paying people to live there too.

Now you know why I am not big on real estate as a method for building wealth—at least not for the middle-income investor. Owning and maintaining real estate involves a lot of work, especially if you have renters. If you get a bad tenant, or if you have a good tenant who falls on hard times, it can be extremely difficult to get payment or to evict them. When it comes to selling an investment property, you have to find somebody ready and willing to pay a price that will give you a profit, and that is not always easy. I'm still looking. Are you sure you aren't interested?

I'm not the only one who has had problems in this arena. One of my clients, a professional basketball player, bought a beautiful mansion with eight bedrooms in a gated community out west, shortly after he signed his first big NBA contract. It was a $2 million house.

Then he got hurt.

Next, he got traded.

Today, he has two houses—the new one he had to buy after being traded to a team in another city, and the old $2 million house in his former team's town.

Once again, the primary problem with investing in real estate is that when you want to sell, there isn't always a buyer ready and willing to pay the price. That isn't the case with stocks and mutual funds. You can always sell your stock or mutual fund at the going rate set by the market. It may be more than you paid originally. It may be less. But at least there is always a willing buyer when you decide to sell.

That can be awfully important if there is an emergency and you suddenly need to get some cash out of your investment. You can sell your stocks, bonds and mutual funds with a simple phone call and have the check in hand within a few days. Try doing that with a house or apartment building. Sure, I have a property that is worth some money, but that doesn't do me a whole lot of good if I suddenly need $5,000 to pay an emergency medical or car repair bill, or, God forbid, pay for a loved one's funeral. Having equity in real estate is a good long-term financial strategy in many cases, but that equity doesn't translate easily to money in your pocket.

Some people might argue that you can borrow against the equity you have in your home, and that is true. It is also true of stocks. Any investment broker will be glad to set up a margin stock account that allows you to borrow against the value of your portfolio in much the same way that a home equity loan works. Some of them even issue credit cards that advance cash to you without selling your stocks.

Another big disadvantage of real-estate investments is that you have to pay property taxes, which can substantially cut into your profits. By placing your stocks in a tax-free individual retirement account (IRA), simplified employee pension plan (SEP) or 401(k) plan you can delay payment of taxes until much later, when, hopefully, you may well be in a lower tax bracket.

I don't want to be entirely negative on real estate as an investment. For one thing, I think it is extremely important that you own your primary personal residence rather than rent, unless it simply does not make practical sense for you. The tax and equity advantages of home ownership are generally much more favorable than paying rent. When it comes to buying real estate as an investment, my advice in general is to leave that to the pros.

MAKING YOUR MONEY WORK FOR YOU

Most of the other excuses I hear for not investing are also poorly thought out. Let's take a couple of interrelated ones. When someone tells me that they are too young to invest, what they are really saying is that they don't feel they have enough money, which is generally nonsense, as illustrated by Denise's story at the start of this chapter.

Remember this: Financial prosperity really has nothing to do with how much money you are making right now. It has much more to do with what you are doing with what you have. Prosperity is a blessing, but it is also a responsibility. The fact is that it makes more sense to begin investing when you are young even though you may not be able to put as much money aside each week. It's a matter of simple mathematics *and* the magic of compound interest; that is, the interest, dividends, capital gains and other forms of return that, *if left in place*, begin generating income on their own.

The longer you allow the returns on your investments to grow, the more money you have when it comes time to cash out. I repeat: *It's not how much you invest that is important. It's how long you invest it and the return (rate of interest) you receive on it.*

If at age 25 Denise had started to invest just $100 a month and saved it at an assumed rate of return of 12 percent, she'd have built up a nest egg of $1,188,242.00 by age 65, even though her own contribution would have been only $48,000. Assuming the same 12 percent rate of return:

- If she'd started at age 30, she'd have to put in $42,000 of her own money to build savings of $649,527.
- If she waited until age 40 to begin saving that $100 a month, she would have to contribute $30,000 to build savings of $189,764.
- And if she'd put off saving until age of 50, she'd have to contribute $18,000 to build $50,458 in savings at the age of 65.

Too young to start saving? Too poor to start saving? I don't think so. The sad truth is that a great many people put off serious investment savings until they are in their forties because by that time they either feel they have taken care of the essentials, like a home and a car and their children's educations, or simply begin to panic about retirement.

It's sad because even though they will be able to save a decent amount by retirement age, those people will never be able to take advantage of the economics of compound interest as fully as young people who begin investing early. Is the message beginning to sink in?

One more example. Economist Roger Ibbotson has noted that one dollar invested back in 1925 would be worth $7.46 today based on inflation alone. If it had been invested in government bonds, it would be worth $17.99. Corporate bonds would have transformed it into $27.18. The stock market would have turned that $1 into $517.50, and only $25.89 of that would have come from price appreciation. The rest of the increase is due to dividend growth and dividend reinvestment.

You may be young. You may not have much money to put aside. But you can still take advantage of time and rate of return. Historically, the best rate of return on investment has been the stock market. A bank will pay you 2 to 5 percent interest for keeping your money in their institution. In the meantime, they are loaning your money out at three times that amount. Is that a good deal for you? Not really. Not when you can invest in a professionally managed mutual fund that can easily pay a return of 15 to 20 percent, and often more.

BULL OR BEAR, YOU WANT TO BE THERE

Ahh, but some of you don't *trust* the stock market, do you? Sure it can go up, you say, but it can also go down! Yes. It happened as I was writing the book: The market plunged more than 500 points in August of 1998. Then it slowly worked its way back up to an even higher level. By the beginning of 1999, the market was at the highest level in history.

When people say they don't trust the stock market, that tells me they are afraid of its volatility. Since 1940, we have experienced twelve bull markets (where stocks in general have increased in value) and eleven bear markets (where stocks have generally declined in value). So yes, the stock market does go up and it does go down. But consider this: The average bear market lasted less than a year and was down 25 to 30 percent, while the average bull market lasted more than *three* years and was up *100* percent. Historically, then, the market has risen over time. This means that patient investors who have not panicked in the short term have benefited over the long run.

As I write this, there are a lot of jitters among investors and investment advisors because the third-longest bull market in history appears to be winding down. Without a doubt, it has been driven by baby boomer investors who are now in their forties and looking to build up their retirement funds. This long-running baby boomer bull market began in October of 1990 and it has already surpassed 2,800 days. Many are afraid it cannot continue, but so far all of the doomsayers have lost out. There have been a few drops, but the bulls always seem to rush back in, buying on the dips and driving the market forward.

In the 1980s, the Dow soared 250 percent to its August 1987 high, before dropping 22.3 percent on October 19, 1987—sometimes known as "Black Monday." In the 1990s, though, the Dow has climbed about 280 percent, including a record three consecutive years with gains of 20 percent or more. What's making some folks jittery is the fact that in the 1920s, the Dow gained 496 percent before plummeting into the Great Depression. But most experts agree that such a huge drop would be impossible in this day and age.

From 1925 to 1998, small company stocks rose, on average, 12.4 percent while Treasury bills had a compound annual return of 3.8 percent. Based on those figures provided by Ibbotson Associates in Chicago, (a premier statistics service) one dollar invested in a small cap mutual fund over that period would be worth $5,116 at the end of 1998, while one dollar invested in Treasury bills would be worth only $15.

Even with the fluctuations in the market and the inevitable downturns, the stock market has proven to be a good bet. Some daredevil types try to play the market's turbulence by buying on the dips and selling on the rises. Even highly trained investors with computer programs at their command have had difficulty outguessing today's stock market. Most people don't have the time, information base or risk tolerance that it takes to play that game. Like most professional investment advisors, I tell clients to invest for the long-term and leave market-timing to the Evel Knievel types.

Taking some of the risk out of the roller coaster

The time-proven best method for dealing with the inevitable volatility of the stock market is to use an investment method known as "dollar cost averaging." To use it, two things are required:

1. Patience
2. Faith

One of the greatest obstacles to successful investing is a lack of patience. You've undoubtedly grown sick of hearing the griping about our culture of "instant gratification" but it's true. We buy cars and other big-ticket items that we can't afford. Then we end up taking out long-term loans to pay for them because we have not saved in advance. When it comes to investing, far too many people demand high returns immediately. As a result, they throw *all* of their money into the market instead of slowly feeding it in over time.

Dollar cost averaging is a method for investing money over time in order to take advantage of the ups and downs of the market, minimizing the risk of getting burned by a sudden downturn. A certain amount of faith is required to believe that the American economic system will continue to thrive, but even crusty old economists are marveling these days at its enduring power and strength.

The dollar cost averaging approach to investing is a simple process in which you invest your money in equal amounts on a regular basis, usually once a month. Let's say you've inherited $30,000 from your Great Aunt Oprah (Hey, we can dream can't we?) but you are afraid of putting it all into the stock market at once. You fear the market might take a sudden dive. It might. That's where patience and faith come in.

Using the dollar cost averaging method you could invest $1,000 a month while keeping the bulk of the money in a bank money market account, which pays at least some interest. The upside of this approach is that it allows you to ease your way into riskier investments so that if the market does drop, you benefit by buying at a lower price. If it goes up, you still benefit because you already have some of your money in the game. One common problem with this plan is that if that investment—a stock, bond or mutual fund—continues to drop, you may be sorely tempted to cut your losses and get out. There are also some potential tax complications with dollar cost averaging if your investments are made outside of a tax-free retirement account. If you buy a stock, bond or mutual fund at different times and prices, it makes it more difficult to determine what you owe the IRS.

I'd advise you to use dollar cost averaging only when investing in tax-free retirement accounts or when the money you seek to put into the market represents a big chunk of your total assets. It is also important to stick with a regular schedule of putting it into the market. Most stockbrokers and investment advisors will invest your money for you according to your specifications. Please note that dollar cost averaging does not ensure a profit and does not protect against loss in declining markets. Dollar cost averaging involves continuous investment in securities regardless of fluctuating prices. Investors should consider their financial ability to continue purchases through periods of high price levels.

That is what I did for Raymond Born, a client and wonderful fellow who went through some difficult times just as he was approaching retirement. Ray was hit with an illness related to his diabetes that left him partially paralyzed. He'd been an active guy, a golfer and socializer, and the illness hit him hard. He was also a guy with very little discipline when it came to saving money. Fortunately, I'd gotten to him about ten years earlier and convinced him that he should start investing his money using dollar cost averaging. He followed my plan and retired with several hundred thousand dollars—enough to buy a house on a golf course in San Diego. I'm pleased to say that at his retirement party, Ray gave a speech thanking me for giving him the discipline and the plan that made his retirement much more comfortable than it might have been. "A lot of the guys I grew up with are still working and they are signed up with your investment program and boy are they glad," Ray told me recently. "They are all going to retire with a bundle of money and like me, they wouldn't have had it if you hadn't talked us into going with your investment program."

CHANGE THE WAY YOU THINK ABOUT MONEY AND CHANGE THE WAY YOU LIVE

At the beginning of this chapter, I listed my ten reasons why African Americans don't invest in stocks, bonds, or mutual funds. Now I'm going to give you

The Reason African Americans *Should* Invest in Stocks, Bonds or Mutual Funds

Are you ready? Here it is:
1. Peace of mind

Go back a couple paragraphs and read again what Raymond had to say about his investment savings and those of his friends. What is he really talking about? *Peace of mind.*

We all have fears about growing old, getting sick, being put out of work by an accident or being hit with unexpected debt. Having an investment plan and money working for you while you work for it gives you a much greater sense of security. Living paycheck to paycheck can be stressful. I've done it. You've done it. A lot of us have no other choice. But stress can kill you. It builds up over time like rust and eats away at your immune system, making you more susceptible to everything from colds to cancer. The good news is that stress over financial matters can be greatly reduced by the knowledge that every week a portion of your earnings is going into an investment that will continue to grow.

My clients often tell me that is the best thing about their investment plan. It makes it easier for them to sleep at night. They know that if they stumble or hit hard times financially, there is a safety net.

George Meyer is a "salt of the earth" kind of guy. He worked as head of a union electrician's shop until age 77 partly because he loved his work and the people who worked for him, and also because he put two kids through college and went $80,000 into debt to do it. George was over sixty when I finally got him to enroll in an investment retirement plan, but he went at it with a vengeance. He put away more than $8,000 a year even as he paid off that big, but entirely honorable, debt. He even opened separate investment accounts for his granddaughter and his great-grandchildren.

Although it took George a while to decide to get into the investment plan I set up for him and his coworkers, he became my best salesman. He preached the value of "Jesse's program" to every new employee and urged all of his friends and family workers to get into it.

Why did he become so enthusiastic? George is a wise man. He realized that it's not about money. It's not about being able to buy things. It's not about having a nice car, a bigger house or a swimming pool in the backyard. It's about peace of mind and what peace of mind brings. I'll let my best salesman tell you in his own words.

Shortly before his happy retirement, George told me this.

"Being in the investment program means that I'll be able to retire and do some traveling to visit my kids and that I'll still be able to give gifts to my grandkid and great-grandkids, but most of all it is a *freedom* thing."

Freedom. That's what having a savings and investment plan is really all about.

Our ancestors fought long and hard for our physical freedom, and it took this nation's only civil war to win it. Since then, we have battled constantly to ensure that our social freedom is protected by law and by the government formed to make and enforce those laws.

The final frontier, then, is financial independence.

You will never know true freedom or peace of mind until you begin building personal wealth and financial security. In this chapter, I identified ten reasons that African Americans give for not investing for the long term, but I could have listed one hundred or one thousand just as easily. I've probably heard *millions*.

All of them are really just excuses. They come from a sense that we don't deserve wealth, freedom, peace of mind. That is a self-defeating mind-set that comes from a sense of scarcity, a belief that there is only so much wealth in this world and we are never going to our fair share.

That is simply not true, nor is it a worthy self-image for our great race . . . a race that has invested heavily in the success of this country, a race that deserves to cash its check on, as the Rev. Martin Luther King, Jr., described it, "the promissory note" of the American dream.

I am not saying that I believe someone *owes* us anything. That "entitlement mentality" serves no one well. At some point in their lives, most Americans rely on some sort of government assistance, whether it be Social Security, food stamps, welfare payments, rent subsidies, student loans, Medicare, Medicaid or crop subsidies. I know that some people have genuine need for some of these entitlement programs and I don't begrudge them one cent of it. But I do worry about them because sooner or later, most of those programs will end or be cut back. There have been a lot of dire predictions in the last few years that the Social Security system is going to go bankrupt when all of the baby boomers hit retirement age. It is not going to happen because it would be political suicide for our congressmen to allow it. Payments may be cut back, however, and most certainly they will move back the age at which people become eligible. It makes sense because we are living longer and staying active now into our late seventies and eighties.

I advise you, as I do all of my clients, not to rely on *any* government programs to take care of you or your loved ones in old age. That is *your* responsibility. I also advise my clients that each of us has the privilege and the right to tap into the most dynamic economy on the globe. This country produces more wealth than any other nation in the world, and African Americans account for a huge percentage of that wealth—$532 billion in 1999 according to The Selig Center for Economic Growth at the University of Georgia. It's time that every black man, woman and child in this country decided that this is *our* country and that its wealth is ours to share in.

"As black people we like to say we make $400 billion a year. We should be ashamed to admit that. The white man doesn't care how much you had and spent. Brag about how much you've kept and invested," the Rev. Jesse Jackson, Sr., said.

Do you know what an abundance mentality is? It's a mind-set that says, "There is enough in this world for everyone and you and I both deserve our shares of it." Forget the entitlements and the excuses. Take responsibility for your financial security. You can begin building wealth for yourself and those you love right now.

Adopting an abundance mentality is the first step toward securing peace of mind and toward reaching the one freedom that we as a people have yet to fully claim: financial freedom. No excuses accepted. No limits projected. Let's get started right now.

Another Day Older and Deeper in Debt   **3**

I hope that by now you are beginning to think that investing in stocks, bonds or mutual funds is a pretty good idea—but you also may be looking at your paycheck and your stack of monthly bills and wondering, *"How?"*

You may be thinking, "I hear what you're saying about this 'abundance mentality,' Jesse, but the pile of bills on my kitchen counter is saying, 'Scarcity Rules!' "

I understand. A great many middle-class people are used to living paycheck to paycheck, and it may seem like there is not a penny to spare. I guarantee you that even if that is the case in your household, I can help you find a way to save money for investments that will enhance your financial security. I will do that by teaching you some basic concepts for saving and budgeting, and by showing you a few money-eating pitfalls to avoid when it comes to handling your personal finances.

African Americans face an even greater challenge than others when it comes to building financial security. It's called racism, and any black man or woman who has ever had to show sixteen different forms of identification in order to cash a check knows what I'm talking about. Financial discrimination is a fact of life for us, and it makes us susceptible to all sorts of scams that inhibit our ability to build true wealth.

I get angry when I drive through a black neighborhood and see people lined up at check-cashing joints to cash their paychecks, Society Security, veteran's benefits or other government aid checks. Those businesses charge you for cashing your checks, while many banks offer free check-cashing privileges. The money you pay for check-cashing could be going into an investment plan that would build wealth. It's a small amount, but as I've shown you already, even a small amount invested regularly can grow rapidly. When you have to pay just to get your checks cashed, it can be difficult to free up money for long-term investing.

Traditionally, African Americans have had difficulty obtaining bank loans for mortgages, car purchases and business start-ups because of entrenched racism and discriminatory practices, such as redlining, by financial institutions. This has impeded our efforts just to pay the bills, let alone build lasting wealth. It also makes us marks for modern-day loan sharks, scam artists and rent-to-own companies. In this chapter, I will help you learn to recognize these predators as well as poor spending and saving practices that can cripple efforts to build wealth. We will look at some of the common money-handling mistakes and explore methods for avoiding them.

Among my many African American clients is a famous and beloved guy who makes more than a million dollars a year. His problem is that nearly everything that comes in goes out. His accountant once told him that his finances resemble a wide-open faucet running into a bathtub with a wide-open drain. Nothing stays in the tub.

The first step toward building wealth is to shut that drain—or at least reduce what goes down it as much as possible. You are always going to have bills to pay, but far too many people throw money down the drain unnecessarily because they don't monitor their spending. I have hundred of clients, most of whom are middle-income wage earners. I talk to plumbers, electricians, carpenters, teachers, secretaries, police officers and other regular people about their finances every day. As soon as anyone finds out I'm an investment advisor, the talk immediately turns to their most intimate financial problems. (It makes me glad I'm not a proctologist.)

From these daily conversations, I have concluded that everyone—and I do mean everyone—lives within their means. That is, everyone spends everything they have, and when they get more, they spend that too. If you make $1,000 a month, you buy a house and a car and groceries and clothes and knickknacks that eat up the whole $1,000. If you get a raise to $1,200 a month, it's not long before you have learned to live within that amount too—by spending every penny.

It's human nature. We spend what we have, then we complain that we don't have enough to save. *Or,* we put money in a bank account and convince ourselves that *that* is our savings. Oh, the little lies we tell ourselves. So often, we do things with our money that we know deep down are not wise. We put our resources in low-return savings accounts or certificates of deposit. We don't pay off our credit-card balances or read the fine print when we sign up with a credit-card issuer. We fall prey to rent-to-own companies and fly-by-night or -by-mail loan agencies that offer quick cash but take a long-term cut out of your finances with astronomical interest rates. These money-handling mistakes add up quickly, most resulting from the fact that people would rather spend money than think about using it wisely and carefully.

YOUR SAVINGS ACCOUNT IS NOTHING TO BANK ON

Often when I ask a prospective client if he or she is saving money for the future, they'll say they are putting $30 or $40 or even $100 a week into a bank savings account or money market account. I have a couple of problems with that answer. You already know my number-one objection: Banks just don't pay much interest on your money even though they charge you plenty when they loan it to you. A *Consumer Reports* survey found that with banks earning near-record profit margins at the expense of their customers, savings accounts have become "some of the worst investment options around." Most banks add to the insult by charging monthly fees to savings-account holders even as they make profits on that money by loaning it out to others. Small savers can actually *lose* money on an account with an average monthly fee of just $2—and that doesn't include the tax charge on the puny interest you're paid.

My second objection is that bank savings accounts aren't really *savings* accounts anyway. Not the way most people use them. In reality, the majority of people use their passbook savings accounts as deferred spending accounts. Be honest. What is the most money you have ever been able to accumulate in your bank savings account? I'd be willing to wager my house in Maywood (it's still for sale, by the way) that most people have never had more than a couple thousand dollars in a passbook or money market account. That money is just too tempting, too accessible.

I'm not saying it's a bad thing to have money in the bank. I recommend that everyone should have at least $1,000 to $2,000 on hand for small emergencies. But a real savings account has two primary characteristics. First of all, it is generally established with specific long-term, big-picture goals in mind, such as paying for a college education, buying a house or funding retirement. That sort of savings account requires discipline. You can't be dipping into it every time the toaster oven blows up. You have to let that money grow by leaving it alone. That is money you invest and then forget about!

Sarai is an accounting manager for the City of Chicago. I met her in 1993 at the church we both attend on the South Side. Naturally, when she found out what I do for a living, she told me about her finances and, just as naturally, I told her she needed help. Sarai had a deferred spending account—I mean, a *bank passbook account.*

"I also had one certificate of deposit worth about three thousand dollars, but mostly my savings were in a bank account," she said. "I thought I had savings, but the truth was, if there was something I wanted, like a new dress, I took the money out of the savings account so I didn't have to wait until payday. I don't think there was ever more than one thousand dollars in there at any one time. As a result, I never got ahead."

When I met Sarai, she was forty-six years young. Her only retirement savings were in her city pension and the government's Social Security system. There was no guarantee that either of those was going to be enough to provide a comfortable life when she chose to retire, so I worked hard on her to start a serious savings and investment plan. Every Sunday, the minister gave her a sermon about the ways of the Lord, and then outside the church, I preached to her about the ways of the stock market.

"Jesse showed me how my money could grow a lot more in a mutual fund and he showed me how to do it without a lot of risk," Sarai said. "He had me start by having one hundred dollars a month taken out of my paycheck and after I saw how much it grew to be in six months' time, I jumped up and down and said, 'This is great!' I really did. Of course, whenever the market goes down, I call him up and whine, but he tells me to relax and hold on. He had to do that quite a bit in the first year, but now I understand that I am in this for the long term and I have to ride out the dips in the market."

Sarai's initial fear of the stock market and, now, her great enthusiasm for it is typical of my clients. She is also typical in that as she has seen her money grow in her mutual fund accounts, Sarai has become a very avid saver. She has learned to put away more than $700 a month and whenever she gets anything extra, such as an income tax return, she puts it into her investment fund too. The last time I checked in with her, Sarai had more than $50,000 in her investment account.

"I've changed my whole way of looking at savings," she said.

CERTIFICATES OF DEPOSIT: AN IOU THAT'S OUT OF REACH

One of the significant changes Sarai made at my urging was to take her $3,000 out of her bank CD. I don't like bank CDs. The problem with them is that they are essentially a promissory note. A fancy sort of IOU.

The CD is a specialized deposit that pays a relatively low but guaranteed return. The interest rate is usually about the same as that of short- or intermediate-term bonds. Lately, it has hovered between 4 and 5 percent. The interest payments are made at regular intervals until the CD comes due ("matures"). Only then do you get the money you deposited, along with accumulated interest—but minus the taxes that you have had to pay on that interest.

In her case, Sarai took $3,000 she'd saved and purchased a two-year CD at her bank. She gave the guys in the suits her money and they gave her a piece of paper saying that at the end of two years she could have her money back. Two years Seven hundred and thirty days. What if Sarai needed her $3,000 *before* that? What if a tree limb fell on her roof and punched a hole in it? What if her car needed a new engine? What if she suddenly had the opportunity to go to Europe for six weeks for only $3,000?

The guys in the suits would not be sympathetic. The only way they'd let her have her money back would be to charge her a hefty penalty that would take a nasty cut out of her $3,000, usually six months' interest or more. To add insult to injury, while your money sits out of your reach in a CD, *you have to pay taxes on the interest it is earning.* Ouch.

There are certain advantages to a CD, primarily that you get a guaranteed return (minus the taxes, of course). I don't recommend them to my clients. If you don't mind putting money where you can't get to it right away or without penalty, I suggest putting your money in a tax-deferred investment such as a mutual funds IRA. At least then you won't be paying Uncle Sam while your money is on the shelf—and the interest paid is often at least twice as much as for a CD.

TURNING OFF THE DEBT TAP

Of all the threats to your financial security, none is more dangerous than debt. When Isaac Singer, founder of the Singer sewing machine company, came up with the idea of "buying on time" in 1856, he never could have foreseen the societal costs it would have. His machines were good but expensive for the hard times he lived in, so Singer devised a plan in which people could buy his machines for $5 down and $5 a month. His plan worked so well, other companies began offering similar programs. In 1916, a fellow named Arthur Morris took Singer's idea and ran with it, creating the installment loan. While such loans have made it possible for many people to purchase homes and cars and other goods and services, they have also contributed to this nation's incredible mountain of debt.

Today, more than 78 percent of the average family's disposable income goes to service their debt. We all fall into the trap of instant gratification. It is a trap set by the lure of credit cards and installment loans that provide easy money in exchange for long-term pain. The process is as simple as it is deadly. It begins when you charge a few big-ticket items on your credit card and only pay off a portion each month. Slowly, your credit-card debt begins to increase so that more and more of your monthly payment is going only to pay off the interest on your debt. Then an emergency arises. You have to make another big purchase and it goes on the credit card too, hiking up your debt even further. Your credit-card issuer notices the increased debt, and like a spider moving in on the fly snared in its web, it moves in on you by offering you an even higher limit on your card. At first you feel relief. Now you can charge even more! And more and more of your disposable income must go toward paying off interest on the debt, instead of paying off the debt itself. Suddenly you are paying hefty "late fees" for failing to make your minimum credit-card payments. The spider is moving in for the kill. Compound interest can work for you and against you. It is your friend when applied to your savings and investments, your deadly enemy when applied to your debt.

WEALTH-BUILDING ENEMY NO. 1:
CREDIT-CARD DEBT

I once knew a young man just out of high school who, upon getting his first job as the manager of a fast-food restaurant, liked to brag to his family and friends about all of the credit cards he had accumulated. He'd walk up to them, pull out his wallet, fan out fifteen credit cards and gloat about having a total credit line of about $50,000.

He wasn't bragging a few years later when he had more than $20,000 in credit-card debt—which kept him from qualifying for a car loan or a mortgage. Credit cards are useful. Credit cards are easy to use. Credit-card abuse will wipe you out. Repeat this after me: *Credit-card debt will wipe me out!*

Before American Express, Visa and MasterCard yank all of my plastic, let me qualify that. It's not so much that the credit card itself is evil or bad—although they are generally designed to keep you in debt forever—it's mostly the way people use them that puts fear in my heart. In this day and age, it is necessary to have at least one credit card because many times there is no other way to purchase some things like concert or theater tickets over the telephone. Have you ever tried to cash a check or get a rental car without a credit card? You might as well be offering yak butter as collateral.

So, I am not advocating that you cut up all of your credit cards, unless you are one of those people who abuses them. If you *are* going to use credit cards regularly, you have to have discipline. You have to budget your credit-card spending and monitor it carefully.

Because credit cards are now showered upon the masses, personal debt in this country is now rising faster than personal-income growth. That's good for the credit-card companies but bad for you and me. Ted is a client who came to me with some serious credit-card debt. He is a blue-collar worker and an easygoing guy whose wife had a purse full of credit cards and no self-control when it came to using them. Worst of all, she didn't keep track of what she was using them for, and she didn't tell Ted either. Of course, he found out when the monthly statements filled the mailbox. Those credit-card bills busted Ted's budget even before he got to the essentials like the gas, electric and food bills, not to mention the mortgage payments.

Since he didn't have the cash to pay off his credit cards every month, Ted fell into the very dangerous trap of simply making the minimum required payment. To quote the great James Brown: *Please, please, please,* if you learn nothing else from this book, learn that you must pay off your credit cards each month.

Paying the minimum is a financial death trap. When you do that, you are charged interest on the balance that remains, and it is steep interest—from 10 to 25 percent and up—and sometimes *double* what certain types of bank loans might cost you. Credit-card companies are very sly about offering low "teaser" interest rates and then jacking them up after a few months. The average credit-card rate is about 18 percent, which is the same as it was fifteen years ago when mortgage rates were twice what they are today. So the card issuers are not doing you any favors. Most of them, in fact, purposefully base their operations in states with weak consumer protection laws.

Paying the minimum on your credit card will get you ahead—a head start toward bankruptcy, that is. If you pay the least amount required each month, odds are it'll take you twenty years or more to pay your card off. If you can't afford to pay off your credit cards, stop using them until they are paid off. Do not allow yourself to get farther and farther behind. Please. Please. Please?

I tell my clients that the key to using credit cards wisely is to use them like checks on your bank checking account. Write down every purchase just like you write down every check, so that you are always on top of how much you're spending and how close you are to going over budget. Don't go over budget. It's also wise to shop around for the best credit-card rates. There is no reason to pay an annual fee for your credit card, and there is also no reason to pay extra for a Gold, Platinum or even a Mother of Pearl premium card. There are plenty of cards now that charge no annual fee. Some even pay you premiums like cash, frequent flyer miles, long-distance minutes or credit toward the purchase of a card. Check *Consumer Reports, Black Enterprise, Individual Investor, USA Today*'s money section and other publications for the best deals in credit cards.

Here are tips for protecting yourself from serious credit-card debt.

1. **Do not pay an annual fee.** No annual fee. No way. No how. There is absolutely no reason to pay one. If your credit-card issuer suddenly starts charging you one, cut their card into small pieces and go elsewhere. Believe me, you won't have to look far.

2. **Watch the annual percentage rate as if it were your favorite niece.** And never let it get out of sight. This is especially important if you tend to carry a balance over, but even those people who make it a practice to pay off their balance every month sometimes slip up or find it necessary to whittle away at a particularly big bill. A low APR (annual percentage rate) can save you a bundle in interest charges over the long run just as a lower mortgage rate can. The magazines and newspapers I mentioned above regularly carry lists of low-rate cards, some of which can be picky about to whom they give cards. If you have a lot of debt, they may not want to help you, even though you are the one who needs it the most. Typical of financial institutions, isn't it?

3. **Remember, everything is negotiable.** If you are someone who makes regular payments but keeps a big balance, you may be able to negotiate a lower interest rate with your card's issuer with just a phone call. You may also be able to get the annual fee waived, or get a higher credit limit (I don't advise doing that, however).

4. **Read the fine print, even if you have to get a magnifying glass.** You would not believe some of the tricks credit-card companies pull to get their hands deeper into your pockets. Most allow the card issuer to change the terms on short notice. Some use a particularly vile ploy called "two-cycle" billing that lets them assess new interest charges based on what you owed the previous month, even if you paid off that bill. If you see the term "two-cycle billing" in your agreement, throw the card in the nearest fire.

5. **Beware the perks.** Credit-card companies are so eager to get their hands on your hard-earned money that these days they'll offer you everything from frequent-flier mileage to travel accident insurance, rebates on gasoline and even on entire cars. Their offers can be enticing, but before you jump into a deal that has you paying an annual fee and a 28 percent APR just to get a free tank of gas every six months, think carefully. Those frequent-flier miles may sound wonderful, and they can be a great bonus, but often the credit cards offering them charge hefty annual fees and often there are pages and pages of restrictions on when, how and where you can apply those frequent-flier miles.

6. **Pay it off. Pay it off. Pay it off.** Because of the high interest rates they charge, credit-card debt is the worst debt you can have. I advise you and all of my clients to get rid of that debt first, to make it a priority to pay off credit cards before spending money on anything else. I'll say it three more times one more time. Please. Please. *Please.*

BEWARE THE FRIENDLY LOAN ARRANGER

One of the greatest obstacles to financial security and wealth building for African Americans is our lack of access to the same sources of capital that most whites take for granted. It's a simple fact that it's far more difficult for us to get home loans, car loans, personal loans or business loans. Racism plays a part in this, without a doubt, but so does economics. Many of the major banks have abandoned black neighborhoods and the inner city altogether because so many working men and women have moved to the suburbs. The return of middle-class African Americans to their old city neighborhoods in Chicago, Cleveland, Detroit and other cities may help reverse this damaging trend, but for now, it is something we have to deal with.

We all have stories of going into a bank or some other financial institution and being treated like we were there to rob the place. Earl Graves is one of the leading African American entrepreneurs in the country, yet he wasn't allowed to cash a personal check at his neighborhood bank because he did not have enough identification with him. Earl, who sits on the corporate boards of both Chrysler and American Airlines, has done millions of dollars in business with that institution. He demanded an apology, and got one from the bank president. Most of us don't have that kind of clout.

Because of our problems in getting access to financing, and our traditionally poor savings habits, African Americans are frequently targeted by what some consumer groups and economists call "poverty predators." These are aggressive home-mortgage lenders, car financiers, rent-to-own companies and other businesses that are part of a "fringe banking system." These fast-loan, fast-buck operators prey on people who cannot get loans at more established financial institutions, whether because of racism, poor credit history or simple lack of understanding on how to go about applying for a loan. The huge increase in credit-card delinquencies and personal bankruptcies has created an enormous market for "subprime" loans, which are loans made to people who cannot get money elsewhere. Subprime mortgage lending is a $125 billion industry. In 1997, 15 percent of home-equity loans were made by subprime lenders, according to a Federal Trade Commission (FTC) report. They also accounted for 8 percent of new-car financing and 14 percent of used-car loans, according to a dealer survey by J D Power and Associates.

In the old days, the people who offered such high-interest loans were known as "loan sharks." Today, they are employees of publicly traded companies that are sometimes owned by larger, more respected financial institutions. Whatever they are, I want you to avoid them like an oncoming freight train. They may talk nice. They may seem like the answer to your prayers. But they are not your friends and they are not in business to help you build wealth. They are in business to rob you blind, according to many consumer advocates.

Some subprime mortgage lenders will even offer you a home-equity loan based not on your ability to pay, but on the equity you have in your house. The monthly payments can eat up your entire paycheck, which means you may fall behind in your mortgage payments, which means you can lose your house. And guess who gets it? That's right, the subprime mortgage lender. It's all perfectly legal, but the National Association of Consumer Advocates calls it "equity theft."

You may think you would never fall into the traps set by these companies, but let me ask you this: Have you ever been tempted to respond to one of those mailings offering to loan you "immediate cash" for home repairs? Mary and Wilton Burton, an elderly couple from suburban Boston, did. They needed to repair holes in the roof of the home they have owned for more than twenty-five years, so they answered the flyer sent to their home by a "consumer finance" company. They received a $2,000 cash loan for the repairs—but the loan origination fee was $3,800. It increased their mortgage payment by hundreds of dollars, to $708. Their fixed monthly income was only $850. According to *Consumer Reports,* the consumer finance company didn't even ask the Burtons what their income was. When the bills began arriving, the couple couldn't pay them.

I cringe whenever I think about what happened next. After learning that the Burtons didn't have the money to pay their mortgage, a loan officer with the consumer finance company visited them and signed them up for a new loan, which charged a 5 percent origination fee and increased their debt to $83,000!

Fortunately, the Burtons had a financial consultant for a nephew. He stepped in and prevented the finance company from foreclosing on their home, but for nearly two years, the Burtons thought they were going to lose their only asset: the roof over their heads. These poor folks had to file for bankruptcy to protect the home that they'd been able to purchase only after saving up for forty years. The finance company is now under investigation by the Justice department and the FTC. Don't let that happen to you!

DRIVING TO FINANCIAL RUIN
WITH A BAD CAR LOAN

Some of the most common, and worst, financial mistakes are made in car purchases. When it comes to buying wheels, too often we don't use our heads. Car loans are a huge burden. Unlike home-mortgage loans, the interest is not tax deductible, and while in most areas of the country your home holds or increases in value over the years, your car begins losing value as soon as you drive it out of the dealership. That new car smell may be the most expensive fragrance you'll ever crave. With new car prices now reaching into the tens of thousands of dollars even for basic American models, obtaining a loan is a necessity for most working-class people. I advise all of my clients in that category to seriously consider buying a low-mileage used economy vehicle rather than a new car, particularly if they can find one that is only two or three years old.

Often, though, the heart and the ego rule in car purchases. While visions of cruising along in that shiny convertible or that powerful luxury car dance in our heads, the car loan salesperson can be picking your pocket.

DON'T GET FLEECED WITH A LEASE

As the cost of a new car has soared into the five-figure range, car dealers have tried to entice buyers with the lower monthly payments offered by leases. The lure is that with a lease you can put less money down, make simple monthly payments and get a more expensive car. They make it so easy. They even let you lease another new car once your current lease expires, or buy the one you were leasing.

The smooth pitch works. In 1997, one third of all new cars that moved off dealers' lots were leased. But, increasingly, consumer advocates are warning that leasing a car can be far more expensive than buying one outright. The Florida Attorney General's office has identified more than thirty ways that consumers can be shafted by car dealers. Chances are you'll never see what hit you, because car leases have become so complicated that it takes a double degree in economics and law to figure one out. In 1998, the Federal Reserve Board, which regulates the nation's banking and credit industry, began requiring auto dealers to divulge basic information on lease contracts, but it can still be tough to follow exactly what you're paying. If you have been tempted to lease, remember a few things. First of all, you can only lease a "new" car, so you're paying for that smell again. Secondly, in most leases, you're paying a high interest rate. In some states, you pay the sales tax twice if you buy the car at the end of the lease. Car leases are baffling, even for financial experts, and that means there are even more ways the buyer can be tricked into paying more. Generally, leasing a car only makes sense if you use it exclusively for business so you can write off your expenses.

Few people can live without cars and few people can afford to pay for one in cash, so a lot of predators are lying in wait. One of the worst scams to come around in a long, long time is the growing practice of car-title lending or car-title pawning, according to consumer protection groups. The companies offering these "deals" charge extraordinarily high premiums, and if you don't make the monthly payments, they can legally repossess your vehicle. In some states, they charge up to 25 percent a month interest, or 300 percent a year, compared to a standard new-car loan that would run you less than 9 percent a year.

Melonie Stewardson, of Crescent Beach, FL, is a single mother of three working two jobs. She contracted for a $480 loan just to get license plates and insurance for her Ford Probe. The loan carried an unbelievable annual rate of 264 percent, with monthly payments of $105, according to *Consumer Reports*. She had to pay a late fee of $100 one month, and the lender *still* repossessed the car—and demanded $900 for its return. When she couldn't come up with the money, the lender sold the Probe to a used-car lot owned by a company employee. Stewardson will probably never be able to get her car back. She either walks, hitches a ride or takes her son's bicycle to work.

Let that be a warning to us all. There are some legitimate companies out there who cater to high-risk customers, but you should always, always be very careful when dealing with them, as well as with the neighborhood bank. Don't ever take out a car loan without knowing what your interest rate and monthly payments are going to be. Compare them to other rates offered in your area. You can do that by calling banks and asking for their rates on auto loans.

If you have to borrow money to pay for your car and you already own your home, the best bet is a home-equity loan. These allow you to borrow against the equity (the difference between what your home is currently worth and what you owe on it) of your house. A home-equity loan is a bit like a credit card that you can pay back either in full or in part. Interest rates for home-equity loans are usually lower than credit cards and most car loans. One of the big benefits is that the interest on home-equity loans is generally tax deductible, so you not only pay a lower rate but you pay less in taxes, too. There is risk, however. You can't sell your home until you pay off home-equity-loan debt, so you should be conscientious in paying this loan off.

THE RENT-TO-OWN TRAP

Cherese Lindsey of Brooklyn Park, MN, fell behind on her payments to a rent-to-own store where she'd gotten her couch and love seat because she couldn't afford to purchase them at a regular store. She knew she was in danger of losing her furniture, but she had no idea that the store's collectors would kick in a door to her house and take not only the couch and love seat but also her television set, her VCR and her microwave oven, reported *Consumer Reports.*

This business is a very profitable one, for those who own the 7,500 rent-to-own stores in this country. For consumers, who spend $4 billion annually in those stores, renting to own can be a quicksand trap. For those hardworking folks who can't afford to pay cash, renting to own may sound like a great deal at first. But many of these stores price their goods at two times to five times the standard retail price. A *Consumer Reports* magazine investigation found that a $140 microwave oven was priced at $360 in a rent-to-own store. The U.S. Public Interest Research Group conducted a seventeen-state survey and estimated that the average annual percentage rate charged by rent-to-own stores was 100 percent, with some charging 275 percent. You can get a personal bank loan or home-equity loan to purchase furnishings for less than 10 percent.

WHAT TO DO IF YOU HAVE BAD DEBT

Debt may be more of a plague upon African Americans than racism in this day and age. It is certainly the greatest obstacle to building wealth.

Here are fifteen early warning signs of debt distress as identified by Debtors Anonymous, which is modeled on Alcoholics Anonymous:

1. Your debts are affecting your home life.
2. Your debts are distracting you from your work.
3. Your reputation is suffering because of debts.
4. Your self-image has gone down.
5. You've given false information to obtain credit.
6. You've made unrealistic promises to creditors.
7. You've become careless about the welfare of your family.
8. You fear that your employer, family or friends will learn the extent of your total indebtedness.
9. The prospect of borrowing more money gives you a feeling of relief.
10. Debt concerns keep you from sleeping well.
11. The pressure of debt has caused you to consider drinking.
12. You've borrowed money without giving adequate consideration to the rate of interest you are required to pay.
13. You expect a negative response when going through a credit investigation.
14. You developed a strict regimen for paying off debt, but then broke it.
15. You justify debt by saying when you catch a break, you'll eliminate it.

If debt is holding you back and weighing you down, you need to deal with it just as you would deal with an illness. I've heard many horror stories from clients who have panicked because of bad credit or problems getting loans. Believe me, the answer does not lie in some storefront "credit repair" operation. Many of those places are predators in disguise.

The only way to truly repair your bad credit is to begin paying off your bills or to declare bankruptcy. For professional help, look to the Debtors Anonymous chapter in your region or to the nonprofit National Foundation for Consumer Credit (NFCC) (1-800-388-2227), which has more than 1,200 counseling locations throughout the United States. For little or no fee, they can help you set up and follow a debt management plan that calls for only one monthly payment handled by NFCC. To qualify for their plan, you must have enough income to meet basic expenses and you must pay approximately 2 to 3 percent on the balance of unsecured debts.

You should keep in mind that the NFCC and its member organizations draw their income primarily from fees that creditors (the people you owe) pay them—commissions on the money they get from you. It's also a fact that restructuring your credit-card payment plan may adversely affect your credit record.

To build wealth, you first have to earn more than you spend, and debt is the primary obstacle to accomplishing that. I have become an expert in helping my clients find ways to cut debts *and* expenses so that they will have money to put into investments. In the next chapter, we'll examine ways for finding your "hidden assets."

Financial Planning 101 **4**

In their best-selling book, *The Millionaire Next Door* (Longsheet Press), researchers Thomas J. Stanley and William D. Danko describe their vision of the millionaires in this country; who they are and how they made their money. Here are the seven common denominators *they* identified among those wealth builders:

1. They live well below their means.
2. They allocate their time, energy and money efficiently.
3. They believe that financial independence is more important than displaying wealth.
4. Their parents did not provide economic outpatient care.
5. Their adult children are economically self-sufficient.
6. They are proficient in targeting market opportunities.
7. They chose the right occupation.

In general, Stanley and Danko found that most millionaires are budget-minded, hardworking, self-employed people who run businesses like trailer parks, paving and construction companies and other non-glamorous enterprises. *Their* average millionaire is a self-employed male who lives in a house that cost $278,000. He is married and his wife does not work outside the home. They have three children and a three-year-old car.

In my opinion, their book is fascinating as a look at the *white* millionaires next door. I would like to profile for you *The Black Millionaire*

Next Door. My research is based on my experiences with African American clients, friends and family around the country, and those next door too. The *black* millionaire next door is typically a woman who is widowed or divorced. She has two children and a net worth of a million or two. She has a lot of equity in her home, a very good corporate or government job and she has been in the same position for ten or fifteen years. She drives a three-year-old car, probably a Mercedes or Lexus, and dresses well. She has credit cards to the finest stores. If she is married, her husband is a professional. She belongs to social clubs and church congregations rather than country clubs. She doesn't buy stock except through her company's retirement plan, and she worries about paying for her children's educations. She does save money, but too often, she doesn't go for a high rate of return. She is more likely to invest in real estate or CDs than stocks and bonds.

I strongly believe that there would be more African American millionaires next door if we spent less of our money on symbols of affluence and more of it on building true wealth. (By way of full disclosure: I own a BMW, but it is several years old.) I understand the tendency toward status symbols rather than wealth building in the black community, but I also believe we must overcome that drive to prove our worthiness so that we can build true and lasting economic power.

The fact is that many people black and white earn far more than a million dollars over their lifetimes. If you work for forty years, from ages 25 to 65, and earn an average of just $30,000 a year, you will have earned a total of $1.2 million. If you average $60,000 a year, you'll earn $2.4 million. Even averaging $20,000 a year over forty years gives you $800,000 in lifetime earnings. A fortune will pass through your hands, but how much will stick? Again, it isn't what you earn, it's what you keep.

SETTING GOALS, COMPOUNDING YOUR EARNINGS

To take control of your financial future, you must first set clearly defined investing goals and develop a plan to go after them. You have to know where you want to go before you can determine the route. It is impossible to make important investment decisions if you don't have these goals to guide you. It also won't work to throw all of your dreams in a pot and say, "Those are my goals, now I have to start saving for them." As I've shown you already in this chapter, each goal has its own unique attributes.

The basic investment goals for most people are:

1. Purchasing a house.
2. Paying for children's educations.
3. Building a retirement nest egg.

I've provided separate chapters on each of those primary goals, but I'm sure you have other, smaller goals, such as saving for a car or a vacation, or that new washer-dryer. I've found it works best to write down your most important goals and then develop an investment plan for each of them. Do it as soon as you have identified a worthy goal. Don't put it off. Procrastination is the biggest killer of dreams in our community. Remember, tomorrow never comes, but the bills do.

The most important step to building wealth is getting started. Nothing happens until *you* take action. Don't worry if you can't do everything at once. Few people can. But you will be amazed at how positive things begin to happen when you begin moving toward your goals. I'm often struck by the fact that when you set goals and go after them, an energy is created. Other people are attracted to those who are actively chasing a dream. They want to see you make it because it means their dreams are attainable too. But you have to invest in that dream; you have to spend time, energy and effort to reap the rewards.

DISTINGUISH BETWEEN YOUR
WANTS AND YOUR NEEDS

Children often claim that they "need" a new toy, candy or bicycle. As adults, we must distinguish between what we need and what we want. Your investment goals must be based on need, not desire. You don't need a $40,000 car or a $200,000 vacation home. You do need basic transportation, a place to live and security in your retirement years. Even as adults, we often delude ourselves that what we want is necessary, but to set goals, you have to focus on what is truly vital for your survival. You'll find that postponing your wants so that you can realize your needs becomes easier as you move toward your goals and see that they are within your grasp. By the way, learning to set aside your wants and first take care of your needs is called *maturity*. It is possible to be mature and enjoy life to the fullest. In fact, it's easier to enjoy life when the bills are paid and your future is secure.

Often the people who come to me are those who have just taken a hard look at their goals and realized that they are way off track. In one recent week, two new clients came to me for that reason. The first was Doris, a lady in her late fifties preparing for her retirement in a few years. An educator for three decades, she did not participate in a retirement plan in her youth, and now she is trying to catch up in a hurry.

A few years ago, Doris did begin putting money into a 403(b) tax-sheltered variable annuity, but she quickly realized that it wasn't going to grow fast enough to provide for a comfortable retirement. She then started investing in a mutual fund as well, but it's not growing quickly enough for her either. Doris is a conservative investor by nature, but her lack of savings and her approaching retirement has forced her to consider more aggressive investments. It isn't a comfortable position for her because she worries about the daily ups and downs of the stock market and its impact on her savings.

Doris is not unusual. She is in a predicament because she did not set her investment goals earlier, nor did she develop a plan to attain them. It isn't easy playing catch-up, especially so late in the game. That is why it is so important to set investment goals when you're in your twenties instead of your thirties or forties. Once you've put your goals on paper, decide which are the most important. Because of the great gift of compounded interest, you should begin investing toward each goal as soon as possible. However, you might want to put the most money toward those goals that you want to accomplish first because there is less time to work with.

I would suggest, however, that you immediately begin taking full advantage of any tax-deferred retirement accounts available to you. If you are still in your twenties or thirties, that may not seem like a priority now, but it should be. The sooner you get in, the more benefits you will derive. You cannot save for a house down payment or for your child's education in a retirement plan because of the tax penalties for early withdrawal. Although recent changes do allow this under certain circumstances, and you can borrow against many retirement plans, in general, however, you should do your best to leave your retirement savings alone so that the money works for you over the long term.

It isn't enough simply to identify goals and prioritize them. You must also set specific time frames for accomplishing each goal, decide what sacrifices you are willing to make to achieve that goal and develop a specific plan that includes keeping that goal in mind every day. The people who get what they want out of life are not smarter than you. They are not luckier than you. They are simply people who set goals and go after them with a "no matter what" determination and drive.

Following is a Goal Planning Sheet that you can use to set your own goals:

My Personal Goal Planner

My investment goal is:

_____

_____

_____

I want to achieve this goal by _____ (the year)

I will need $ _____ to achieve this goal on time.

A. Annual inflation rate anticipated _____%

B. Annual investment growth rate anticipated _____%

C. Subtract A from B to get growth rate adjusted for inflation _____%

Present amount available to invest $_____

Future cost of goal adjusted for inflation $_____

Additional capital required $_____

Additional lump sum required $_____

Monthly savings required $_____

BE PREPARED FOR EMERGENCIES

Before you begin building wealth toward your specific goals, I urge you to first set up an investment plan for one goal that may not have occurred to you: an emergency fund. Many of my clients have been forced to rack up high-interest credit-card debt or, even worse, dip into their retirement accounts to pay for emergency medical care, funerals or car or home repairs. It worries me when this happens because it not only cuts into their retirement savings, it also costs them dearly because of the penalties for early withdrawal.

To save you from this burden, I strongly suggest that you make it a priority to build up three to six months of living expenses in an emergency fund. You should do this in an account that is easily accessible, probably a high-yield money market account. Remember, this is not a "mad money" fund. It is for emergencies only. No trips to St. Thomas. No nights out on the town. Most wealth builders did not start out with huge incomes, but they were blessed with discipline and patience. You will enjoy the vacations and nights on the town much more when you know that your financial future is secure.

DETERMINE YOUR RISK TOLERANCE

After you've set your goals, you need to develop an investment plan for achieving those goals. The first step in doing that is to determine your risk tolerance. Remember your old investment foe, *inflation?* To stay ahead of inflation, you generally must invest your money in things that have higher risk than bank savings accounts. It's a fact that the investments that give you the highest rate of return, or profit, are usually those that carry the highest risk. Low-risk, low-return investments include your bank savings account, CDs, government bonds, U.S. Treasury bills, money market funds, fixed annuities and the equity in your house.

Next up on the risk scale you'll find blue-chip stocks, which are usually those of established, brand-name companies like Microsoft and Coca-Cola, whose shares are widely held by investors; and high-grade corporate and municipal bonds, utility common stocks, mutual funds, Ginnie Maes and Fannie Maes. (I will define these terms later.)

One more notch up the risk scale are speculative investments such as common stocks, real estate, lower-quality corporate and municipal bonds, real estate partnerships, over-the-counter stocks and penny stocks. And finally, the riskiest investments of all: commodities, tax shelters, precious metals, oil and gas partnerships and equipment leasing partnerships.

Throughout this book, I'll be offering you investment options based on the amount of risk you are willing to accept. Even though stocks, bonds and mutual funds in general have increased in value over the long term, some investments experience more ups and downs (volatility) than others. The more volatile they are, the more risk.

If the value of an investment rises and falls like a yo-yo, it is judged to be riskier than one that climbs slowly, even if the yo-yo asset outperforms less volatile assets over the long term. This is because history has shown that the more volatile returns have a greater chance of losing value. On the other hand, if you take the long view as an investor, stocks are almost guaranteed to outperform anything else over a span of ten years or more; so if you fret too much about short-term risk, you may lose out over the long run.

THE RISK METER

When I am trying to determine the risk tolerance of a new client, I have the person take a little "Risk Meter" quiz. You might find it helpful too. The first thing to consider is that your investment may or may not outpace the rate of inflation. Secondly, you need to assess your tolerance for market risk. Generally investors who choose investments with lower inflation risk have a better chance of outpacing inflation, but those willing to accept higher market risk (with more market fluctuation likely) can generally expect higher rewards. Every individual has his or her own level of risk tolerance. When clients call me and tell me they can't sleep because they are worried about their investments, I tell them to sell off their investments until they can rest comfortably. That's one very simple way of determining your risk tolerance. Here's another: Get a pen and paper and take this test to determine your investment comfort level. Remember to be honest in your responses. There are no right or wrong answers.

The Risk Meter

QUESTION 1: Imagine that you are thinking about buying a home. Your inclination when weighing your options on financing the home is to:

A: Go for a monthly payment that fits your current budget even if it involves putting down a larger down payment.

B: Put down a small down payment that fits into your current budget but leaves some money invested.

C: Stretch to fit the mortgage payment into your budget, confident that your income will increase.

D: Go for the biggest mortgage you can possibly afford, and borrow the down payment.

QUESTION 2: Ten percent of your savings are in a mutual fund with high market risk. It climbs steadily six months, then falls 30 percent in one month. Your response would be to:

A: Sell it as quickly as possible.

B: Sell half of it.

C: Hang in there.

D: Buy more shares.

QUESTION 3: Just after your first child is born, you set aside $15,000 to buy the kid a new car as soon as he or she reaches age 18. When you realize that in eighteen years the car would actually cost $30,387 because of inflation, you decide to:

A: Give up on the idea.

B: Make the kid raise the other half by getting a job.

C: Double the amount you put aside.

D: Invest the $15,000 in a mutual fund, hoping that it will double over the long term even though you know it could possibly drop in value or increase less than the desired amount

_____

QUESTION 4: When do you expect to retire?

A: Less than five years

B: Five years to ten years

C: Eleven years to twenty years

D: Twenty-one years or more

Risk Meter Scorecard

Total your points from the risk quiz according to the key below. Your score will indicate the type of investor you are in terms of risk. For each answer, give yourself the point equal to the letter it represents:

A=1, B=2, C=3, D=4
Total Risk Meter Score

- If you scored between 12 and 16 you are an Aggressive diversified investor willing to accept significant market risk to gain maximum investment growth.
- If you scored between 8 and 12 you are a Moderate investor who generally seeks returns that may or may not outpace inflation.
- If you scored between 4 and 12 you are a Conservative investor who seeks to avoid market risk even if investments may not keep pace with inflation.

WATCHING THE CLOCK

As a stockbroker, I know I cannot help anyone invest if they don't have specific goals. So, I am certain that you won't be able to put together your own investment plan without determining what your goals are, and what your comfort zone is as far as risk. How much risk you are willing to take as an investor depends a great deal on the *time factors* involved. If you have a lot of time to invest and build wealth toward a goal, then you should have a greater risk tolerance. If you have only a few years, then your risk tolerance should be less because the closer you get to your investment goal, the more you want to protect what you already have.

For example, if your goal is to save $20,000 for a house down payment within three years, I would advise you not to invest in high-risk mutual funds, even though they provide the opportunity for high returns. Why? Because while the stock market has historically climbed upward over time, three years is simply not enough time for it to correct itself adequately if it should decline. I wouldn't want my client to risk the $10,000 already saved for the house payment over such a short time span. If that same client was looking ten years down the road, then I might feel more comfortable with a higher-risk mutual fund.

That is why it is so important for you to know exactly what your investment goals are, so that you, or your advisor, can determine what risk levels are appropriate. "I want to be rich and retire when I'm thirty-five" doesn't cut it as a specific goal. That's a dream, and it's a fine one, but it is not a goal. Here are examples of some specific goals that can help you determine your risk level and plan an investment strategy:

- "I want to have at least $150,000 saved by the time my eight-year-old daughter reaches college age." (This person has a moderate risk tolerance.)

- "I want to have $30,000 for a house down payment in five years." (Lower risk tolerance.)
- "I want to have $250,000 in savings when I retire in thirty years." (Higher risk tolerance.)

In the case of someone saving for an eight-year-old daughter's college education, I would recommend a moderate-risk mutual fund, probably one that goes for "aggressive growth," because the time frame is moderate. Over that length of time, they can handle some risk because stocks have traditionally gone up in the long run.

In the case of the person saving for a house down payment in five years, I would recommend a lower-risk growth and income mutual fund because of the limited time span. These funds contain a wide range of stocks designed to give steady returns with limited risk.

Finally, the person who is looking at retirement in thirty years should be relatively comfortable in a higher-risk mutual fund, such as a "sector" fund that concentrates on a specific but promising area such as health care stocks, drug company stocks or Internet stocks. Those high-risk investments hold the promise of high returns, particularly if you are willing to hold them long-term.

Every time you make an investment, you are betting that the rewards will be greater than the risk. In general, the riskier the investment, the greater the opportunity for rewards; otherwise, you wouldn't be willing to accept the risk—not if you know what you're doing, anyway.

FINDING THE RIGHT BALANCE

If you jump on a stock, bond or mutual fund that you don't know much about, or one that doesn't offer a return worth the risk, then you have weighed the scales too heavily on the side of Risk. On the other hand, if you invest too cautiously by keeping your money in low-risk passbook savings accounts or in stocks, bonds or mutual funds that offer a low return, your investments will never get off the ground and you won't be able to reach your Goal.

Nearly seven out of ten investors are so afraid of risk that they keep their savings in low-return CD and Treasury notes, according to a survey by The Gallup Organization and the Employee Benefit Research Institute. They may sleep better because they think their investments are safe, but one day they'll wake up and realize they're a lot poorer than they would have been if they had been willing to accept a little more risk in exchange for higher rewards. People who are unwilling to take some risk are forgetting that other factors can weigh in and tilt the balance for them. The biggest spoiler for the overly conservative investor is inflation. If your investment is making less than the rate of inflation, then you are losing ground.

Let's say you purchase a "no-risk" ten-year, $10,000 Treasury note that pays 6.9 percent. You'll earn a guaranteed $690 a year on that $10,000 note. But if you are planning to use the interest income to meet your living expenses, you will probably lose ground. If you are in the 28 percent tax bracket (as a married couple with a taxable income of $39,000 a year filing jointly would be), you would get to keep just $497. Then, when inflation jumps on the scale, things really get thrown out of whack. If inflation runs 4 percent, by the end of that ten-year period, you'd need $735 to buy what $497 would have bought you on the day you purchased the note. At that rate, you would have lost money on your investment.

Now, let's take a look at some basic investment principles that will help guide you toward wise wealth-building strategies, so that the next time someone goes looking for that millionaire next door, they'll see a lot more people who look like you and me.

One of the investment professionals I deal with regularly is a guy who knows as much about taking it to the hoop as he does about taking it to the bank. M. L. Carr is now an executive vice president with Putnam Investors in Boston. But he is much more well-known in that city and around the country as a former NBA player, coach and general manager for the Boston Celtics. M.L. was a great athlete, and he is also a wise man. His wisdom comes from his depth of experience in the world. He is famous and wealthy today, but none of it came easily. "Early in my career, I was cut from three teams. I worked as a prison guard for a while and sold cars too. I didn't start making big money until later in my playing career, so I knew that there was no guarantee that the money would always be there," M.L. told me. "My goal was always to keep building my nest egg for the day when I'd no longer have a big paycheck. As a veteran player, then as a coach and a general manager, I often told younger guys that even a birdbrain builds a nest because he knows that eventually winter is coming."

I have a number of professional athletes among my clients. I also look after the investments of a large group of black professionals who each make more than $100,000 a year. Many of these affluent people grew up comfortably because their parents were professionals or money-smart themselves. But those who come from the middle class or backgrounds of relative poverty often remark to me that one of the most difficult lessons they have had to learn upon becoming successful is that having money does not guarantee wealth.

M.L. says that he often saw athletes make the same mistake. "The traditional mentality has been that once a player starts getting his paychecks, he buys cars, maybe a home for his parents, and then puts the money in a bank so he knows where it is. There wasn't much of an effort to understand the value of investing for the long term, but that has changed some in more recent times as a lot of the older guys have tried to warn their younger teammates about mistakes they've made or that they've seen other players make."

There are many sad cases of famous athletes, musicians, actors and others who have suddenly been showered with money only to lose it all because they have not handled it wisely or because they have trusted the wrong people. That is why it is so important to begin building wealth, however slowly, as soon as you start earning money. More than any racial community in this country, African Americans at all levels of society are on a earnings roll. Now we need to get on a roll in building lasting wealth.

Thanks to a booming economy in the late 1990's, the poverty rate for African Americans hit 26.5 percent in 1998, the lowest level since the government began collecting data in 1959. That's wonderful news. It means that more low-income blacks are leaving the welfare rolls and finding jobs. The most recent census figures show that the median income in households headed by blacks rose 15.5 percent between 1993 and 1997, while for whites it was only 6.5 percent. The black middle class is also growing at a faster rate than ever before, and so are the ranks of professional African Americans in the most affluent classes. We shop in Nordstrom as well as Wal-Mart. We drive Mercedes and Land Rovers too. But a comfortable lifestyle and a good-paying job are only the first steps to building wealth.

"Blacks should be buying stocks, bonds and mutual funds instead of overpriced homes, BMWs and fancy clothes. . . . Frankly, it's time for our community to have faith and embrace sound and sensible investment strategies that will help us accumulate and build real wealth," according to Michelle Singletary, columnist for *The Washington Post*.

After all, if you die, you can't pass your job on to your children. It is not a transferable asset. It won't buy you anything lasting. It can't be used to start a business or finance a community project. Neither can that nice car, or the fine clothes in the closet. Real wealth can do those things and more, and to acquire real wealth, you have to continuously make more than you spend. Investing in stocks, bonds and mutual funds is a time-proven way to do that. When you invest in the stock market, you take advantage of three basic investment tools that are your gifts from the money gods: time, compound interest and rate of return.

TIME CAN BE YOUR BEST FRIEND OR YOUR WORST ENEMY

Investing is a method of putting what you have into something that will make it worth even more. It's a way of making one plus one equal three. You get more because an investment takes advantage of factors that add value. Life gives us two gifts: opportunity and time. When it comes to building wealth, time really is a great gift. The more time you have, the greater the opportunities to build on what you have. Even if you have never saved a dollar in the past, there is still time to begin building wealth if you invest wisely. This is especially true if you put time together with two other factors, *rate of return* and *consistency*.

Let's take a simple example. Suppose your parents had deposited $1,000 on the day you were born. We'll assume a modest 6 percent rate of return. If you left the account untouched until you turned sixty-five that $1,000 would have become $44,000—without you ever having added another penny. Unfortunately, most people don't have parents with that kind of financial foresight. But time can still work on your side.

It can also work against you, of course. A one-dollar bill is worth less today than it was ten years ago because of inflation. You can't buy as much with that dollar today as you could then. Time and inflation have diminished its value. But if you had used that dollar to purchase something that would increase in value over time, you would have been investing wisely. Let's say that ten years ago you used that dollar to purchase one share of stock in a small start-up technology company that today is an industry leader with stock valued at $80 a share. In that case, you would have used time to your advantage.

One of the biggest mistakes people make in their finances is assuming that they don't have enough money to begin saving and investing. Don't get locked into that mind-set. Remember that time and compound interest can work in your favor. Almost everyone with an income can find some way to save. Even $10 or $25 a week can grow into a sizeable amount over time. You don't have to put aside $500 a month to build wealth. It's true that the more you put away the better, but there is nothing wrong with starting small and gradually increasing your weekly or monthly savings as your wages increase. When you are young, you can save small amounts and still end up with thousands of dollars. If you wait until you are older to begin saving, you have to put much more into the savings and investment plan because you don't have as much time to work with.

So, time can either be your best asset-builder, or it can be a pain in the asset. If you are young, start investing for the future now. If you have children, you need to think about putting money aside so that time can work for them. The most important thing is not how much you invest, but that you begin to invest as early in your life as possible and that you keep investing consistently.

COMPOUNDING YOUR WEALTH

I gave you a brief explanation of the wonders of compound interest in Chapter Two, but it might be beneficial to give you a bit more before we get deeper into the basics of building wealth. Remember the parents who deposited $1,000 at 6 percent interest when their child was born? At that rate, the annual interest would be $60. When you multiply $60 by sixty-five years, it comes to only $3,900. Then how did the child have $44,000 to withdraw at age 65? *Compound interest.*

Here is how it works: The first year of the deposit, the 6 percent interest added $60 to the $1,000 investment, making it $1,060. In the second year, the interest was calculated on $1,060, so the interest amount credited was $63.60, bringing the total in the account to $1,123. As the account grew each year after that, the interest payment was calculated on the total in the account, which included the past interest payments.

Compounding the interest is how the $1,000 grew to $44,000. With that sort of power, it is often amazing how fast a few hundred dollars can grow into thousands, tens of thousands and even hundreds of thousands. Money market funds and CDs pay in the range of 5 percent, while the average historical rate of return for the U.S. stock market is 10 percent. It is possible to earn 20 percent or more by investing wisely in stocks, bonds or mutual funds.

Even if you are earning a relatively low rate of return, it is possible to double and triple your money over time. At 7.1 percent, you double your money in ten years. That is how true wealth is built. If you have the discipline to save and the willpower to let the factors of time and compound interest work for you, then your savings will grow into lasting wealth.

DON'T UNDER-RATE THE RATE OF RETURN

"Rate of return" is another name for the interest rate you earn on your savings. When you are looking for a mortgage for your house, you want to negotiate for a low interest rate, but when you are investing your money, you want the highest rate of return possible. The difference of a few percentage points can have a significant impact on your rate of return, particularly over an extended period. Many people don't realize the dramatic effect of a higher rate of return. It makes sense to think that if you could earn a 10 percent rate of return instead of 5 percent, your money would double. But that isn't the way it works. You have to factor in the power of compound interest. The 5 percent difference adds up to much more over time, and can mean thousands of dollars to you and your family.

Let's go back to the parents who deposited $1,000 at 6 percent interest for their child. If that money had earned only 3 percent more all those years—or 9 percent—the child would have had $226,000 more in the bank upon reaching age 65. Had that $1,000 earned 12 percent interest all those years, the lucky kid would have had more than $1 million more.

Now you can see why the rate of return, or interest rate, you get is so important. Your main objective in saving is to accumulate as much cash as possible. You can reach the same objective in one of two ways: save more money and accept a lower rate of return, or save less and get a higher rate of return. It only makes sense to put less of your own money into the investment plan by getting a higher rate of return, and that is why high-return stocks, bonds and mutual funds are generally more appealing to investors than lower-return passbook savings accounts, CDs or savings bonds.

THE FORMULA FOR BUILDING WEALTH

When you combine the three essential elements of time, compound interest and rate of return, you have almost all that you need for building wealth. The other crucial elements are a goal and the discipline to stay focused on that goal. Far too many black folks view wealth as the accumulation of nice things instead of the accumulation of real assets. They feel that if they have a nice home, a good car, nice clothes and some cash in the pocket, they've got wealth. African Americans aren't the only ones who fall into this trap, of course, but we are particularly susceptible to it because for a long, long time, we were denied access to any kind of wealth at all. It's understandable that people who grew up with very little would yearn for nicer things and buy them when they first get the opportunity. It may be good for the self-image, but spending your money on material things can be a real handicap to building true and lasting wealth.

Conspicuous consumption will eat up the money that could one day give you substantial wealth. I've shown you many ways to cut back on spending, but you can also preserve more of what you earn by protecting as much as possible from those two money-eaters, taxes and inflation.

THE WEALTH DESTROYERS: TAXES + INFLATION

Even if your investments earned a high rate of return in a given year, you can't truly claim any profits until you figure in your tax rate and the impact of inflation on your earnings. Uncle Sam always gets his share. Often, investors forget to figure in the tax, and that can come back and bite you where it hurts the most—in the bank account.

You can calculate your after-tax return by first determining the percentage of return that you earned. Take that percentage number as a whole number (not as a percentage) and multiply it by the tax rate. If you earned a 10 percent return and you are taxed at 33 percent, the amount of tax you would pay is 0.10 multiplied by 0.33, or 3.3 percent. Next, subtract the 3.3 percent from the 10.0 percent. You have 6.7 percent, which is your after-tax return, or how much you really earned.

When considering how to invest your money, you should always keep in mind the tax implications because that impacts your true earnings. In general, you should try to put your money in as many tax-free or tax-deferred investments as legally possible. Don't get me wrong. I love paying taxes because when you owe taxes, it means you made money. The more taxes I pay, the more money I have made. I want to make this country prosperous by paying taxes because I know I will prosper with it. On the other hand, there is no sense in paying more taxes than you are required to pay. That means taking full advantage of the legal methods of investing that allow you to defer paying taxes on income, or those that allow you to avoid paying taxes all together. As I take you through various forms of investing, I will show you the tax advantages and disadvantages of each.

INFLATIONARY PRESSURE

While I advise my clients to play fairly and legally when it comes to their investments and taxes, I also tell them that they are free to figure out any way they can to beat inflation, which is the second major impediment to building wealth. Inflation can work for you, and it can work against you. It is working for you when you buy a house for $100,000 and then, five years later, sell it for $175,000 because the market has become inflated. It works against you when you take that $175,000 and try to buy a bigger house in the same neighborhood. Inflation also works against you by eating into your savings.

If your mutual fund provides a nice 15 percent after-tax return but inflation rises at 10 percent, then you are only 5 percent ahead. One of your goals as an investor, then, is to always stay ahead of inflation. It doesn't do any good to simply hold on to what you already have during times of inflation. Putting your money in a savings account that pays 2 percent interest in a time of 3 percent inflation means you are losing one percent of your savings every year. I don't think that's what you want to do. To at least maintain your purchasing power, your savings must keep pace, or better yet, stay well ahead of inflation.

You can track inflation by checking the Consumer Price Index (CPI), which the federal government reports on every month. You can find the CPI in the business or financial section of your newspaper, or on line at the Bureau of Labor Statistics home page (http://stats.bls.gov/news.release/cpi.toc.htm).

ASSET ALLOCATION

Another enemy of investors is market volatility. The 1990s have proven to be a highly volatile period for investors. After the longest bull run in market history, the inevitable correction hit and stocks plummeted; then the market went on a wild roller-coaster ride, sometimes dropping hundreds of points one day only to rise hundreds more a few days or weeks later. A primary weapon against short-term volatility in the stock market is asset allocation. This is an important concept to keep in mind as you read the rest of this book.

When you invest in only one type of security or asset, you're limiting your ability to increase your wealth by putting all of your eggs in one basket. When you diversify your assets, you're investing in a variety of stocks, bonds or mutual funds so that your entire portfolio has a greater chance of increasing in value over time. The time-proven way to do this is by allocating assets—or distributing your money—among different *types* of investments. The theory is that not all stocks, bonds and mutual funds drop in value at the same time. Some may even rise when others fall, so there is wisdom in spreading your money around in a variety of assets rather than in one particular stock, bond or mutual fund.

Nearly 92 percent of a portfolio's performance is due to asset class selection, according to a 1991 study reported in the *Financial Analysts Journal.* The rest of a portfolio's performance depends on your individual selections and the timing of the purchase of assets. It's not as complicated as it may seem. In fact, it may be easier to think of this as the "don't keep all of your eggs in one basket" concept. I will go into more detail on asset allocation and diversification as it applies to specific investment goals in later chapters.

It is important that you allocate all of your investments, even those that you have in retirement plans, savings bonds and IRAs. The overall determining factor in how you allocate your assets is your age. I will provide a few basic ground rules. Remember that these are not set in stone. Everyone's situation is unique. Everyone has his or her own risk tolerance. These are just the basic guidelines that I use when I first consider how to allocate a client's assets for long-term savings. The guidelines vary for specific investment goals; I will cover that in chapters devoted to saving for a home, for college and for retirement. Don't worry if you don't understand all of the descriptions for different types of stocks; we will cover that in later chapters.

FOR THE TWENTY- TO THIRTY-YEAR-OLD INVESTOR

From your twenties to your early thirties, you can afford to be aggressive because you have a lot of time to take advantage of the stock market's general upward climb. That means you can take on more risk than those with a shorter period to let their investments work. You should be willing to accept short-term fluctuations as you pursue long-term maximum growth.

As your investments reach $5,000 to $10,000, you could comfortably invest 70 percent of your assets in growth stocks or mutual funds, 20 percent in growth and income stocks or mutual funds, 5 percent in capital preservation equities like money markets or CDs, or even cash, and 5 percent in income-producing funds.

Now to give you a little broader reference base. I've seen other asset allocation recommendations for people in this age bracket that offer these guidelines.

Investors in their twenties and thirties

10%	large company stocks
25%	midcap stocks
15%	small company stocks
30%	international stocks

15%   intermediate-term corporate
bonds

5%   convertible or high-yield bonds

This recommendation, which comes from the folks at *money* magazine, advises young investors to put no less than 80 percent of their money into stock funds. They note, and I agree, that if you feel comfortable putting all of your investments in stocks or mutual funds at this young age, by all means do it. As they note, "You have nothing to lose but a few more years of your working life. You have nothing to gain but an earlier retirement."

This allocation should offer annual returns around 9 percent based on past performance, with the possibility of returns of 25 percent or more; or, the worst case scenario, 7 percent or less.

FOR THE THIRTY- TO FORTY-YEAR-OLD INVESTOR

Men and women in this age bracket usually have started taking on more responsibilities by starting families and buying homes, so the general guideline is to reduce risk somewhat, but not too much because they still have a long way to go, hopefully. I recommend allocating 60 percent of your assets into growth stocks or stock funds, 30 percent into growth and income equities, 10 percent into capital preservation income. *Money's* advisors are a little more conservative. Here is their breakdown:

Investors in their thirties and forties

10%   large company stocks
25%   mid-cap stocks
10%   small-cap stocks

25%   international stocks
20%   intermediate corporate bonds
10%   international bonds

Again, those who may not have children, or plan on only one or two, and do have an affordable mortgage might want to keep even more invested in stocks if they feel comfortable with a bit more risk. Your goal should be to get average annual returns of about 8.75 percent, with the possibility of earning more than twice that in the good years, but, hopefully, not less than 5.75 percent at the worst.

FOR THE FIFTY- TO SIXTY-YEAR-OLD (AND BEYOND) INVESTORS

Now is the time to begin getting more conservative in order to protect your assets from year-to-year fluctuations. For people in this age group, many of whom are looking to retire within five to fifteen years, I advise allocating 30 percent of assets in growth stocks or funds, 30 percent in growth and income equities, and 40 percent in capital preservation income (stocks and bonds).

The greatest risk here is getting too conservative and then outliving your investment savings. People are living longer and living better into their seventies, eighties, and even their nineties, so you can't write off your investments once you hit age 65. You should take the positive approach and keep your money where it will keep on growing.

Money advises that those in their fifties and sixties follow this model:

Investors in their fifties and sixties

20%   large caps
15%   mid-cap stocks

5%   small company stocks

20%   international stocks

40%   municipal bonds or treasury notes

Your goal is to get an average annual return of around 7.5 percent, with the possibility of earning as much as 20 percent a year or as little as 4.5 percent a year.

The concept of asset allocation is among the basic rules of investing. A great many novice investors make mistakes simply because they've never learned some of the more basic rules and guidelines. It's not their fault, they just haven't been exposed to them, just as a young musician may make very basic mistakes until someone takes an interest in teaching her the essentials. To help protect you, here are a few more.

INVESTING IN THE DREAM

Here are some basic guidelines for investing:

1. Max out your tax-deferred retirement plan contribution as soon as you can and stick with it until you retire.

If this book were a song, this would be one of the refrains. I say it so much to my clients and prospective clients, I'm surprised they haven't named me "Max Out" Jesse Brown. Later in the book, I will go in depth on the benefits of 401(k), Keogh, 403(b), SEPs, and other tax-deferred retirement plans. Just keep in mind that before you stash any of your savings or wages in stocks, bonds, mutual funds, annuities, CDs, passbook savings accounts, shoe boxes or sock or underwear drawers, you should first be maxed out on your contributions to your retirement plan.

Money in these plans grows faster than just about anywhere else because it is not taxed; it's allowed to compound unmolested until you retire. Let's say you save $5,000 a year for thirty years and earn 8 percent interest each year, but pay taxes of 28 percent. At the end of the thirty years, you would have $288,585—not bad, not bad. *But*, if you had put that $5,000 into a tax-deferred retirement plan, earned the same 8 percent interest, and *not* been taxed at 28 percent, you would have $611,729 in your bank account. Much, much better, don't you think? If your employer throws in an annual matching fund contribution, which many do, there would be even more awaiting you just as you are ready to retire to the beach, golf course, fishing pond or living room couch.

If your employer doesn't have a plan, you should lobby for one. If you are self-employed and don't have your own tax-deferred SEP or similar plan, you would be wise to establish one. These plans often feature matching contributions from your employer at the most; at the least, they protect your investment savings from high taxes. This amounts to *free money*, which is one of the favorite things known to humankind, at least in the places where I hang out.

2. Keep your investment goals in mind and at least four times a year, check your investments to make sure you are still aligned with those goals.

Things change rapidly in today's global economy. You can't afford to put your money into investments and then leave them unattended. Even supposedly "safe" stocks like Coca-Cola and IBM have taken major hits in recent years. If you are saving long-term for retirement, you can probably ride out volatile periods in the stock market; but if your goals are shorter-term, such as saving for a house or for college, then you have to monitor more closely. Make it a point to study your asset allocations every three months to make sure they are still serving your investment goals.

3. Play it smart by planning and investing for the long term.

The best long-term defense against risk is to have a good long-term offense: an investment plan. The history of the stock market shows that the longer you hold on to your stocks, bonds, mutual funds and Treasury bills, the less volatile they become. Jumping in and out of the market by constantly buying and selling increases the risk levels dramatically and is best left to those professionals who can afford to play the stock market as if it were a dice game. "Market timers" and "day traders"—or those who try to buy at the highest price and sell at the lowest—are playing a gambler's game, and stand to lose in several ways. Each time they sell a stock for a profit, they must pay capital gains taxes. I tell all of my clients that they should invest for the long term but protect themselves by sheltering their money in money market funds or bonds as they get nearer to reaching their goals.

Investors who buy stocks and hold on to them do significantly better than those who try to predict the market's ups and downs and trade their holdings constantly, according to Dalbar Inc., a Boston investment research firm that analyzed ten-year stock-market performance trends for successive years beginning in the first quarter of 1984. Between 1986 and the end of 1995, those who stayed in the market saw their portfolios increase 300 percent in value. Those who tried to outguess the market gained just 96 percent. If your portfolio had a balance of about $18,000 (the average for mutual-fund holders), that difference in performance would have totaled more than $36,000, according to *Consumer Reports*.

4. Don't take a sucker's bet.

Avoid hot tips from amateurs. My friend Wes had just started investing in the stock market when he fell for one of the oldest ploys in the book. A friend of a friend of a friend of a stockbroker told him about a hot "penny stock" in a high-tech company that he could buy cheaply, wait just a short time and sell for a big gain. To his credit, Wes did call the stockbroker, who lived forty miles away. The broker faxed him a lot of promising information about the company, which allegedly was about to corner the market on a new technology. Wes got so excited, he bought $2,500 in shares and then talked his father and his brother into buying another $1,500. Well, the stock shot up in value for a few days, and then did a quick dive, never to rise again.

After several months, Wes called the stockbroker—only to learn that he had left the firm. When he told me about it, I didn't have much sympathy. Wes had fallen for a typical stock scam, and although he had called the stockbroker, he hadn't checked out the broker's reputation. Although I don't know for certain, I suspect that the broker owned a large stake in the company, and spread the word that the stock was going to go up in order to drive up the price so he could sell his own stock at a profit and then get out. Unfortunately, this sort of market manipulation happens a lot. That is why you should never buy stock on a "hot tip" from a friend or even from any stockbroker whom you don't have an established relationship with.

Certainly there have been some low-priced or "penny" stocks that have soared and made a lot of money for investors, but such purchases should be made only when based on solid information from trustworthy sources. I advise most amateur investors to stick with the stocks of well-known and established companies or mutual funds ranked high by Morningstar.

Wes might be able to write off the loss of his $2,500 as a "learning experience" but the fact is that if he had invested that money more wisely, it could have grown into a substantial sum. Instead, it was lost forever. That's a heavy price to pay. Just as you should avoid hot tips like a poke with a hot stick, I'd also advise you to beware of any stock tips or investment opportunities offered to you by a phone telemarketer or in the junk mail. You are just asking for trouble if you respond to those solicitations. Although I'm a professional stockbroker and financial advisor, I believe one of the best ways you can increase your personal awareness and knowledge of investing is to join or start an investment club. I'll offer you information on how to do that in the final chapter.

It is also wise to shy away from any stocks, bonds or mutual funds that you simply don't understand. Multibillionaire Warren Buffett, probably the most successful and famous investor in history, refuses to buy high-tech stocks because he doesn't understand them. Now, some high fliers may contend that Warren is missing the boat with that policy—and he may be—but he is comfortable with more down-to-earth stocks and you should be comfortable with your purchases too. In coming chapters, I'll give you the information you will need to more comfortably make decisions in buying and selling stocks, bonds, annuities and mutual funds. But I still caution you to never rely solely on information relayed to you by nonprofessionals, or professionals who don't have a stake in your success.

5. Select your financial advisors carefully.

The financial planning industry is largely unregulated. While the majority of people in the business are ethical and professional, there have been financial planners who have taken advantage of unsophisticated investors, particularly young people and the elderly. There are more than 500,000 licensed financial advisors in this country, according to *Consumer Reports*. Just 10 percent or so are qualified to give financial advice, meaning they have five years' experience and a clean record working with clients, according to a study by DALBAR Inc. Only about 4,000 are fee-only financial planners, who don't earn commissions from the sale of products they recommend.

You should look for a financial advisor or stockbroker in the same careful way you look for a doctor, a lawyer, a preacher or a plumber. Ask for recommendations from people you know and respect. Don't put your trust in them just because their company has ads on television or a half page in the Yellow Pages. Check out their reputations. Ask for the names of clients. Do your homework.

Many investment professionals working for big companies will try to get you to put your investments into a managed or "wraparound" account, which they may sell as a professionally managed account. Be very careful. These often carry steep management fees, sometimes more than 3 percent per year of assets under management. If the stocks in your account earn 10 percent in a year, then 30 percent of your earnings go to the account manager—and that's *before* the government gets to take its tax bite.

In the chapter on mutual funds, I will tell you about no-load funds, which may be the best choice for nonprofessional investors because they have no sales commissions and are managed by professionals. Keep them in mind, and remember to trust in your common sense and to keep a lot of distance between any financial advisor or stockbroker who promises you big returns or claims an ability to predict the future.

TAKING MEASURE

Before you begin to consider any stock, bond or mutual fund investments, then, you should go through the steps I've covered in this chapter and the previous one. Here is a review before we move on to an explanation of stocks, bonds, annuities and mutual funds.

1. Determine your investment goals (home, college, retirement, etc.) and the amount of time you have to save for each goal.
2. Make sure you understand the difference between the things you want and the things you truly need.
3. Understand your risk tolerance.
4. Know how you want to allocate your assets among stocks, bonds and cash based on risk tolerance, how much you need to meet your goals and how much time you have to build wealth.
5. Decide how you are going to stay informed on your investments, whether by staying on top of market news and your investment per-

formance yourself or with the assistance of a stockbroker or financial advisor.

6. Cross your fingers. A little good luck is almost better than compound interest.

Section II   **Understanding Stocks, Bonds and Mutual Funds**

A race which cannot save its earnings can never rise in the scale of civilization.

—Frederick Douglass

The Basics of Stocks and Bonds 6

Like the Rev. Martin Luther King, Jr., I have a dream. My dream is that African American men and women from all economic levels could have ownership of thriving businesses so that they could share fully in the wealth of this country. I can remember the days when black business districts thrived in areas like Atlanta, Chicago, Miami, Brooklyn and across the country. Before integration, you could go into black neighborhoods all over the United States and find store after store owned by African Americans and run by African Americans. When you purchased goods in these stores, you knew your money was going to go home with African Americans and contribute to the long-term wealth of your community.

We needed integration just as the country needed it. But we lost something too when we integrated. We lost our sense of community and we lost some of our handhold on the American dream. When the doors to white businesses opened to African Americans, we somehow got the impression that the white man's ice was colder. We joined the nation's economy, but often it was to the detriment of our own businesses. It set us back. It made it harder for black men and women to build wealth as business owners.

Today, African Americans are starting businesses and growing them faster than any other racial group. That's a great, great thing. But even now, many blacks simply do not have the money or the skills to start a business, and it's rare for one person to own multiple businesses. The demands are just too great. Investing in the stock market is one way that each and every African American can buy back in. You can reinvest in the dream by purchasing the stocks of great companies. Not all companies issue stock. Those that do are said to be *publicly traded*. Those that don't are known as *privately held* companies. If you hear about a company *going public*, it means that the business is going to offer shares for the first time.

I have many clients who make less than $30,000 a year, and yet they own shares of Coca-Cola, IBM, Microsoft, General Electric, Disney, and many other multibillion-dollar publicly traded businesses. When those companies thrive, my clients do better too. And if those companies begin to move in a direction that my clients don't like, they have a vote and a voice as shareholders. The Rev. Jesse Jackson, Sr., understands the power of investing in the dream. He has called for African Americans to purchase stocks in this nation's biggest companies so that through our stock ownership we can wield greater economic power. Stocks, bonds and annuities offer a way for everyone to invest in the dream.

When you shop at Walgreens, Marshall Fields, Osco, The Gap, Sears or Toys "R" Us, you are supporting businesses and corporations. You are investing in them and taking an active role in the economy. You have a stake in that economy. It determines the quality of your life. If the economy grows stagnant and goes into a recession, the quality of your life can be impacted adversely. I like to think of investing in stocks as taking an even more active role in the economy. Of course, when you make any purchase, whether it's a car, a house or a new hip-hop CD, you should do your research and know exactly what you're getting into. That is especially true with investing in the stock market.

I'd been working on Marvin to invest in the stock market for a long time in order to get more out of his savings. He was too conservative in his savings, putting most of his money in low-return CDs and bank passbook savings accounts. Finally, he seemed to get the message. I ran into him one day and he was excited. "Jesse," he said, "I think you finally got through to me. I want to start investing in a stock."

I was glad that he'd seen the light, but the reference to "a stock" gave me concern. It seemed like maybe the light was a little narrow beam in this case. Sure enough, Marvin had come up with a "sure thing," two words that give most investment advisors the willies.

"I have two teenagers and they are always at McDonald's or wanting to go to McDonald's, so I want to invest in the place where all my money is going anyway," said Marvin. "The place is always packed. They have a system that is working."

McDonald's is not a bad stock. At least it's a start, I thought. "Are you sure you want to put all your money in just one stock?" I asked.

"Oh, I don't want to buy McDonald's stock," said Marvin. "I want to buy stock in the company that provides the hamburgers to fast-food places. That way if one of the restaurants goes down, there will be another going up."

Marvin thought he was on to something. It wasn't a bad idea to invest in the primary source of product for a huge industry; it was just that Marvin wanted to put everything he had in one stock. And that's never a good idea. I tried to explain to him the value of diversification, that if he spread his money out more, he'd lessen the risk.

I advised that it was fine have some money in food stocks, but it's wisest to diversify, so that if one industry gets hit your risk isn't so great. If you own stock in food companies, oil companies, Internet companies, banks and builders, you have greater opportunity for steady growth over the long term.

Marvin didn't hear any of that. He was on a mission. He got on the Internet and found the name of one of the largest processors of frozen hamburger patties in the business. I told him to invest $1,000, not his entire $10,000, but he informed me that I was the broker not the boss. "Have it your way," I told him. And so while I had a pickle, Marvin went for the super deluxe biggest of the big burgers, putting all of his savings into the stock of a company that provided beef patties to hundreds of fast-food franchises. Based mostly on his teenagers' great hunger for Micky D's, he jumped on what he figured was a meaty money train.

Well, Marvin had not counted on his money train being derailed by a tiny little bacteria known as E. coli. This tiny group of cells makes people sick, especially people who have eaten hamburger containing the bacteria—or people who have invested in the companies who make the hamburgers that make people sick.

I'd already read the story in the paper and was waiting for his call when it came. It was Marvin's turn to have a pickle. "Did you see the story?"

"Yes, Marvin," I replied. "Are you ready to sell, or would you rather wait until all of your money disappears?"

The discovery of the E. coli bacteria in the company's hamburger patties resulted in the largest meat recall in the history of the USDA. The plant was temporarily shut down, and during the investigation, it lost its contracts with the fast-food franchises. The stock took a dive and it hasn't been seen since. Neither has a big chunk of Marvin's hard-earned savings.

PUTTING STOCK IN COMMON SENSE

From an early age we hear, "Don't put all of your eggs in one basket," but for many of us, the only way to learn is the hard way. Marvin learned about diversifying his stock investments the hard way. He lost thousands simply because he didn't follow some very basic rules of investing. It is vital that you know these rules and follow them when you invest. It is one sure way to lessen the risk and increase the rewards. An educated investor, or one who invests with a stockbroker, bases his or her investment decisions on a number of specific factors. Not everyone uses the same exact formula, but there are certain basic pieces of information that should be taken into account when buying any stock—if you are investing instead of gambling.

Louis Hureston of Rockville, MD, understands the value of following wise investment practices. He earned $15,000 in just one year trading stocks by tapping into the vast resources offered on the Internet. Using his personal computer and modem, he began trading stocks on the Internet in 1994 after taking a buyout plan from his job as an electrical engineer. "I nearly lost my shirt the first time I traded," he said. But as he learned to use the resources of the Internet to find in-depth information on stocks, his selections began to pay off.

Within just two years he was getting a 50 percent return on his investments by using America Online and Prodigy to tap into investment news groups and company information. He used an on-line discount broker to make purchases and sales and to get additional information on particular stocks. Still, he did his own homework, spending ten hours a week gathering information, tracking stocks and and charting their performance. He would follow companies for weeks before deciding which stock to buy. Intelligence gathering is the most important aspect of home trading, said Hureston.

After learning how to successfully trade online himself, Hureston now uses a trusted broker to whom he has given "complete authority."

"Now I'm a fifty percent return without putting in all that effort," he noted. He advises novice investors to learn as much as they can about the stock market themselves before putting complete faith in a broker. "I was out of college nearly fifteen years before I got to that point where I trusted a broker to make each and every stock pick for me," he said.

BUYING INTO THE DREAM

When you invest in stocks you are really investing in the American and global economies. Total stock returns in this country have averaged 13 percent over the last fifty years. Investing in stocks and mutual funds is an incredible method for creating wealth. It is something you should not be missing.

When you invest in Coca-Cola, IBM, Microsoft, Wal-Mart or General Electric, to name a few of the most widely held stocks, you are buying into a product and brand name known around the world. The stock in these and other top U.S. companies represents far more than a hand of cards in a blackjack game. These companies employ millions. They are responsible to stockholders. They don't leave anything to chance.

It's also true that there is more information available today on these companies, their dealings and their financial health than ever before, thanks largely to the Internet. Sorting through all the information can be daunting for amateur investors and even professionals. But the availability of information on individual stocks and on market trends and news from the financial world has made investing far more of a science and far less of a gamble—if you take the time to educate yourself. Keep in mind, however, that while the Internet has opened up the information super-highway to millions of individual investors, it has also become a thoroughfare for swindlers, con men and pranksters of all sorts. Billions are lost each year in on-line fraud.

It is especially important that you be extremely skeptical of any investment advice or tips offered in Internet chat rooms or E-mail. Anything that sounds too good to be true most likely is exactly that. Be very wary of any tipster who claims you have to act immediately or you will miss the opportunity. Don't be a cyber-sucker. Rely on stock information only from trusted sources and always, always do your own homework. If you are tempted to follow an on-line tip, first call the smartest investor you know and run the idea by her or him. You can also run questionable investment tips by the folks at the National Association of Securities Dealers website (www.investor.nasd.com) and also at www. stockdetective.com.

If you are a novice investor, or even someone who has purchased mutual funds and stocks, I recommend that you read magazines and newspapers devoted to wise investment strategies. There are scores of good magazines aimed at the amateur investor. Their stories are not overly complex and they can give you a good, basic understanding of key investment principles. You should be careful when reading their tips on hot stocks or mutual funds, however, because magazines have long lead times before they reach the newsstand, and in the modern stock market, things change quickly. Don't take what they say as gospel; always check with several sources before making a decision to buy or sell. Some of the best magazines for average investors are *money, SmartMoney, Individual Investor, Worth, Kiplinger's* and *Black Enterprise.* I'd advise subscribing to at least one of these magazines and making it a point to check the others on the newsstand or at your local library. The more good information you have, the smarter you can be about building wealth for you and your family.

INVESTING IN STOCKS

Let's say you wanted to start a business, a hot dog stand, but you didn't have all the money needed to build the stand and stock it with dogs and buns and mustard and ketchup. What might you do to raise the money? While lending to small businesses has improved in recent years, it's entirely possible that you might have to raise the money yourself by offering to sell shares of your business to friends. In exchange for giving you 10 percent of the money you need, you give each friend a share in 10 percent of your business.

When you sell shares in your business you are, in effect, selling *stock* in your company. Instead of getting a loan or issuing bonds, which put you in debt, selling shares is a way to raise money without going into hock. When companies need financing to grow, they issue securities or stocks, which are then sold to investors. If your hot dog stand looks like a sure money-winner because of your granny's secret relish recipe or because you have exclusive rights to the hot dog concession for Wrigley Field, then your friends and neighbors and even some of your sworn enemies might be so eager to buy stock in your company that they will bid the price up.

It's also generally true that as a company's earnings go up, so does the price of its stock. Investors look for companies whose earnings are likely to keep going up over time. How much? If a company is able to earn $1.50 on a stock whose book value is $10, that is a 15 percent return. That's considered a good return these days, especially when compared to what you can get in a bank passbook account or from a CD or Treasury note. With a return like that, investors are likely to keep buying, while sellers hold on for the uphill ride. When that happens, the price of the stock is bid up until it reaches a level that might encourage those who own the stock to take some profits.

All of this takes place within the magical, mystical, money-centered world of the stock market. In this chapter, I'm going to feed you a lot of basic material on how stocks, bonds and the stock market work. If this book were a meal, you would now be staring at the vegetables. This may not be the most fun section, but it's essential if you want to grow into a thoughtful long-term investor. (Don't make me do the "Here comes the airplane, open the hangar" thing, please.)

Stock exchanges were born in the early days of trading for crops and other commodities. European traders gathered at fairs in the Middle Ages, but since cash was hard to come by, they had to come up with a different method for exchanging goods. The traders developed a system of credit based on drafts, notes and bills of exchange.

The stock market in France traces its origins to the thirteenth century when Philip the Fair (I am not making this up) became the first *courratier de change*, or stockbroker. At first these early stockbrokers met at trade fairs, taverns and coffeehouses, but by the nineteenth century stock exchanges were housed in their own buildings. The first stock exchange in the United States was established in Philadelphia in 1791. New York's first stock exchange formed the next year but it wasn't like the one you see on CNBC. Twenty-four merchants and brokers did most of their trading under a shade tree at 68 Wall Street. The New York Stock and Exchange Board was not formally organized until 1817.

TRACKING THE MARKETS

Even if you've never been involved in the stock market, you undoubtedly have heard stock market updates and reports on the radio and television. Investors and other market watchers track how the overall stock market is doing by checking the market yardsticks, or *indices*. The 100-year-old Dow Jones Industrial Average (the Dow) is the most recognizable of these yardsticks. The Dow is an average of 30 bellwether stocks listed on the New York Stock Exchange (NYSE). Among those blue-chip big company stocks are IBM, General Electric, AT&T, Coca-Cola, Disney and McDonald's. Notice that each of these represents a different sector of the economy, such as computers, appliances, telecommunications, soft drinks, entertainment or food. Because these are major companies in diverse sectors, the average of their performance is considered a good measure of how the overall market is faring.

When you hear "The Dow was up ten points today," the inference is that the stock market as a whole was up. That doesn't mean that *every* stock was up ten points, but only that there was an upward trend in these big blue-chip stocks whose performance is generally indicative of the overall market. The performance of the Dow has been generally upward since this index was first used in 1885. Then, it was 86. It surpassed 5,000 in 1995, and in 1999, as I write this, it has soared over the 10,000 mark!

The Dow has two stepsisters (neither of them evil as far as I can tell) that serve as measures of two important stock sectors. The Dow Jones Transportation Index and the Dow Jones Utilities Index are yardsticks for transportation and utility stocks in the United States. Professional investors and firms also follow a benchmark developed by the Standard & Poor's Corporation known as the S&P 500 Index. It tracks the performance of 500 stocks: 425 industrials, 25 railroads and 50 utility companies. Since the beginning of this century, the stocks in the S&P 500 have averaged an annual return of 9 percent. If your stock portfolio had the same record, you would have outperformed corporate bonds, Treasury bills and inflation over that period—one more example of why the stock market offers the best opportunity for building wealth.

The *Wall Street Journal*, which covers the stock market like your hometown newspapers cover events in the community, has reported that since 1926, the odds of losing money in the stock market over one year have been about 30 percent, but over ten years, the risk is just 4 percent. So, if you have long-term investment goals like saving for retirement or college or that dream getaway home in the North Georgia mountains, time is on your side. However, if you have more immediate goals like saving for a new car or a down payment on a home, you face greater risk.

TALKING SHOP ABOUT STOCKS

At its most basic level, the stock market is simply a method for entrepreneurs to finance their businesses by selling shares to speculative investors. The "shares" or "stocks" of the businesses are "secured" or given value because they allow the holder to claim a share of the company's assets or profits. So, if you sell your cousin Alfonso ten shares of stock in your *Something to Relish* hot dog stand company, he should get 10 percent of the profits, or at least ten hot dogs. This is known as *capital appreciation*.

On the other hand, if customers decide to eat soy burgers instead of your hot dogs, Alfonso will have the dubious honor of sharing in the downside, or risk, of running a business. The value of his investment will drop, an occurrence also known as *capital depreciation*.

A share of common stock represents a share in the ownership of a company, which means that as a shareholder, you get one vote for each share you own when it comes time to elect the company's board of directors. In the past board members sometimes were nothing more than a collection of yes-people selected because their kids belonged to the same Scout pack as the CEO's, but more and more board members are professionals who have a lot of clout. They decide policy matters, who runs the day-to-day company and how to spend profits. Board members also have control over decisions on whether their company will pay *dividends* (a portion of the company's income shared with investors that is usually paid four times a year), repurchase stock or pump profits back into developing the business.

If you own *common stock*, you share directly in the success or failure of the business issuing the stock. The value of your investment goes up and down with the value of the company. If you have a *preferred stock*, however, the dividends are fixed so you may get some of your investment back even if the company goes in the tank. It is possible that you may not get any additional rewards even if the company has a banner year. If a company goes bankrupt or otherwise fails, preferred shares are paid first, so they are thought to be a safer investment but they also tend not to gain as much value. Generally, private investors prefer common stock and big investors go with preferred stock.

When you listen to or read about the market news, you will hear and see all sorts of names for stocks. Here are some of the most common terms. Keep in mind that some stocks may fit into several categories. For example, Coca-Cola can be considered a large-cap stock, a blue-chip stock, a defensive stock and an income stock. It is also true that a company stock might jump from one category to another if its circumstances change.

TYPES OF STOCK

Blue Chips
This is an unfortunate name with gambling connotations for a category of stocks that most investors consider to be less of a roll of the dice than nearly all other types. Blue-chip stocks are those of high-quality, well-run and proven companies. These companies are usually leaders in their industry groups and deliver products and services with a high degree of brand recognition. Most investors feel these stocks are a great bet for building wealth over the long term. They are also

often expensive stocks to purchase because so many people want them. In rocky times, you will often hear that "investors flocked to blue chips in a flight to quality," meaning that people bought these high-quality stocks because their companies have solid foundations and will weather down times better than most. Most investors consider IBM, Microsoft, and General Electric to be examples of blue-chip stocks.

Growth stocks

I recommend these stocks particularly to investors with long-term goals and also to high-income investors with taxable portfolios. (By the way, a portfolio comprises your stock holdings or one group of holdings. I read an interview once in which a financial reporter asked singer Willie Nelson about his portfolio. "Never wear one," Willie replied.) Growth companies generally pour their profits back into their businesses rather than paying dividends, which are taxed unless the stock is held in a tax-deferred retirement account of some sort. Currently, the hot growth stocks are the Internet, high-tech and bio-tech companies and drug companies like Cisco Systems and Pfizer.

Many avid investors and investment clubs concentrate on growth stocks with consistent revenue and earnings performance because they have a philosophy of holding stocks for the long term. They believe that if a company continues to increase sales, earnings and dividends, the price will climb over time. They do monitor the company carefully, focusing not so much on the day-to-day price fluctuations of the stock but more on the fundamentals of the company itself.

Growth stocks carry more short-term risk traditionally because they are fairly volatile—their prices can rise and fall with market developments. They are often the first and hardest to fall when investors get nervous. If you don't have long-term goals, you probably don't want to overload your portfolio with growth stocks. But it is certainly wise to have some growth stocks in credible companies because these stocks, particularly the blue-chip growth stocks, deliver consistently high rates of growth in sales and earnings.

There is a subset of this category, known as *speculative growth stocks*. These are generally new or emerging companies with less than five years of history. They have high growth rates, high price-earnings ratios, great expectations and sky-high risk. Owning a few speculative stocks is not a bad idea, depending on your tolerance for risk. Some of the leading stocks of today were once speculative stocks; many investors reaped enormous profits, but you have to do your homework on these stocks because they can appear like comets, burn brilliantly and then fade over the horizon.

Large-cap, mid-cap, small-cap and micro-cap stocks
These terms refer to stocks according to the size of the companies and how many shares of stock they have issued. Large caps generally are those with more than $5 billion in total market capitalization (the amount of stocks or shares issued by the company). Mid-cap companies have $500 million to $5 billion. Small-cap stocks are generally defined as those with between $100 million and $500 million. Micro-cap stocks are generally those with less than $100 million in shares issued.

The late 1990s saw a divergence between the values of large caps and small caps. For most of the decade, investors flocked to the high-flying big caps, but when the market hit a wall and crumpled in August of 1998, investors began looking for relief in small cap stocks, which have been known to take off under similar circumstances. In late 1998, many were predicting that small cap stocks were going to outpace the high-priced larger stocks.

Income stocks

These are usually steady companies with a strong performance history in their industries. Often they are blue chips that pay higher than average dividends. Seasoned investors have a mix of these in their portfolios as a calming influence, particularly if they also have more volatile growth stocks. I recommend income stocks to investors who have low risk tolerance. Retired people like them because they are relatively stable investments that provide regular dividend payments to pay expenses each month. These stocks often remain stable and sometimes even rise in value when the rest of the market hits rough water. Examples of income stocks might include Time Warner, ConAgra and TCI Communications. (Keep in mind that things can change rapidly, so any stocks I mention are intended to serve merely as examples, not recommendations.)

Many income stocks are also considered *defensive stocks*. These are not shares of companies that make bulletproof vests, fighter jets, car alarms or underarm deodorant. These are stocks of companies that make products that are considered essential for everyday living. They are known for holding their value even in down times, so investors tend to "seek refuge" in these stocks in down markets. Utility companies that provide phone service, electricity and gas are viewed as defensive stocks; so are the biggest food companies and drugmakers. Coca-Cola has traditionally been a favorite refuge of investors in times of market volatility, although it has gone through a bit of a rough time recently due to problems in its foreign markets.

Value stocks

This is a category for bargain hunters. Value stocks are usually shares of good companies that have gone through hard times or cyclical downturns and have the promise of bouncing back stronger than ever. They have solid foundations generally, but the environment has been bad. Sometimes this category includes a small company in a hot industry, so it is priced cheaper than its competitors but has the same potential for growth. In the late 1990s, oil company stocks were considered value stocks because their prices were down due to cheap oil, yet there was an expectation that when oil prices increased, so would the value of those fundamentally sound companies such as Exxon and Chevron, Schlumberger and Noble Drilling.

International stocks

In times of high stock prices in the United States bargain hunters often look to international stocks. They can be a good way to reduce risk in your overall portfolio mix with U.S. stocks; however, I don't recommend that amateurs buy foreign stocks unless they plan to do careful research or get assistance from a financial guide with a solid background in global markets. The truth is, most major American companies are involved in overseas markets and many foreign companies are heavily involved in the U.S. economy, so it is really one huge global ball game.

That said, investing in foreign stocks will give you an appreciation for the stability of the U.S. marketplace, as many investors discovered when the Asian markets hit a wall in the late 1990s. Savvy traders can do quite well with international stocks, but staying on top of market developments in Seoul, Tokyo and Caracas is not easy. You can purchase shares in blue-chip European companies such as Daimler-Chrysler, Zurich Insurance, British Aerospace and others that carry considerably less risk than smaller companies in less stable nations.

Cyclical stocks

In contrast with defensive stocks, these stocks tend to thrive in good economic times but lose value when economies falter. Their earnings are closely linked to the general economic environment. They usually reflect the ups and downs of the business cycle. Big ticket durable goods are their fare. Big construction companies, airlines, newspaper and paper companies, chemicals, steel, aluminum and automobile manufacturers tend to be cyclical in nature.

These are not stocks for investors who like to operate on cruise control. Nor are they for the faint of heart. Experienced investors like them when the economy is strong but avoid them in downturns. These stocks are for active traders. If you don't pay attention, you could miss a cyclical downturn and find yourself on the downside of the roller-coaster ride. Growth stocks can be expected to bounce back from a downturn within five years or so, but cyclical stocks often take much longer to stage a recovery.

You don't have to have a PhD in economics to be successful with cyclical stocks but you *do* need to keep a close watch on the Big Picture. Even many investment clubs stay away from cyclical stocks because they are so "high maintenance." It is important with these stocks to understand how they are doing in relation to the overall economy. While car and clothing sales may rise quickly when the economy surges, other companies are considered "later-stage cyclicals," meaning they are slower to rev up. Steel companies and chemical manufacturers fit into that category.

There are opportunities to pick up some great stocks in good companies in this category, but to invest wisely and pick up bargains, you have to understand where a company is in its cycle. If you are able to spot early signs that a business is picking up or slowing down, you have an advantage in this stock category. In fact, I tell clients who are involved in the steel, airline or automotive industries that they have an edge when it comes to investing in cyclical stocks in their businesses because they are in a position to know where business is headed. If the company announces plans to build a new factory or distribution center, chances are it is a good time to invest. If they are announcing layoffs and plant closings—well, you get the picture.

Tech stocks

This is a term you hear a lot these days, so I have given it a priority. It refers to a category of company stock just like *utility stocks* and *transportation stocks* refer to their categories. Tech stocks, though, are particularly hot these days, with many magazine and newspaper articles trumpeting the latest hot tech stocks. Tech stocks are those generally related to the Internet and also to computer makers and their suppliers. Tech stocks are known for their high volatility. They are often new and unproven companies that rise out of nowhere and attract millions and even billions in investment. Some have risen only to fall but many, including Microsoft, amazon.com, America Online, Intel, Netscape and others have become stalwart companies in the global economy.

If you are involved in the Internet, work for a high-tech company or have a deep interest in this cutting-edge industry, I think tech stocks can be a fascinating investment. But be wary of those companies that suddenly appear out of nowhere. Many have failed because their managers are technical wizards without business backgrounds. Investing in this category demands that you do your homework, or that you seek professional advice.

Penny stocks and IPOs

Turn on all of your BS detectors when shopping in this category. Penny stocks usually sell for less than $5 per share, and for that low, low price, you get high, high risk. They are often new companies or companies that have hit rock bottom. If you receive a telephone or mail solicitation to buy a penny stock, do not do it. Buy them based only on professional advice or rock-solid information.

IPO stocks are initial public offerings, which are companies offering publicly traded shares for the first time. Most IPOs have no track record of performance. This is a highly speculative category and if you find yourself tempted to purchase either a penny stock or an IPO based on information from a friend of a friend, or a guy who knows a guy, I have just one word of advice: STOP! You should only buy stocks in this category based on well-founded information.

Certainly, there have been millions earned from IPO stocks in companies that made it big. Microsoft and America Online were once IPOs, but picking the next big winner out of scores of unproven entries is a gambler's game. Of the nearly 3,500 companies that went public from 1993 to 1998, more than half were priced below their initial offering price by the fall of 1998, according to one study. This is a category that you should invest in only if you can afford to lose *all* that you invest. Don't say I didn't warn you. And if my warning isn't enough, here's what a *Fortune* magazine report from November of 1998 had to say regarding "The Ugly Truth About IPOs": "The fact is that the typical IPO of the last decade proved to be at best a mediocre investment—and at worst an outright wealth destroyer."

THE BASICS OF BONDS

When you buy stocks you become a part owner in the companies issuing those stocks, so you have equity in those businesses. When you buy bonds, however, you are actually making a loan to the company issuing the bonds. That is why stocks are known as *equity* securities and bonds are known as *debt* securities.

Bonds pay a fixed amount of interest on a regular basis, which can make them attractive compared to stocks, which carry no guarantees at all. If you buy a five-year, 6.5 percent bond from the Pepsi-Cola Company, then you are actually lending your money for five years at 6.5 percent interest to the folks at Pepsi. You are guaranteed a 6.5 percent rate of return on your money; however, if interest rates increase to 8 percent on new bonds while you are still waiting for yours to mature, then the comparable value of your bond will make it less attractive to buyers. The downside is that bonds do not generally increase in value over time as much as stocks and that, with the exception of U.S. Savings Bonds, they are usually not sold in increments of less than $1,000.

Who buys bonds? Individual investors, banks, money market fund managers—anyone who wants to gain a slightly higher rate of interest but needs to get to the cash in a short time. Investors who have a very low risk tolerance like U.S. Treasury bills, which are considered to be very safe, but again, pay a low rate of interest compared to investments with a bit higher risk. Foreign governments with economic problems often invest in U.S. Treasury bills, which should make you proud to be an American—at least until the next impeachment trial.

Bonds generally pay a bit more interest than federally insured instruments such as CDs because the bond buyer is taking on more risk. Many services (Moody's is probably the largest) help buyers assess the riskiness of any bond issue by rating them. I tend to view bonds as a way of "renting but not owning." I feel they can be an important part of your portfolio if you are interested in owning them, but I don't emphasize bonds much with my own clients because I don't think they pack the same punch as stocks and particular mutual funds.

When clients inquire about bonds, I tell them about the *Rule of 72.* This rule helps investors determine the most important thing they need to know: how much they need to earn on their investments to get the return they will need to meet their goals.

The Rule of 72 is a hypothetical formula based on compounding a fixed rate of return over long periods. However, the returns of most investments fluctuate so that the time it takes for an investment to double or quadruple in value cannot be predicted with certainty. It is a rule of thumb that can help you compute when your money will double at a given interest rate. Its name comes from the fact that at 10 percent interest your money will double every 7.2 years thanks to the power of compounding.

The formula is simple: You divide the annual interest you expect to get into 72. For example, if you get 6 percent on an investment and that rate stays constant, you can determine when your money will double by dividing 72 by 6. In this case, your money will double in 12 years. (I hope you weren't saving for a new car).

You can also compute the interest rate you'll need if you know you will need to double your money in a specific time frame. For example, if you want to buy a Mazda Miata in two years and you need twice the money you have saved now, then you can determine the rate of return you'll need on your investment by dividing 72 by 2 to get 36 percent. If you think you can get that return on your stock portfolio or with mutual funds, please call me. I'd like to hear how you do it. I don't think you can get that rate of return on bonds because they just do not perform as well as stocks and mutual funds.

HOW BONDS WORK

The price of a bond is a function of prevailing interest rates. As interest rates go up, the price of the bond goes down, because that particular bond pays less interest when compared to more current offerings. As rates go down, the price of the bond goes up, because that particular bond pays more interest when compared to current offerings. The price also fluctuates in response to the risk perceived for the debt of the particular organization. For example, if a company is in bankruptcy, the price of that company's bonds will be low because there may be considerable doubt that the company will ever be able to redeem them.

On the redemption date, bonds are usually redeemed at *par*, meaning the company pays back exactly what the bondholders paid. Most bonds also allow the bond issuer to redeem the bonds at any time before the redemption date, usually at par but sometimes at a higher price. This is known as *calling* the bonds and frequently happens when interest rates fall, because the company can sell new bonds at a lower interest rate and pay off the older, more expensive bonds with the proceeds of the new sale. By doing so the company may be able to lower their cost of funds considerably.

TYPES OF BONDS

Corporate bonds

Companies often issue bonds when they need to fund a large project such as a big equipment purchase or a new office building. If the bond issuer gets in financial trouble and declares bankruptcy, its bondholders must be paid off before its stockholders. If the organization defaults on its bond payments, any bondholder can go to bankruptcy court and request that a judge place the company in bankruptcy.

Debenture bonds are those backed by the corporation's general credit. *Asset-backed bonds* are backed by corporate assets. In the United States a, corporate bonds are often issued in units of $1,000 and are sold through brokers. Those that are top-rated are considered nearly free of risk of default. They are fully taxable, unlike tax-free government bonds, but they have a higher yield.

Municipal bonds

City governments and their various departments or agencies often issue bonds to fund the construction of major projects such as schools, sewers or primary streets. These projects require big sums of money, and rather than lend it from a bank, the organization may chose the less expensive path of issuing bonds. In going this route, the company or government body must agree to pay a set rate of interest on the bonds when it redeems them on the agreed-upon redemption date. When municipalities issue bonds, they are usually in units of $5,000. Interest payments are usually payments made every six months.

U.S. Treasury Notes and Bonds

These are issued by the U.S. Treasury Department and other federal agencies for periods from two to ten years (intermediate) and ten to thirty years (long term). They are sold for $1,000 or more through brokers or directly—and commission-free—from the U.S. Federal Reserve Bank. These are considered to be a safer investment than corporate bonds but they have a relatively low rate of return. Treasuries, as they are known also, are not taxable by the issuing state, and some states do not tax bonds of other government bodies.

U.S. Savings Bonds

These can be purchased for as little as $25 and come with a guaranteed rate of return if you hold them for five years. You can buy up to $15,000 in these bonds in one year from banks. Some companies also offer them through payroll deductions. You don't pay taxes on these until you redeem them; if you use them to pay college costs for a child, you may not have to pay any tax at all.

U.S. Treasury Bills or T-Bills

These are relatively expensive but a very popular form of short-term investment because they carry very low risk, although they offer low return. They can be reinvested for up to two years without making a new application. T-bills are sold by brokers in lots of $10,000 for 13, 26 or 52 weeks. The interest paid on them is the difference between the discounted buying price and the amount paid at maturity.

Agency bonds

These are federally supported mortgage-backed bonds sold by "Ginnie Mae," the GNMA primarily, but other federal, state and local agencies can sell them too. They are perhaps the most popular form of bond investment because they can be bought from banks or brokers in lots of $1,000 and up. They carry higher risk but provide a higher return than Treasury bills.

Bearer bonds

These were made illegal in the United States in 1982 and included coupons that were used by the bondholder to receive the interest due on the bond; this is why you will frequently read about the coupon of a bond (meaning the interest rate paid).

Convertible bond

This is a bond that can be converted into stock shares of the company that issues the bond if the bondholder chooses. Investors buy convertibles if they think a company is growing and that there's potential for the stock price to rise. The question is whether that potential is worth the lower interest rate. The conversion price is usually chosen so as to make the conversion interesting only if the stock has a pretty good rise.

There are a few terms that you need to understand to talk about convertible bonds. The *bond value* is an estimate of the price of the bond based on the interest rate paid if there were no conversion option. The *conversion premium* is calculated as price minus parity dividend by parity, where parity is just the price of the shares into which the bond can be converted. The *conversion ratio* specifies how many shares the bond can be converted into. For example, a $1,000 bond with a conversion price of $50 would have a conversion ratio of 20.

Investment grade bonds

This is a term referring to high-quality bonds that have been ranked high in safety by independent ratings services such as Standard & Poor's and Moody's. These ratings services and others measure the financial stability of the company or agency issuing the bonds and then rate them from triple A to D. Bonds rated *Baa* (no sheep jokes) or higher by Moody's or *BBB* or higher by Standard & Poor's are considered to be investment grade. The higher a bond's rating, the lower the interest it is required to pay to attract investors.

Junk bonds

These high-risk bonds carry potentially high returns but also a slight probability of default. They are offered by companies with low ratings, sometimes even no rating at all. Junk bonds got a bad name in the 1980s because some high-profile junk bond traders such as Michael Milken got in hot water with the government. These can be good investments but probably not for the amateur or casual investor with a low or moderate risk tolerance.

Zero coupon bonds

These are deeply discounted bonds sold by companies or government agencies. They don't pay interest; instead, the value of the bond increases to its full value when it matures. So, you could pay $35 for a zero coupon bond that is worth $50 when you cash it in after seven years. The downside is that you have to pay taxes on the interest every year, even though you aren't getting the money, unless you have the bonds in a tax-free retirement account. If interest rates increase during the life of the bond, they really aren't worth the investment.

Shopping for Stocks

7

Joey and Pat Brooks are the sort of hardworking entrepreneurs who revitalize my faith in this country and the people in it. Twenty years ago, Joey started his own moving business with just an old pickup truck in Evanston, a lakefront suburb just north of Chicago, where he grew up. Today Joey's Movers and Messenger Service is a very successful family business with a fleet of bright blue moving vans and more than $1.5 million in annual sales.

As a lifelong entrepreneur, Joey, 38, is a take-charge guy. He is also a concerned husband and father of five who wants to leave a legacy for his family. So, a few years ago, Joey took it upon himself to begin investing in order to build some lasting wealth outside of his business. He is a very busy man and he didn't really have time to study the financial markets or to learn about investment strategies. He just dove in. He'd buy a stock here and there based on tips he'd heard or things he'd read. He bought some bonds too, putting together a hodgepodge of investments.

Then he became interested in initial public stock offerings, in which investors attempt to buy a new stock just as it opens on the market at its initial price, hoping to cash in if it rises quickly in value. Some investors have made killings in the IPO market. But a great many have also seen their investments crash. Joey saw his crash in a ball of flames. Shortly after that, I helped him put together an investment strategy for both himself and his wife and children. Together, we've set up a plan with clearly defined goals and parameters, and a disciplined approach. "All my kids now make regular payments into their mutual funds and they mail the money in themselves," said Joey. "I encourage them to invest, but they have to have a plan. Everyone should have a plan."

Some people get into the stock market for the wrong reasons. They let their emotions or the hope of making a quick buck lure them into investing before they've properly educated themselves. Others don't invest in the stock market at all because they don't understand how the process itself works. After all, it is not quite the same as going to Wal-Mart or Nordstrom to pick up lawn chairs or a cardigan sweater. *I'd like 100 shares of Cisco Systems, please, and do you gift wrap?*

Investing in stocks is not like any other business exchange. It can be intimidating and it often punishes those who get in out of greed or excitement over a hot tip. Before you jump in, you should understand how the stock market works and what traps can await the unwary.

STOCKS FOR SALE

The stock market may sound like a place down the street where you and the neighbors can pick fresh shares in American companies, but it is really a whole chain of markets or exchanges where stocks can be bought and sold. In this country, the places to shop for stocks are the New York Stock Exchange; the American Stock Exchange, which consists of the Chicago, Boston, Philadelphia and San Francisco exchanges; and NASDAQ (pronounced *NAZ*-dack) which is the acronym for the National Association of Securities Dealers Automated Quotation system.

The New York Stock Exchange (NYSE) and the American Stock Exchange (ASE) are listed exchanges, which means that brokerage firms supply them with specialists who handle all trades in a specific stock. The specialists match buyers with sellers in the auction market where they can see who has blocks of stocks to trade. It's sort of a monetary matchmaking system for buyers and sellers of stocks. Think of it as *The Dating Game* meets Monopoly.

The NASDAQ exchange, NASDAQ Small Cap and the OTC Bulletin Board comprise the Over-the-Counter market in which brokerages (stockbrokers like me) act as sales agents for stocks. The brokerages are all linked over a computer network managed by NASDAQ.

Within these marketplaces, stock shares are traded from one person to another. When you hear stocks referred to as *liquid*, it doesn't necessarily mean they are offered by Pepsi-Cola, Coca-Cola or Anheuser-Busch. Stock liquidity means that shares can flow from seller to buyer just as easily as cash can change hands.

You can make money in the stock market by selling stocks for more than you paid or by receiving dividend payments that are your share of profits from the company issuing the stock that you own. Dividend payments vary depending on how well the company has done in a given year. Some don't issue any dividends. Others pay regular dividends and point to it with pride. A company that pays high dividends, above 1.8 percent or so, is generally worth a good look. They don't pay dividends if their business is in trouble, or if they think their stock isn't going to keep growing in value.

Owning a stock is a bit like being a fan of a local high-school team. You want the company issuing the stock to do well because that usually means the value of your stock increases. If you own stock in Pepsi-Cola, for example, you may stop buying Coke just as a show of loyalty. You will probably find yourself cheering every time there's a news story reporting favorably on a Pepsi product, or getting irate when a waitress tells you that the restaurant only serves Coke. One of the things I like about investing in the stock market is that it gives you a greater sense of being an active participant in the economy. That's a good thing, because we *are* the economy. What we buy and sell and own and save has an impact. We should do all that we can to get the full benefit of being part of the world's most dynamic economic system.

African Americans may well want to purchase stocks in companies owned and operated by blacks. At the very least, I'd advise you to *not* purchase the stocks of companies who have shown little inclination to hire and promote African Americans. *Black Enterprise* magazine in recent years has published its *B.E. Black Stock Index,* which is a good guide to the top-performing stocks of companies that are owned by African Americans. Among them are American Shares Hospital Services (AMS); Ault, Inc. (AULT); BET Holdings (BTV); Broadway Financial Corp. (BYFC); Caraco Pharmaceutical Labs (CARA); Carson, Inc. (CIC); Carver Bancorp (CNY); Envirotest Systems (ENR); Granite Broadcasting (GBTVK); Pyrocap International (PYOC) and United American Healthcare (UAH).

I would advise you not to invest in any of these companies from the *B.E. Black Stock Index* unless they meet the standards you've set for your portfolio. If you don't think they meet your specifications, put your money elsewhere, by all means. However, if they compare favorably with other white-owned businesses, I think it would be a wise investment for you, and for the future of African Americans everywhere, to put your money in these black-owned businesses so that they may grow and create more jobs, and more lasting wealth in the community.

PRICING STOCKS

There is no set cost for stocks. They range from so-called "penny stocks" that can sell for under a dollar to stocks that sell for hundreds of dollars. The prices go up and down with the fortunes of the company, the economy and, sometimes it seems, with each shift of the wind. The *price-earnings ratio (P/E)* measures the level of a stock's price relative to (or divided by) company earnings. The overall P/E of U.S. stocks has hovered around 14 for most of the last 100 years, meaning that stock prices per share, on average, are selling at about fourteen times their company's earnings per share.

There is no perfect P/E ratio but the higher the ratio is the more unlikely the price will justify its returns. A P/E ratio of 25, for example, indicates that buyers are willing to pay twenty-five times the stock's current earnings to buy a single share. Stock shoppers who look for bargains generally look for companies whose P/E multiples are below that of the S&P 500. If the stocks in the S&P 500 on average are showing P/Es of 20, then the bargain hunters will look for those stocks with P/E ratios in the range of 16 and lower. But remember, there are stocks with high P/E ratios that can be good buys, particularly if they are in a particularly hot sector.

The serious investor always pays attention to the P/E ratio. It is a reflection of investor confidence in a stock. It's as important to know the P/E ratios when choosing a stock as it is to know the profit margins when buying a business. Many investors compare a stock's P/E ratio to its growth rate. If the two figures are equal or close to equal, the stock is probably trading at a decent price. If the P/E is less than the growth rate, it may be trading at a bargain price.

The P/E ratio is one of the surest measures for checking out the real potential of those too-good-to-be-true stock tips passed on by your brother-in-law's second cousin who knows a guy who plays basketball with a stockbroker's monkey's uncle. If a company's P/E ratio is out of whack with the historical and current averages for the market—say a P/E of 200 when the historic mark is about 14 and the current overall P/E for the market is 20—then you need to check further into the stock and the basis of its appeal.

It is a fact that desirable stocks in growing companies have higher P/Es, but they also carry higher risk. The bigger these balloons get, the louder and more destructive the bang will be. The pressure for these companies to keep getting bigger and bigger and bigger can cause them to self-destruct. Generally, the price of a stock reflects its market value (not necessarily its profitability or intrinsic value), which is how much investors are willing to pay for it. It works like an auction. Let's say there's an old lamp up for bid. It may have cost only a dollar originally, but if a few bidders decide it is an antique, they may bid up the price well above its original value. That's what has happened with many Internet-related stocks. Amazon.com, the pioneering on-line bookstore, has stock shares worth millions and millions even though the company itself has yet to turn a profit. Its value as a stock soared because of its popularity and the company's perceived potential, not its profits. In just three years' time its shares rose from around $7 to $321 at the end of 1998. But it was a roller-coaster ride and more than a few investors took some hard falls along the way. It is also true, however, that many investors made a very good return by getting in early and riding the stock to the top.

MANY FACTORS IMPACT A STOCK'S VALUE

A stock's price is also affected by the financial health of the company, which is measured in terms of its *assets, debts and earning capabilities.* The price can be impacted further by the number of shares issued, the overall economy, the mood of the stock market as a whole, interest rate changes and the investment community's general perception of the company and its stock. Some company stocks such as those of amazon.com are prom queens. Others are outcasts. And it is not at all unusual for today's prom queen to become tomorrow's outcast, which is why anyone investing in stocks should take the time to make regular checks on how their holdings are doing. The *Wall Street Journal, Barron's,* CNBC, CNN, your local newspaper's stock pages, and a wide variety of on-line stock monitoring services offer ample opportunities for checking up on your stocks throughout the day.

The value that *you* place on a stock in your portfolio is measured on its return for you relative to the price you purchased it for and also how much it has paid in dividends. Here is a simple formula for measuring a stock's return over one year:

$$\frac{\text{Current Price} + \text{Dividend}}{\text{Purchase Price} + \text{Commissions or Fees}} - 1 \times 100 = \text{Return}$$

To use the formula, follow this example: Let's say you own 100 shares of a stock that currently trades at $30 a share and pays a dividend of $1.00 per share annually. Your purchase price a year ago was $20 a share and the commission was $100. Here's how you would figure the return.

$$\frac{3000 + 100 = 3100}{2000 + 100 \quad 2100} = 1.47 - 1 \times 100 = 0.47 \text{ (or 47 percent)}$$

If a stock's yield (its dividend divided by its current price) is above that of the S&P 500 value, investors may begin to circle.

CREATING A PRACTICE PORTFOLIO TO PROTECT YOUR ASSETS

Every investor and every investment advisor has favorite theories about picking stocks. Even the most famous of stock pickers, Warren Buffett and Peter Lynch, have unique and distinct styles. I don't claim to be a genius at picking stocks but I do know the fundamentals. Just as a good basketball coach, who may not have been a great player, can teach his team to prepare them for a game, so can I help you with the basics and, hopefully, help you get started.

Picking stocks really is not a hobby or a sport. It can be fun and rewarding, but it is nothing to play at if you're putting your money and your financial future on the line. It takes a great deal of research and analysis—and even then there are no guarantees, not even for professional stockbrokers. In later discussions, I will present to you a lot of information on both mutual funds and investment clubs. I strongly advise you to begin your training in stock selection in those two forums rather than striking out, literally and figuratively, on your own. Novice investors should not put money into individual stocks until they have developed a system for stock selection that they're comfortable with. That said, if you insist on purchasing stocks on your own right away, I suggest that you spend at least six months working with a practice portfolio. How do you do that? Track the performances of your selections for at least six months before you actually start making stock purchases.

I know you may want to jump in right away. I don't blame you— it's exciting—but it can also be very costly. I'd rather you *learned* with play money and *earned* with real money. There are lessons that you have to learn on your own, and there is no sense risking any of your hard-earned money until you reach a point where you have confidence in your stock-picking abilities.

There are many ways to build a practice portfolio. For those who know how to surf the Net, there are a number of on-line services that allow you to track stocks in a personal portfolio without actually spending any money. America Online's personal finance page and Quicken.com are two of the most popular services. For those without access to the Internet, I'd suggest using your local newspaper's stock listings as a re-source. You can keep track of the stocks by keeping a practice portfolio in a notebook. Even after you've done that, I encourage you to put only about 10 percent of your portfolio in pure stocks for the first year or so.

Why? Well, I believe that only a fool tests the water by jumping in with both feet. Beginning investors too often fall prey to the temptations of the marketplace. They fall in love with a product or a company or a particular sector of stock and begin buying with their hearts rather than their minds. How many people buy a car that really doesn't fit their needs just because they become enamored by the flow of its hood, the growl of its exhaust or the supple feel of the Corinthian leather? The same thing happens in buying a stock. I know of an investment club formed by a group of golfing buddies that put a big chunk of its money in Callaway golf stock even though they could see by the stock charts that it was headed south. It was an emotional thing. And it cost them.

The primary reason people make bad investment decisions is not lack of knowledge, but because they're blinded by emotion. I'll make a prediction that at some point early in your experience as an investor in the stock market, you will sell a stock that you bought "for the long term" because it seems to take a dive. Then you will kick yourself later as it climbs back up and exceeds the price you paid for it. I can make that prediction because it happens to every investor sooner or later. We all fall prey to our emotions. To be a successful long-term investor, you have to devise an investment strategy that fits your goals, and then stick with it regardless of the emotional roller-coaster ride caused by market turbulence.

INVESTMENT STYLES

What do you need to know about a stock when making your picks? Mostly, you need to know where to go for information, and then you need to know what information is significant. There are primarily two types of investors:

Technicians

When you hear a stockbroker or individual investor refer to "looking at the technicals," it means that they are trying to predict how a stock will do by using charts and graphs that show how that stock has performed in the past. They look for patterns and buy and sell stocks according to the trends they see. You'll hear them make comments like, "That stock hit a double bottom last week" or "It broke a triple top," which refers to the stock's performance on their charts. They pay less attention, in general, to a stock's book values, dividends and earnings. Also known as "chartists," these analytical stock pickers make their decisions using tools such as the 200-day moving averages, which are the arithmetic averages of the past 200 days of stock closing prices. When stock prices head above the 200-day moving average, the tech-pickers buy. When prices fall below the average, they sell.

Technical traders are known for jumping in and out of stocks frequently; that can get expensive if they're paying a broker each time they buy and sell. Taxes can also be a problem if your portfolio is not in a tax-deferred retirement account or IRA. I don't really recommend technical trading, particularly for novices, because it is *so* technical and because it's almost a full-time job tracking the ups and downs of stocks each day. It can also be hard on the nerves for those with specific investment goals.

Fundamentalists or Value Investors

Unlike technical traders, these investors take a more hands-off, long-term approach. They make their decisions based on a stock's *fundamentals*, or basic performance data, including the company's earnings, the dividends it pays shareholders and book values. As value-seekers (and aren't we all?), they buy stocks in what they perceive to be solid, growing companies, and then they hold on to those stocks for the long term in the belief that the value will increase even though there may be short-term dips. The secret here is to do your research thoroughly so that the companies you pick really are long-term winners.

Dart-throwers

More properly known as *efficient market hypothesizers*, these investors believe that randomly selected stocks have every bit as much chance of doing well as those selected by the experts, pros and gurus. They feel that you might as well select stocks by throwing darts at the stock listings. The *Wall Street Journal* plays along by occasionally running a feature known as the *Investment Dartboard*, which tracks a randomly selected portfolio.

STOCK-PICKING PROS

If you spend any time at all reading, watching or talking about selecting stocks, you will most certainly hear the names of Peter Lynch and

Warren Buffett, two of the most successful stock pickers of all time. Both are one-man industries, and both are billionaires. Neither would ever admit to picking stocks by tossing darts.

Lynch is the guru with the white hair and the golden touch. From 1977 to 1990, he managed the Fidelity Magellan mutual fund, which was the star of that era, outperforming the rest of the market by more than 10 percent. If you had put $1,000 in Lynch's fund in 1977, he'd have turned it into $21,000 over those thirteen years.

Lynch has written a number of books on stock selection methods. Essentially, he believes that the best place to look for stock picks isn't necessarily the *Wall Street Journal, Investors Business Daily* or any of the other standard guides. He favors your local shopping mall. Lynch's theory is based on common sense, but be careful not to oversimplify it. Basically, he says that the average consumer is drawn to companies with good products and service. If you find yourself making repeated trips to Toys "R" Us, Wal-Mart, Barnes & Noble, Safeway grocery stores, or Best Buy, then you might also want to consider investing in those companies for the long term, Lynch says. If you see every kid on the block wearing tennis shoes by Nike, riding bikes by Schwinn, and playing Nintendo, then those too are stocks worth investigating.

Please note that Lynch doesn't say you should rush out and buy stock in these companies without checking out their fundamentals. He strongly advocates that you do your homework, but, in general, he holds that a company's stock value is closely tied to its success in reaching its customers. So those brand-name businesses that are thriving in your communities are worth more serious investigation.

While Lynch looks like a stock market guru, Warren Buffett looks more like your neighborhood grocer. No doubt about it, he can put bread on the table. Buffett is one of the richest men in the world, with an estimated net worth of more than $16 billion depending on how the stock market is doing on any given day. Buffett has made a lot of other people very wealthy too. In Omaha, NE, where he lives and runs the world's most expensive (and closed) mutual fund, Berkshire Hathaway, there are said to be at least thirty families worth more than $100 million—and I'd dare to say nearly all of them thank the Lord for Warren Buffett at least once a day. In fact, in a city of 345,000 residents, it is estimated that there are as many as 15,000 millionaires. Nearly all of them are regular people who entrusted their savings to Omaha's most famous investment professional.

Many invested with Buffett when he was fresh out of business school in the 1950s and early 1960s. He started his small investment partnership to test his theories on the stock market. They have tested very well. Originally, a share in his partnership cost $43. Today a single share in his Berkshire Hathaway fund is worth around than $80,000.

Buffett follows a very sophisticated investment philosophy but it boils down to this: Find good companies that are well-managed, undervalued and recession-proof; then buy their stock and don't sell it until you absolutely have to. He also believes in investing in businesses that he understands, so Buffett has been a rather noticeable no-show in the Internet stock frenzy. Like Lynch, he is drawn to big brand-name companies such as Coca-Cola, Gillette and McDonald's because they have global appeal and long-term growth. He places a high priority on good management and efficient operation too, and he likes companies that generate a lot of cash, which is why he buys himself an insurance company every now and then.

On the surface, this all sounds rather simple. However, you have to keep in mind that Buffett, Lynch and other professional stock pickers do an incredible amount of research before purchasing stock in a company, and they keep a close watch on every aspect of its business once they buy it.

TAKING MEASURE OF A STOCK'S VALUE

The boom in the stock market in the 1990's has triggered an even bigger boom in investment advisory services of all sorts. From on-line brokers to investment newsletters and magazines to Internet chat rooms, the Tower of Babble never babbled like this. Frankly, you could drive yourself crazy unless you tune out most of the financial wizards and focus on one or two reliable and proven sources of information.

One of the best and most popular tools for individual, professional and club investors is *The Value Line Investment Survey,* which can be found at most local libraries and at www.valueline.com on the Internet. I advise all novice investors to use this highly regarded service. "Value Line's ranking system has such an impressive long-term record that even skeptical academics have conceded that it beats the market," reported the *New York Times* in a recent story on finding solid investment advice.

Value Line provides a treasure trove of information in a format that is easy to read and understand. It does most of the heavy lifting for you—providing key information on more than 1,700 publicly traded companies—so you won't get a headache trying to select stocks for your portfolio. Here are the key factors that *Value Line* considers important when analyzing stocks. Whether you use this service or not, these are important factors to understand and weigh when making your selections. Many of them are based on common sense, but some involve complex economic principles. Don't feel badly if you don't understand these terms immediately. As you pay more attention to the stock market and individual stocks, it will slowly start to make sense. It's like learning a new language: The more exposure you have to it, the quicker you pick it up. *Value Line* offers a synopsis of each company, and you can usually get a good grasp of its potential from that. Remember, give yourself time to develop a comfort level by using a practice portfolio to buy and sell without risking any of your hard-earned money.

Industry Rank

The general rule is to go with stocks that rank in the top one third of their industry, preferably in the top twenty.

Timeliness and Safety Ranks

Using a rating scale with 1 being the highest and 5 the lowest, *Value Line* has been ranking the *Timeliness* of stocks since 1965. This is a measure of how individual stocks are expected to grow in the next twelve months. Those stocks ranked 1 are projected to be the best relative price performers in the period. Those ranked 4 or 5 are expected to perform below average. In general, I'd advise that you look for stocks that rank 1 or 2.

Changes in a stock's Timeliness ranking can be caused by new earnings reports, changes in the price movement of the stock relative to the market, a combination of earnings and price factors or shifts in the relative position of other stocks. *Value Line*'s analysts usually have about 100 companies with the top rank for timeliness. It's not a bad idea to pick a dozen or so from that group that appeal to you and then see how they fare in the other categories provided.

The Safety ranking (1 is the safest, 5 is the riskiest) is *Value Line*'s judgment of the risk level of a stock. The rating is derived from the stock's Index of Price Stability relative to the 1,700 other stocks considered, and from the Financial Strength rating of the company. The company considers this ranking, which it has provided since 1966, particularly important in periods of market decline. "If you think the market is headed lower, but prefer to maintain a fully invested position in stocks, concentrate on equities ranked 1 or 2 for Safety. Also, at the same time, try to keep your list ranked as high as possible for Timeliness," *Value Line* urges its subscribers. I agree.

Beta

The *Beta* is a relative measure of the historical sensitivity of a stock's price to overall fluctuations in the market. The Beta is determined by comparing the selected stock's performance in relation to the type of stock, bond or index it should most likely mirror. The person doing the analysis selects the Beta, sometimes called "the benchmark." A Beta of 1 means the stock price is likely to move up and down at the same rate as the market. A Beta of 1.50 indicates that a stock tends to rise or fall 50 percent more than the market. The Beta is generally listed with other measures of performance.

Aggressive investors will be drawn to stocks with a higher Beta, in the range of 1.6 and above, because stocks in this category are likely to move up more quickly in a rising market. However, those same stocks are more likely to take a dive in a downward market. Conservative investors will generally be more comfortable with stocks in the Beta range of 0.90–1.10. Some professional investors place a great deal of importance on a stock's Beta, while others claim it has no validity at all. Philosophy professors dazzle each other with theories on the existence or nonexistence of God. Economists debate whether or not "Beta is dead." I believe Beta has value as a measure, but certainly not the *only* measure of a stock's volatility and risk. I invite you to form your own view on how much emphasis to put on this rating by tracking the performance of your stocks.

Debt

This is a measure of how much a company owes. Generally, you should look for companies that have less than 35 percent of their assets in debt. It's common sense. The less debt a company has, the less chance that the business will go under. Being particularly thorough analysts, the folks at *Value Line* examine a company's total debt, long-term debt, debt due and total debt due in five years. All you have to remember is this: high debt, bad; low debt, good.

Earning Per Share (EPS)

The EPS is determined by dividing a company's profits by the total number of shares issued. *Value Line* has a much more complicated explanation, but that's the bottom line. It lists a stock's EPS for fifteen years prior and projects what it will be for the coming two years. Investors with long-term goals should select companies with a yearly growth rate of 15 percent or higher. This is an EPS typical of growth stocks whose prices are likely to at least double in five years.

Cash Flow and Stock Price

Cash flow is the money a company still has in the safe after paying dividends and other expenses. *Value Line*'s analysts project a range for a stock's price over five years based on cash flow and an estimate of future earnings. It's wise to look for a stock whose price is projected to at least double in five years' time. Having a good cash flow is important because it allows a company to weather the inevitable challenges that all businesses face. A company without much cash flow is probably a poor pick, while one that is cash rich can generally be considered a good bet, if all other fundamentals look solid.

Price-Earnings Ratio (P/E)

I've already explained this to you as one of the most important measures of a stock's potential to grow in your portfolio. In case you were reading with your eyes closed earlier, the P/E ratio is established by dividing the most recent stock price by the last six months of earnings plus earnings estimated for the next six months. This ratio gives you an idea whether a stock's price is on the mark or out of whack. My general rule is to look for a current P/E ratio that is below the company's average P/E ratio for the last five years.

The overall P/E of U.S. stocks has hovered around 14 for most of the last hundred years, meaning that stocks on average, are selling at about fourteen times their company's earnings per share. The P/E ratio that is higher than a stock's ten-year median P/E could indicate that it is overvalued. Beware stocks with especially high P/Es because they are susceptible to sharp declines if future earnings fail to measure up to investors' expectations. If a stock's P/E ratio is lower than the growth rate, it may well be a bargain. Merry Christmas. You should always consider the P/E ratio in relation to a company's growth, which is also measured by the thorough stock watchers at *Value Line.*

Margins

Value Line examines both the *operating margin* and the *net profit margin* of companies issuing common stocks. The operating margin is determined by looking at operating earnings (before deduction of depreciation, depletion, amortization, interest and income tax) as a percentage of sales or revenues. The net profit margin is a reflection of the net income before nonrecurring gains and losses as a percentage of sales or revenue. You can compare these figures for companies you are researching with those of other companies in the same industry. The higher the margin, the better. High margins indicate that the business has strong management and an edge over its competitors.

Percent Earned on Net Worth

This factor is calculated by dividing a company's annual earnings by the shareholders' net worth or how much of the company they own. The higher the percentage the better. A strong company will consistently double this percentage over the years.

Income and Total Return

Some investors look for stocks with a high annual income. Others hunt for stocks whose price will increase in value so they can be sold for more than the price paid. It's probably best for most investors to add those two figures together to get the *total return rate* for a company, and make their judgments based on that figure.

Sales
This is the most common measure of a company's size.

Insider Decisions
Everybody loves being on the inside, and more and more stock-picking services are providing information on what company executives are doing with their own stocks and stock options in their companies. This is a very intriguing area to look at, but you have to be careful. There are many reasons for company insiders to sell stock. The CEO may want to buy a new Mercedes. The CFO may have a daughter about to enter Princeton University. An executive vice president may be trying to unload some stocks before her divorce is finalized. Or it may be that they all think the company is headed for trouble. You can't really draw any solid conclusions unless all of a sudden *everybody* in the company is selling huge blocks of stock. That is definitely a red flag.

On the other hand, there is generally only one good reason for insiders to be *buying* more stock and that is because they believe it's going to go up in price. If a company's executives are stocking up, you might want to consider doing the same.

Target Price Range
This is the projected average annual price range for the next three to five years based on *Value Line*'s earnings and P/E ratio forecasts. The midpoint of the range is its estimate of the average annual price three to five years ahead. The percentage appreciation potential and the estimated annual total return are computed from the projected low and high prices from three to five years ahead.

Technical Rank

Value Line's own ranking of a company's estimated stock price performance relative to the overall market in the next three to six months, based on a complex analysis of the stock's relative price performance during the past fifty-two weeks. *Value Line* urges investors to limit their purchases to stocks with Technical ranks of 1 (highest) or 2 (average). The company emphasizes that it considers the Timeliness rank to be a superior measure for investment decisions.

STEP-BY-STEP STOCK PICKING WITH *VALUE LINE*

When it comes to selecting stocks for your portfolio, *Value Line* suggests following these steps:

1. Read *Value Line*'s summary and opinion of the economy and the stock market, and its current advice on investment strategy contained in the "Selections & Opinion" section.

2. Check its ranking of industries in order of Timeliness in the "Summary & Index" section. Note the top six industries shown to be most timely in the current market.

3. Check the 100 stocks given the highest ranking of 1, and the top 300 stocks ranked 2 in Timeliness by *Value Line*. They appear in both the "Ratings & Reports" section and in the weekly "Summary & Index" section.

4. Pick at least six or more stocks in the listing for the top six industries. Next, pick at least four or more stocks from either those with Safety ranks of 1 or 2 within the top twelve industries, or those that are ranked 1 or 2 for Timeliness or Safety, even if the industry isn't top ranked. (To narrow the list, follow steps five through seven. Keep

in mind that you should diversify the stocks in your portfolio. The recommended number to have in industries and sectors is 10.)

5. Read the industry comments that precede each stock's report to get a handle on the big picture and the long-term growth patterns of earnings and values for stocks in the industries you are interested in.

6. From the stocks selected so far, choose those that also conform to your risk tolerance levels. Rate them according to how they match your tolerance. Remember that a low Safety ranking may be more acceptable when the market is undervalued because riskier stocks are typically depressed in such times. Since they are likely to be more volatile, they are also more likely to rise faster when the market begins to move upward.

7. Finally, look at the stocks that are still on your list and note those that meet your dividend requirements. You can find a stock's dividends for the coming year in the "Summary & Index" section and also on the "Ratings & Reports" pages.

STOCK SLEUTHING

Remember that it's tough to find a stock that meets *every* one of your requirements, so you will have to make some concessions or do some trading off. The final decision may come down simply to which stocks make you feel most comfortable. Picking stocks is difficult, time-consuming detective work. It requires you to be part investigator, part mathematician, part business analyst, part economist and part fortune-teller.

A little old-fashioned luck doesn't hurt either. Often, good luck is nothing more than being ready when opportunity presents itself. To prepare yourself to invest in a company's stock you need to have a good handle on all facets of the company, including its management, profitability, growth, stability, market, competition, dividend payments, potential legal problems and public relations risks, as well as the economic factors that impact it and any developments in legislation or technology that will affect its business.

If you have access to the Internet, I suggest you take a look at the engaging web page of the Stock Detective, Kevin Lichtman, who is an expert at sniffing out "stinky stocks." Often humorous, but also well-researched, his reports can be found on his entertaining website at www.stockdetective.com.

Lichtman, a former stockbroker, has such a knack at finding "pump and dumps" and other stock swindles that the Security and Exchange Commission's (SEC's) investigative unit is suspected of monitoring his website. There is some evidence of this as many of his selected stinky stocks have found themselves targeted by the Feds. He hones in on suspect stocks particularly when he sees that a company seems to be spending more money and effort promoting their stocks than in building business. His theory is that heavy stock promotion and stock fraud often go hand in hand.

THE ANNUAL REPORT OFFERS CLUES YOU CAN USE

Lichtman has a wealth of experience and a great many sophisticated resources to do his stock detecting. As a rookie on the stock beat, you'd be surprised how many good sources are at your disposal too. When checking out a stock, one of your first stops should be the company's annual report. I won't carry this analogy so far to call the annual report "the scene of the crime," but it *is* the place where you will find basic information to help make your case on whether to invest in the company's stock or look for another suspect. You can get annual reports by requesting one from the company itself or by going to its web page on-line. Other good on-line sources for company information include:

- The Annual Reports Library at www.zpub.com/sf/ar;/index.html
- The SEC at www.sec.gov
- Hoover's Online Company Profiles at www.hoovers.com
- Zacks Investment Research at www.zacks.com
- America Online's Personal Finance Page at www.aol.com
- Companysleuth.com

Keep in mind that slick-looking annual reports are designed to impress stockholders and potential investors, so you have to be wary when reading the sections written by top executives. Some will try to gloss over problems and emphasize the good news. Savvy stock detectives look for the real skinny in the footnotes stuffed at the very back of most reports. I give them close study whenever I am considering a stock. The National Association of Investment Clubs also encourages its member clubs to go to the fine print for getting the inside dish on how a company really does business, earns profits and handles its cash. Buried there, under the innocent-sounding heading "Contingencies," you'll find reports on lawsuits or environmental issues that might do serious damage to a company's bottom line.

Like an archaeologist studying hieroglyphics, you can learn to translate the footnotes. One thing that you can pick up early on is to note just how much information is contained there. Companies that really care about informing their shareholders will offer thorough explanations of the material that is footnoted. Those that would rather keep you in the dark don't do much explaining at all. If an annual report includes a definition of financial terms and a long-term history of sales, profits and assets, you can conclude that they are trying to keep you informed. A key consideration when reviewing the stock of any company is how much the business owes, what interest rate they are paying on loans and when the loans are due. You can find this information in the annual report footnotes as well.

It's not easy to decipher the footnotes, but if you make a practice of reading them regularly and comparing one company's footnotes to another's, you'll slowly begin to get a picture of what's contained in them, and what to look for. If you have questions, feel free to call the company's investor relations office or its public relations office. It's their job to answer your queries. If they refuse to answer legitimate questions asked in a courteous manner, then you should consider ditching their stock.

WARNING SIGNS AND TRADING TRICKS

Like a father sending a son or daughter off to college, I feel there are a few things I should tell you about the ways of the world before you run into them and wonder why I hadn't warned you. Some of these are common practices of which you should simply be aware. Some are practices you might want to consider yourself. And others are things I wouldn't advise you to try or get involved in until you have gained a lot of experience in stock trading—and maybe not even then.

The Buyback Maneuver

Chances are, you'll be reading or hearing about this frequently when you become tuned in to stock market news. It's likely you'll hear or see a report that says something like this: "The Tribune Company announced that it will buy back ten million of its shares in the next quarter."

What does that mean? Well, it doesn't mean that your shares in Tribune Co. will go shooting skyward, nor does it mean they will collapse. In general, if a company can't keep its stock price up with a solid profit report, it will often announce a buyback as a show of confidence in its own business. It's a common way to try and boost stock prices and get investors interested in a stock again. Companies also do it if they think their stocks are at a bargain price—or if they want investors to think that. Big blue-chip companies, such as IBM, often have a buyback program in place permanently. In truth, companies often announce huge buybacks and then in reality buy back very few shares, or even none at all.

When you hear that a company is buying back shares, it is not a sign that you should rush in and buy some too, even though that's what they would like you to do. It's far better that you ask why the company isn't investing its cash into making their business better. After all, companies sell stock to raise cash to improve their businesses, don't they? Buyback programs generally don't do a company a whole lot of good because the company has to use its own cash or borrow to buy its own stock. Most of the time, it would be far better to use that money to increase profits.

Making more with your money with a steady drip, drip, drip

Many companies send out dividends each quarter to investors. While retirees often count on those payments to pay their living expenses, I advise most clients to reinvest those dividend checks so that they can be used to purchase more stock in the company. This can be done automatically through a Dividend Reinvestment Plan, known as a DRP or "Drip." Commissions on Drips are usually small or nothing at all, but there may be a service charge. You owe tax on the reinvested amount unless it is in a tax-deferred account. You will get a separate tax statement from your broker at the end of the year for any Drip plan investments.

Buying on margin

This is the practice of borrowing money from your broker to finance a portion of a stock purchase. You buy on margin by depositing cash or securities in a margin account to fund your share of the purchase. You can then borrow up to half the cost of any transaction. Note that you do pay interest on the borrowed money but usually at less than the going market rate. A margin account allows you to leverage a relatively small amount of your own money to make a big purchase. The hope is that if the stock does well, your return will be greater.

Confused? Here's an example: You decide to purchase $1,000 worth of Jesse Brown, Inc., (a major growth stock due to my heavy investment in pizza) with $500 out of your personal piggy bank and $500 from your broker B.A. Usury. Since you are a lucky sort of person, the stock increases in value to $1,500. You then sell it and repay the loan plus interest and you still have a $500 profit to stick back in ol' piggy. If you hadn't had the margin loan from your broker, you would've had to either come up with the cash yourself or bought less of the stock and made less profit.

Reality check: It is also possible that once you'd gotten the margin loan and bought JBI, it might have *decreased* in value, in which case you would have had to repay the loan *and* eat the loss. Brokers protect themselves in these situations by making you deposit extra funds in your margin account when the value of your stocks fall below a certain point. If you can't meet that *margin call*, then you have to sell the stocks and take the loss.

As you might have already guessed, I think buying on margin to be one of those tricks best left to the sophisticated investor with deep pockets.

Selling short

Most of the time, investors buy a stock expecting that the price will go up. The technical term for this is "buying long." There are stock market players who "short" stocks by having a broker "borrow" shares of a stock that they think is going to drop in price. You have to have a margin account to sell short. When the price drops, you cover your short position by then buying the stocks for less than you sold them. Next, you give the stocks to your broker, replacing the ones you borrowed and taking your profits.

Let's say you sell short 100 shares of JBI at $10 a share and then buy 100 shares a week later for $7. You make $3 profit per share, minus the interest you owe your broker plus commission costs. As in buying on margin, there is the upside/downside risk that the price of the stock may go up instead of down, leaving you to cover your short position by paying more for the stock than you sold it for. This gives you the opportunity to then lose even more than you had invested. I don't recommend this for novices, veterans or even those people who knocked my books out of my hands in junior high school.

Are you feeling a little overwhelmed? Investigating stocks can be complicated; there are so many different factors and theories. If the formulas and math involved in trading stocks cause you to have disturbing flashbacks to high school algebra, you may not be ready to pick your own stocks. That's okay. My advice is to start slowly anyway, and one way to do that is to seek professional investment advice through a financial advisor or stock brokerage firm.

SELECTING A STOCKBROKER

Most private investors do their trading through a brokerage firm, dealing with the brokers either in person, on the phone or over the Internet. To make a trade, you call your broker, who, for a fee, makes the deal. Within a few minutes, the stockbroker makes the trade via a computer link to his firm's representatives on the floor of the stock exchange where the stock you want is traded. In some ways it's like a typical flea market. The broker representing the buyer says that his client is willing to pay the "ask price" of the stock. The broker representing the seller says he is willing to put out a "bid price." The difference between the bid and ask prices is called "the spread," and the buyer has to pay that difference, which is then split between the two brokers as their profit for putting the transaction together.

The birth of low-fee Internet brokerage firms has revolutionized the brokerage business. On-line brokers generally charge much less, as little as $7 a trade in some cases. The more traditional brokerage firms argue that their higher fees are justified by the higher level of service they provide, the keener interest they take in your portfolio and the higher quality of their research departments. Those lines have become muddied even more as many of the larger brokerage firms have started their own online divisions.

Can a stockbroker be relied on to provide well-analyzed, well-thought-out information and recommendations? It depends on the broker. On the one hand, a stockbroker is in business to sell you stock. Would you trust a used-car dealer to carefully analyze the available cars and sell you the best car for the best price? Then why would you trust a broker to do the same? The *New York Times* recently reported that roughly two thirds of all brokerage recommendations are "buys." The message is that brokers are in business to sell you stocks, not to talk you out of making bad investments. That doesn't mean you shouldn't use a broker or that you should never trust their advice, but it does mean you should pick your broker as carefully as you choose your clergyman—or at least as carefully as you pick a plumber.

The major question today is whether an individual investor should make his or her own stock picks and trade with a discount brokerage firm, or pay a higher fee for the services of a full-service brokerage firm who will help pick stocks and mutual funds according to the investor's specifications, buy them for him or her, monitor them and advise when to sell or increase the holdings.

I wish there was an easy answer, but it's really up to you and what you feel comfortable doing. Naturally, as a stockbroker I have something of a bias for the full-service brokerage firm, but if you have the time, energy and enthusiasm for making your own stock selections, I say more power to you. But please don't start putting a lot of your money in stocks until you've developed your skills to a high degree.

Let's take a look at the kinds of firms that are out there and what services they offer. Let me note right off, however, that the Internet is changing the way this business works on almost a day-to-day basis. Basically, most brokerages take a commission every time you make a trade. They add their fee onto the money you pay when they buy and they subtract their fee from your payout when you sell. The fee rate varies depending on the size of the trade. It's usually 1 percent with a large trade, 2 percent with something midsize (in the $2,000 to $5,000 range) and more on smaller trades. Discount and deep discount brokers sometimes charge a flat fee for every trade, or they use a sliding scale.

A broker's commissions cut into your profits, so you have to balance out the benefits with the costs and make certain you're getting your money's worth. The money that they take from your investments is money that is not working for you, so the broker had better be providing at least basic services. All brokers are responsible for taking your orders and executing them (by doing the trading for you), keeping track of your investments and handling the stock certificates for you and keeping records showing how many shares you own, when a stock splits and what dividends you have coming, if any.

Here are some of the basic types of brokers now operating. Keep in mind that the bigger brokerage companies have extended their reach to cross into several categories in order to hang on to their market share.

Wire-house firms

This term is a bit outdated these days, but it's still the common way to describe the major national and international brokerages that you've probably seen advertised on television and in magazines. Salomon Smith Barney, A. G. Edwards, Merrill Lynch, Morgan Stanley Dean Witter, Paine Webber and Edward D. Jones are a few of the more well-known wire-house firms today. That name, by the way, traces back to the old days when only the big brokerages were "wired" for high-speed trading. These big full-service brokerage firms will do it all for you—for a fee, of course. Along with investment advice and stock trading, they do financial planning for retirement, college, home purchases, funerals, you name it. They will set up tax-deferred retirement plans or IRA accounts. If you have money, believe me, they've got a plan for it.

A good full-service broker pays attention to the stocks you're interested in and lets you know if there is any possibility of a hostile takeover or merger with another company or any other activity that could impact your decision to buy, hold or sell.

Regional firms

These are also full-service firms, but they don't have offices all over the map. Some may grow into national firms given the chance and enough money, but for the time being, their names are often longer than their list of offices. Some top-quality regional firms include Legg Mason Wood Walker, based in Baltimore, MD, and Wheat First Butcher Singer, based in Richmond, VA.

Independent brokers

These are individual brokers who have a securities license (at least, they'd better) but mostly prefer to work outside a large brokerage firm. You'll find them listed in the Yellow Pages, or they'll find you by calling and asking if you'd like to invest through them. Don't invest with anyone you haven't checked out thoroughly. Independent brokers know that they have to win your trust, so they will probably want to meet you in person, buy you lunch and work to build confidence. However, beware that some "independents" *are* affiliated with larger brokerage firms and use those firms' research divisions to help them make decisions. Be careful here. There are many fine and trustworthy independent brokers, but don't give your money to anyone without thoroughly checking them out.

Discount brokers

These lower-cost, lower-service brokerage have been sprouting up on the Internet like dandelions in the spring. They can save you money but along with having to fret about commissions, access and accuracy in their trades, you also have to worry about computer crashes. Look for an on-line brokerage that maintains its own equipment as a sign that they will be on top of any problems.

Charles Schwab, which has tripled its client base on-line in the last two years, is one of the pioneering discount brokers, but Charlie has been getting plenty of competition on the Internet from competitors like Fidelity Investments and Waterhouse Securities. While you might pay $100 or so to buy 100 shares of stock from a full-service broker, you'll pay less than half that for a discount broker. Their service is generally limited to buying and selling what you tell them to buy and sell. Normally they don't offer you advice on selecting stocks but they may provide market information and financial services such as money market accounts. Chances are low that they will take you out to lunch or invite you to play a round of golf. There isn't much human contact with discount brokers.

Deep-discount brokers

You'll be lucky to make contact with anything other than a computer or a website with these low-low-low cost and no-frills brokerage firms: Nearly all of them operate on-line. Some are divisions of larger, full-service brokerages. Unlike a full-service broker, these brokers won't do anything to save you from making mistakes. They are also notorious for poor customer service because they often get more customers than they can handle. Deep discounters charge as little as $7.95 for any and all trades or $5 for a trade of 1,000 shares or more. Among the deep discounters are E*trade at www.etrade.com; eSchwab at www.eschwab.com; and Datek at www.datek.com. There are many more, and the cast changes regularly. You can see a list of active on-line brokers at www.smallcapinvestor.com.

The deeper the discount, the fewer the services offered. Novice investors need those support services, so I recommend the discount and deep-discount brokers only to sophisticated investors. Anyone just starting out should look to a full-service broker to help steer clear of the inevitable rookie mistakes.

ON-LINE INVESTING

On-line stock purchases now account for more than 190,000 trades a day; the volume doubled between 1997 and 1998. Investors are obviously big on on-line trading. It's fast, it's easy and it's generally cheaper than making a call to your friendly stockbroker. But as with any fast-starting, rapidly growing business, there are problems to watch out for and trouble spots to navigate around.

Buying and selling stocks on the Internet is generally regarded as safe as long as the brokerage you are dealing with is a bona fide member of the National Association of Securities Dealers. Their members carry insurance up to $10.5 million. I don't know about you, but that would cover what I keep in my trading account. Most on-line brokerages have automated E-mail and telephone confirmation systems that are considered highly reliable. Deposits and withdrawals are generally made from accounts kept with the broker or by check. Nearly all on-line brokerages use encryption software to guard the privacy of trades.

Trading on-line is relatively easy if you are familiar with on-line shopping at all: Go to the page or website of your broker, go to the registration form, print it out, fill it out and send it in along with a check. Some firms will allow you to fill the form out on-line and submit it via E-mail. Once your form has been received, the broker will give you an account number and a password. When you're ready to trade, you fill out another on-line form and submit it by clicking the buy or sell options.

No doubt about it, on-line trading is convenient, relatively safe and popular. There are a few things to keep in mind, however.

- Be certain that you type in the correct symbol. A slight miss on the keyboard can get you 100 shares of Key Production Company (KP) rather than Coca-Cola (KO). Almost no on-line brokerage will order a stock without your confirmation of your purchase order, and most send you a confirmation form that lists the full name of the company. Make sure you make sure, because getting your orders canceled can be a very big hassle once they are made.
- Don't take anything for granted. One of the most common complaints of on-line traders is that their brokers are slow to execute trades. A slow response can be expensive if a stock is moving up quickly in price. If your on-line broker is slow to make a trade, let them know that you are unhappy; if it seems to be a continual problem, you may want to change brokers. You should also monitor how quickly your broker sends out confirmation notices and how accurate the broker is in keeping records of your account. Keep your own records so you can double-check their math.
- Read the fine print, and make certain that you know when your broker stops taking orders. Many on-line brokerages cut off trading at certain times during the day. If you execute a trade in these periods, it may appear that it was accepted but it won't be made by the broker's traders and you won't own the stock. Reading the fine print of an agreement is a pain, but this is *your* money we're talking about, isn't it?

CHOOSING A BROKER WHO SUITS YOUR INVESTMENT STYLE

If you are not fully confident of your stock picking skills and think you'll need a lot of personal guidance, I'd suggest you go with a full-service broker, at least until you become more comfortable. You can look up brokers in the phone book but that doesn't tell you much about the quality of their work. First off, ask friends who they use or who they've heard good things about. If you have coworkers who are investors or belong to investment clubs, ask them for the names of reputable brokers in your area.

When you meet with a full-service broker, ask the broker what he or she can do to help you increase your wealth over the long-term while meeting your financial goals. Ask them about their firm's research department and whether they are primarily technicians or fundamentalists. You can find ratings of brokerage firms and their skill at picking stocks in a number of places. Zacks Investment Service at www.zacks.com offers a wide range of services, most of them for a subscription fee. Many investor magazines do regular rankings of brokers and their services. *SmartMoney* magazine, which has a website affiliated with the *Wall Street Journal*, its parent company, recently ranked the full-service firms in its annual survey and the overall winner was A. G. Edwards, based in St. Louis. Next was Merrill Lynch, which had earned the top ranking for three years in a row. Tied for third were PaineWebber and Smith Barney, and in last place was Edward D. Jones.

SmartMoney made its judgment by looking at the quality of each firm's stock picking advice, the fairness of its rate structure and commissions, its selection of mutual funds and the range of services and products it provides, along with how well it informs its clients—on web pages as well as by other means—and, last but not least, whether it stays out of trouble with government regulators, customers and others.

Rating the on-line brokerages is a bit trickier, since new ones tend to spring up every week. Five years ago, there was not a single discount broker on the Internet. Now there are more than fifty. The big brokerage firms and financial service companies have waded in. American Express and Charles Schwab are forces to be reckoned with. But they have plenty of competition from deep-discount challengers such as Ameritrade, which charges a flat fee of $8 for equities trades.

Like credit-card companies that offer low, low start-up rates and then hike them once they have your business, these discounters often add fees or tack on costly requirements, so make sure you read the fine print. Ameritrade, for example, requires that you put $2,000 in an account with them to begin trading and you have to hold a minimum balance there to keep your account open. Other discounters, such as SureTrade and First Flushing Securities, have similar rates but no such requirements concerning a starting or minimum balance.

It can be extremely difficult to get a real person on the phone when dealing with on-line brokers. They are required to use registered brokers to take orders, but to cut costs, they usually keep a skeleton staff. There have been published reports of reporters waiting for a half hour and more just to get a broker on the phone at these brokerages. You can find rankings of on-line brokers at *SmartMoney*'s subscription site and also at similar sites maintained by www.onlineinvestor.com, www.nasphq.com and www.financialweb.com/smallcapinvestor.

A good broker can help you, not by giving you daily stock tips, but by helping you select stocks that fit your investment strategy and providing you with research on the companies issuing those stocks. Of course, you can find stock research elsewhere too. *ValueLine* has its own research department, as do many other consumer groups, such as the American Association of Individual Investors and the National Association of Investment Clubs.

I make it a point to pay attention to the investment decisions made by the people who manage the most successful mutual funds. Many of them have solid track records and excellent resources. You will find interviews with them in most of the investing magazines and in the investment sections of major newspapers. You will also find interviews occasionally with the people who manage large pension funds. They too have serious research departments, so their stock picks are carefully considered. Remember, however, that investment professionals are unlikely to give away any really hot tips in magazine or television interviews. After all, people pay them for that sort of information, so why would they hand it out for free? Move cautiously, and do your own homework before jumping on information provided by them in the media.

Be very wary also of investment advice and stock tips offered in Internet chat rooms, unsolicited E-mail or telephone solicitations. The growth of on-line investing has attracted sharks and con men who prey on unsophisticated investors. There are more and more cases of shady brokers taking advantage of new investors too. The Stock Detective reports that a broker in Maryland not only stole $343,999 in life savings from an elderly customer with disabilities, he also made more than $24,000 by trading stocks in the nursing home patient's accounts without permission. Never give a broker permission to trade in your name without checking with you first. It's best to deal only with brokers you know personally, but if you don't have that luxury, or if you prefer to trade with discount brokers on-line, there are several ways to check them out with regulatory agencies.

The Central Registration Depository (CRD) system, which is owned by state regulatory agencies and the National Association of Securities Dealers (NASD), keeps records of brokers' complete employment history, the states in which they are registered, even their test scores. They also have records of disciplinary actions, court judgments and arbitration awards concerning registered brokers. Much of the information is not generally available to the public, but you can try to get the disciplinary histories of registered brokers and brokerage firms on a telephone hotline by calling 800-289-9999, or by going on-line to www.nasd.com.

The U.S. Securities and Exchange Commission (SEC), which polices the securities industry, offers help through its Office of Investor Education and Assistance (202-942-7040), and at its website at www.sec.gov. In truth, however, you will probably get more help and prompter action from the state attorney general's office in your state capital. Most of them have divisions assigned to investigate complaints against brokers and brokerage firms. The Stock Detective's website at www.financialweb.com/stockdetective offers a list of state investment watchdog agencies.

Stock "churning," or buying and selling frequently without the investor's permission, is one of the most frequent complaints against brokers lodged with the NASD. If you discover that your broker has been doing this, you can't sue, thanks to a 1987 Supreme Court ruling and the fact that you signed a waiver of your right to sue when you signed with the broker. But there are ways to seek justice if you believe your broker has done you wrong. You can hire a lawyer who specializes in securities disputes by calling the Public Investors Arbitration Bar Association (PIABA), based in Oklahoma City (405-360-8776).

The PIABA has a list of securities lawyers around the country. A lawyer can take your case to arbitration, at which one person or a panel hears testimony and reviews the evidence. The New York and American Stock Exchanges offer arbitration, as do the NASD and the American Arbitration Association. A high percentage of these cases are settled even before they reach arbitration; but when they do get that far investors prevail in about 54 percent of the complaints filed and typically recover about 40 percent of their losses, according to a survey by the *Securities Arbitration Commentator*, a journal based in Maplewood, NJ.

Arbitration can be costly and there are no guarantees. Many consumer advocates urge investors to use NASD's mediation system instead. A neutral party works with both sides to reach a settlement agreeable to both. The fee is $600 for each four-hour session. You can call NASD at (212-858-4000) to learn more about this service.

8

Craig Johnson likes to say that he has taken his liberal arts degree "to the max." The fifty-one-year-old Chicagoan has worked as a newspaper reporter and photographer, a television commercial producer, a radio jingle writer, an insurance claims adjuster, an electrician and, most recently, a salesman of silk-screen prints. He is also one heck of a skier. Craig and his wife Denise have skied all over the world. In fact, Denise is the past president of the Sno-Gophers Club, an African American ski club in Chicago.

For all of their many talents and skills, Craig and his wife decided the one thing that they were not good at was picking stocks. After Craig's mother passed away in 1991, she left him a bit of money. Craig and Denise talked about how to invest it wisely, and at first, Denise felt a bank CD was the best way to go. Craig convinced her that the stock market would produce a better return. An avid reader of the *Wall Street Journal*, Craig had educated himself on the stock market; but even so, he didn't feel comfortable wading through all of the vital information on individual stocks. Instead, he called me and asked for help in picking mutual funds. "I talked to different friends who dabble in the stock market and even though I know a little about investing in stocks, I just wasn't comfortable picking them myself. The fund managers are professionals who are paid to study companies and evaluate them, so I felt better looking to mutual funds," he told me. "I'd rather buy four or five funds and let them sit until I'm ready to retire."

As I noted at the beginning of this book, one of the reasons I left the big brokerage firm where I started back in 1986 was that I didn't like selling investments in bits and pieces. I became a stockbroker to help people build wealth by investing. Back then I felt more like a shoe salesman than a real investment advisor. I didn't want to be a pitchman for "hot stocks" or in-house investment vehicles. I wanted to take a far more holistic approach in which I helped people define their goals and set up specific, step-by-step plans to achieve those goals. I'd become a big believer in the value of professional investment management for regular investors like the Johnsons. That's why so many investors have found mutual funds appealing. They offer both professional management and diversification, which are two of the best ways to protect the investments and build wealth for people from every walk of life.

A mutual fund is an investment vehicle that puts a pool of investors' money into the financial markets, giving them much greater leverage. Each fund (except for index funds, which I will describe later) is managed by a professional or team of professionals whose careers ride on the performance of the fund. The manager's job is to diversify the investments within the mutual fund to reduce risk from market swings while building wealth. They do this in a balanced stock fund, for example, by purchasing shares of stock in a wide range of companies in various sectors of the economy, so that if business slows down—say, in the retail market—the investors will still have stock investments in other sectors that may fare better and help balance out the bottom line. Each individual investor in the mutual fund owns shares in proportion to how much each has invested. Your shares increase or decrease in relation to how the rest of the fund is doing.

A mutual fund is like a toolbox with a wide assortment of tools. Each one is unique, but all of them can work together for a common purpose. Typically a mutual fund will hold anywhere from ten to several thousand stocks, and often a mix of bonds, futures and options. The median mutual fund contains about fifty stocks and other equities.

Let's look at one fund picked at random just to give you an idea of what a mutual fund contains. I won't give you the fund's name because I don't want to endorse one fund over another in this book. This particular fund is considered an aggressive capital (or cap) growth fund that seeks long-term growth. It is a highly regarded fund with average risk and high returns, according to Morningstar, the independent mutual fund ranking service, which gives this fund its highest ranking of five stars.

By the way, this is also a very popular fund. Investors have poured more than $3.5 *billion* dollars into it. (This can be both a good thing and a bad thing, which I will explain later.) What is the big attraction for this fund? It is a good performer, averaging returns that are generally above the S&P 500 measuring stick even in down years. Its top holdings include many of the most popular brand-name stocks owned by institutional and individual investors. Some are so diversified they are virtually mutual funds themselves. Its top holdings include:

1. Pfizer, a leading drugmaker whose products include Viagra, Ben-Gay and Visine.
2. Philip Morris, a tobacco and consumer products company whose products include Marlboro cigarettes, Kraft foods, and Miller beer.
3. Merck, the top drugmaker in the United States.
4. Coca-Cola, one of the world's top brand names.
5. Intel, the dominant computer-chip maker.
6. Johnson & Johnson, the global maker of products ranging from Tylenol, Band-Aids, AcuVue contact lenses, Reach toothbrushes, drugs and birth control.
7. Fannie Mae (formerly the Federal National Mortgage Association) is a public company created by the U.S. government to buy mortgages from lenders and resell them.
8. American Home Products makes health care and agricultural products ranging from Advil and Robitussin to herbicides and insecticides.
9. General Electric, the fifth largest U.S. corporation, owns everything from NBC to companies that make aircraft engines, appliances, industrial materials and lighting.

Now you may be getting an idea of why mutual funds have become so popular. Where else would an average individual be able to purchase shares in so many of the biggest and best-run companies in America? I'd like you to note something else. On the day I wrote this particular part of the book, one share of Pfizer was selling for $112; one share of Philip Morris was going for $55; and one share of Merck was $156. Yet, on that same day, the per-share price of this mutual fund was *$41*, though like many funds it had a minimum investment price of $2,500. Still, that's not a bad deal, particularly since this fund has been averaging returns of more than 20 percent over the most recent four years.

Mutual funds are now this nation's most popular investment vehicle, with more than $5 *trillion* put into this form of security. In 1998, mutual fund assets surpassed total bank assets for the first time in our nation's history. Why? Because they offer a simple, convenient and relatively inexpensive investment option for those people who may not have the resources or confidence to manage their own investment portfolios.

BENEFITS OF INVESTING IN MUTUAL FUNDS

Full-time professional management

Most people simply don't have the time, training or temperament to manage their own investments. With mutual funds, professional managers are on the job full-time, monitoring the market and making well-informed decisions on whether to buy, sell or switch securities in their mutual fund portfolio. They do in-depth research, even making personal visits to companies and interviewing their customers and suppliers before buying stocks. They also read the signs to determine if the market is about to take a dive or whether it is going to soar, and they adjust their holdings and strategies accordingly. (That's why it is important to consider *who* is managing a mutual fund before you decide to buy into it.)

Diversification

I've already told you a few stories of investors who made the mistake of putting all of their money into only one or two investments. That's a high-risk strategy in my book. Yet, I understand that it can be daunting for the individual investor to build a diverse stock portfolio. With a mutual fund, that is done for you by professionals who purchase a wide variety of stocks and bonds and other securities. In a diversified fund, no more than 5 percent of a fund's assets can be invested in any one security. That makes for a much safer investment. Keep in mind, however, that there are no guarantees that your mutual fund won't drop in price if there is a decline in the stock market. If you have a diversified mutual fund portfolio, however, you probably won't be as hard hit as someone who has invested in only a few select stocks.

Marketability

With many fixed-income vehicles, such as variable annuities and CDs, you have to give up access to your money for several years to get the maximum rate of return. With a mutual fund, you get the potential for growth *plus* you always have access to your money. If you decide to sell your shares, the mutual fund company will buy them back at the current market value. Mutual funds are required by law to mail a client's redemption check within seven days from the time they receive their request.

Tax reporting

Your mutual fund company sends you an annual statement showing your income and capital gains, if any.

Automatic reinvestment

The money earned by your mutual fund is automatically reinvested in new shares of the fund, allowing your investment to grow without interruption.

Convenience

Tracking your investment is as easy as reading the daily newspaper. All major newspapers have a daily listing of fund performance. You also receive a fund statement whenever you make a transaction, as well as an annual report on your fund's progress. Fund families (a group of different funds offered by one company such as Putnam, Fidelity, Vanguard) allow you to move money back and forth among funds as your goals and strategies change.

Affordability

You can purchase mutual fund shares with low minimum investments of $1,000 to $2,500 and sometimes even less with retirement accounts. It doesn't matter how much you invest, your assets are managed with the same care that all others are given.

Watchdogs

Mutual funds are regulated by the SEC, and each fund's claims regarding expenses, fees and operating costs are checked by independent accounting firms. If you have a complaint about a mutual fund, you can take it to the SEC.

Variety of objectives

There is a mutual fund for every temperament and investment objective, from aggressive to conservative to those in-between:

Equity funds are for the most aggressive investors willing to face higher risk for the potential of higher return.

Balanced funds are for the middle-of-the-road investors who want to combine equity investments with income investments such as bonds.

Income funds are for the more conservative investors who want current income with only moderate risk.

Index funds generally are low-cost, low-risk funds that track the performance of a particular market index. They generally are not actively managed and have low turnover so they don't generate a lot of taxable income.

Potential for growth

Historically, mutual funds have far outperformed more conservative investments. There is some risk, but in return mutual funds offer a far better potential for growth than investments such as bank savings accounts, CDs, bonds and other more conservative securities.

THE GOOD AND BAD OF A BOOM

In the mid-1980s, there were only about 1,000 mutual funds. Now, there are more than 9,000 and the numbers grow almost daily. The extended growth in the U.S. stock market and the dawn of the baby boomer generation's peak earning years have created an enormous demand. Please note that while the benefits of mutual funds are considerable, there are bad funds and bad deals out there too. The fast rise of this industry has led to many abuses and sometimes poor regulation. There are funds that have exaggerated their rates of return or otherwise misrepresented their value. Others have inflated their fees or tacked hidden costs onto the charges paid by investors.

After the mutual fund industry performed poorly in the roller-coaster economy of 1998, there was a backlash of criticism that success had spoiled mutual fund companies. As funds have gotten bigger and bigger, amassing billions and billions of investors' dollars, the fund companies increasingly have become content to live off the fat rather than build investment muscle, according to critics. They point to the fact that in late 1998 only about 25 percent of the mutual funds were beating the market. There was no little truth to their criticisms. Many mutual funds were guilty of overcharging for their services and not adequately protecting their investors from taxes. That's why it is important for you to know how these funds operate, how to monitor their performance and where to find in-depth information on funds that interest you.

More and more investors complain that while mutual fund companies have become enormously profitable, they haven't cut their fees. I believe you can get great value when you invest in a well-managed mutual fund. In general, you also have less risk, less stress and better access to information on your investments than with a portfolio of individual stock. But the mutual fund professional managers have to be paid and their expertise does come at a price. As a stockbroker, I charge a commission fee when I buy and sell stocks for my customers. Mutual fund companies do the same, charging fees that are deducted from the assets of the funds you purchase.

Those investors who dislike mutual funds cite these fees as a primary reason for scorning this form of investment. Often, however, those critics are professional or very experienced investors who have the time, skill and resources to manage their own stock portfolios. That is a luxury that most working people do not have. If you do choose to join the millions of people who think mutual funds are one of the greatest forms of building wealth ever available in this country, you should take the time to educate yourself on both the pitfalls and the benefits.

THERE IS A PRICE FOR PARTICIPATING

The fees charged by mutual fund companies are fairly complex, but it is important that you learn the basics—because if you don't pay attention, they can eat into your savings. Here is a list of the standard fees charged by mutual funds.

Front-End Load: Also called Class A shares, these are fees charged at the initial purchase point, even before your money is deposited into a fund. An average front-end load ranges from about 4.5 to 5 percent of your investment. These loads usually decrease as an investor puts more dollars into a fund. If you don't use a broker to purchase, you normally don't pay a "load." So keep in mind that in general, a loaded fund of any kind is something you should avoid under most circumstances.

Back-End Load: These are fees paid when an investor sells out of a fund. They are sometimes referred to as Class B shares. The idea is to encourage you to keep your money invested for the long haul. So, often, the longer you stay with a fund, the lower the load.

Level Load: These funds, also known as Class C shares, charge small front-end loads, small back-end loads and have higher than normal expense ratios. With these funds, you don't have to pay costly up-front fees but you can get hit with high yearly expenses.

Expense Ratio: This refers to the total percentage of assets deducted from a fund each year to pay for service fees as compared to the average net assets of the fund. The expense ratio varies a great deal from fund to fund. A fund that earns 20 percent but has an expense ratio of 2 percent will pay you only 18 percent. That's a sizable bite out of *your* investment. Look for funds with a low expense ratio, around 1.4 percent or less.

12(b)1 Fees: These fees are levied to cover a fund's marketing and advertising costs. Nobody likes them—and for good reason—but about half the funds on the market charge them. This is just a slightly sneakier way for mutual fund companies to take some of your wealth away from you. Savvy mutual fund investors look for funds that aren't heavily promoted in all the magazines, newspapers or on television. They are looking for the small funds that will grow into big funds, so that their investments will grow with them. For that reason, they see high 12(b)1 fees as a bad sign, and as another charge that eats into *their* wealth The good news is that these fees cannot legally be more than 1 percent.

Management Fee: If you want professional management of your investments, you have to pay the piper, often in the range of between 0.25 and 1.5 percent of your earnings. As a fund's assets grow, the management fee is supposed to diminish. It doesn't always work that way, so look for those with reasonable management fees compared to the performance of the fund.

TO LOAD OR TO NO-LOAD, THAT IS THE QUESTION

One of the great debates among mutual fund investors is whether to purchase a *loaded fund* (which is sold only through stockbrokers who help select funds appropriate for your needs) or a *no-load fund* (which you can purchase directly after selecting the funds yourself). There is no doubt that load fees and other types of fees can put a dent in your earnings. A 5 percent load on each $1,000 you put into a mutual fund reduces your initial investment to $950. On the other hand, many conservative investors prefer to have a broker select their mutual funds for them. You will have to make your own choice here, but my advice is that if you purchase a loaded fund, it is up to you to make sure you are getting your money's worth.

The controversy over the relative value of these two types of funds is a long-running one. It's like the Cubs vs. the White Sox or the Yankees vs. the Mets. Each side has strong opinions, some of which are well-grounded in reality, some of which are not. Most consumer groups are fairly adamant in advising investors to skip loaded funds. *Consumer Reports* noted that from 1995 to 1998, "no-load funds were nearly twice as likely to outperform the S&P 500 Index as funds that burden shareholders" with load fees. The magazine also noted that 12(b)1 fees "are even more insidious . . . (they) hit shareholders year after year for as long as they own a fund."

While many individual investors shy away from loaded funds, if your broker is giving you good advice and attentive service, it can be well worth the additional cost to have peace of mind, particularly for the novice investor. But again, a loaded fund has to perform exceptionally well to make up for the cost of its fees. Most fund families offer loaded and unloaded versions of their funds, and most of the time there is little or no difference in their performance. There's no sense paying for the loaded fund if that is the case. Understand that there are alternatives that don't cut so deeply into your investment.

More than half of all funds are loaded. Some load funds perform magnificently and may well be worth the additional expense, but there aren't many of them. If your financial advisor or stockbroker has you invested in loaded funds of any kind, you should make sure there is a very good reason. One case in which it really doesn't make any sense to pay a load is with short-term bond funds because they're all pretty much alike and offer similar returns, so you might as well buy a no-load.

There are those who argue that every mutual fund is managed by a professional working for the fund, so having a broker oversee the fund isn't necessary because you might well be paying twice for the same service. In the end, it's really up to you and how comfortable you feel picking your own mutual funds. If you have the time and inclination to teach yourself, more power to you. In this chapter, I'll try to give you most of the basic information you'll need to make your investment decisions wisely, no matter what type of fund you select.

WHAT TO LOOK FOR WHEN BUYING A MUTUAL FUND

There are now more than three times the number of mutual funds as there are stocks traded on the New York Stock Exchange. Shopping for a mutual fund is rapidly becoming more difficult than picking stocks. For the novice investor, I'd suggest first looking for recommendations from friends, professional investors, newspaper columnists or stories in consumer-oriented investment magazines such as *Mutual Fund, Individual Investor, Black Enterprise, money, Kiplinger's, Worth* and similar publications.

These sources are good for tipping you off, but you should still do your own homework. Remember that many investor magazines are full of ads from mutual fund companies. The publications derive substantial income from that advertising. I'm not saying that any respectable journalist would purposely slant a report to favor an advertiser, only that you should take the responsibility of doing your own research, too. Don't ever buy a stock or mutual fund solely on the recommendation of any single source.

Once you've found a mutual fund that appears interesting, I'd suggest that you check it out at fund directories such as Morningstar (www.morningstar.net) or *ValueLine* (www.valueline.com). You can find their guides at your local library, or you can subscribe to them for a fee. These two independent references rate mutual funds according to risk-adjusted performance, or how the fund has performed in relation to the volatility of the stocks in its portfolio. They are valuable consumer services used by professionals and amateurs alike.

Their rating systems are complex, and they aren't perfect. Critics claim they arrange funds in overly broad categories and that they don't pay enough attention to the funds' operating expenses. Morningstar, however, recently did a study showing that a statistically significant majority of funds that received four- and five-star ratings in 1987 were still ranked that high ten years later.

BRAIN BREAK

Are you starting to *see* Morningstar stars whirling around your head? Suffering from information overload? Mutual fund fever? *ValueLine* vertigo? I don't blame you. And I don't advise you to try to pack all of this into your head at one sitting. Believe me, there is no pop quiz tomorrow.

My goal is to give you the basic material and let it sink in over time as you begin to watch the stock market, read investment magazines and talk to other investors and stockbrokers. As a novice investor, you may find all the information bewildering, but the more you study these reference guides, you will develop a greater feel for how your selection measures up against similar funds.

Here are some of the criteria that researchers for Morningstar, *ValueLine* and other professionals look for in judging the value of a mutual fund. You don't have to memorize them, just tuck them in your memory bank for later reference.

Long-term profitability

That's why you invest, so naturally, you want a fund that will increase in value and help you meet your investment goals. Historically, stock mutual funds have compounded at a rate of 10 percent annually, according to *Mutual Fund* magazine. That is the average of all classes of stock funds, although some, such as small-cap funds, have compounded at a higher rate. Others have been lower.

While it's true that many mutual funds are only a few years old, the novice investor probably should look for those that have been around at least five years and have an established track record. Look for those that are ranked in the top one third of their peer group by Morningstar. Be wary of any fund that boasts about its performance over just one or two years. That's not long enough to show that the fund managers can handle the ups and downs of a volatile market.

An experienced and proven management team

The disclaimer that comes with most mutual fund material warns that past returns are not an indication of future performance. That's true. But a fund that has performed well over the long term in the past has a greater likelihood of doing well if the same management team remains in place. Morningstar's ratings, which are also available on America Online, will tell you how long a fund's managers have been on the job. Investment magazines frequently have stories that identify the best mutual fund management teams.

In recent years, the top-ranked mutual fund managers have become the celebrities of the finance pages. That might be entertaining, but it can also be dangerous. Just as you can't believe all you read about the Hollywood stars in the tabloids, you should be wary of the hype over "star" mutual fund managers. Success can spoil them too. Many well-regarded mutual fund managers in recent years have started their own funds. There is no guarantee that they will succeed on their own, and often, but not always, the funds they leave have difficulty. So, you should pay close attention to who is running the show at your mutual fund. Consistency of performance is a key in selecting mutual funds, and having a strong manager or management team leads to consistent performance.

Cost efficiency

Fewer than half of mutual fund buyers take the time to determine what they're being charged for buying and owning a fund, according to one recent survey. Big mistake. Would you buy a suit, or even a pair of socks, without asking the price? Before choosing between funds, make sure you know the relative costs of owning them because management fees, up-front loads and other costs can be a serious drain on any future profits.

You can often tell how efficiently a mutual fund company is run by its *expense ratio*, which is the percentage of *your* investment that pays for the salaries, annual statements and other costs run up by your fund's managers and their bosses. The average expense ratio of all stock funds is 1.34 percent. International and aggressive growth stock funds generally have higher expenses, mostly because their research costs are more. With an average annual equity market return of 10 percent, the typical fund takes about 13 percent of the portfolio's return for expenses. Your defense against this is to shop for low-cost funds by checking the rankings. The expense ratio is one of the measures provided in both the *ValueLine* and Morningstar analyses of mutual funds. Here are a few other key measures that can help you compare your mutual fund prospect to others:

Beta: This is a measure of a fund's volatility compared to the rest of the market. For a stock mutual fund, the beta is measured against the S&P 500, which is equal to 1.00. A mutual fund with a beta higher than 1.00 means that the fund has experienced greater volatility than the market in general, while one with a beta less than 1.00 indicates that the fund has been less volatile. Experts consider the beta less of a factor for consideration with international, metals and specialty funds because they are less likely to track with the S&P 500. Remember, as I noted in the chapter on stock selection, that economists are split on the merits of beta as a measure for selecting stocks, so don't rely solely on this one factor.

Standard Deviation: This is a good measure of a fund's risk. A fund with a standard deviation of 10 can be expected to produce an annual return that is within 10 percentage points of its average annual return two thirds of the time. The higher the number is, the more volatile the fund's return has been.

R-Squared: A measure of how closely a fund's performance tracks with the market as a whole. An R-Squared of 100 means that the fund is exactly as diversified as the S&P 500.

Return on Assets: The after-tax and after-debt-service profitability of the companies a fund owns. Funds that score well by this measure are usually those with a high earnings growth rate. This is generally considered a measure of a company's operating efficiency.

Price/Earnings Ratio or *P/E:* The weighted average of the price/earnings ratios of the stocks in a fund's portfolio. Anything around 20 is good, 30 is even better.

Price/Book Ratio or *P/B:* The weighted average of the price/book ratios of all the stocks in a fund's portfolio. Book value is the total assets of a company, less total liabilities. Again, anything in the 20 to 30 range is enticing.

Net Asset Value or *NAV:* This is what one share of a fund's stock is worth, so it's the figure you're looking for when you read the mutual fund listings in the newspaper or on-line. It's determined by adding the values of all the fund's holdings and dividing by the number of shares.

Turnover ratio: In basketball, this refers to how many times you flub the ball, kick it out of bounds or bounce it off your foot. In the mutual fund game, it's an indicator of your potential tax exposure if your mutual funds are kept in an account that is not tax-deferred. A turnover ratio of 100 percent indicates that over the course of a year, the entire value of the fund's portfolio would have been traded, generating taxable gains. This generates additional expense within a fund, which means you lose wealth-building power. In general, you want to invest in a mutual fund in which the manager makes good stock selections and sticks with them for the long-term rather than buying and selling frequently, which is also known as *churning.*

TYPES OF MUTUAL FUNDS

All funds are either closed-end or open-end funds. An *open-end fund* is the most common variety. It has an unlimited number of shares available. Both existing and new investors may add any amount of money they want to the fund. The more that investors put in, the bigger the fund grows. Investors buy and sell shares either by dealing directly with the fund company or through a broker. The price fluctuates in response to the value of the investments made by the fund, but the fund company values the shares on its own. Investor sentiment about the fund is not considered. An open-end fund may be a load fund or no-load fund. A *closed-end fund* has only a limited number of shares available. Its shares are bought and sold through a broker just like a stock, and they are traded on the major exchanges. The price fluctuates in response to the fund's performance and what people are willing to pay for it. Shares often trade at a discount, unless the fund gets hot for some reason.

Stock funds

As opposed to bond or money market funds, these funds primarily contain the stocks of companies, although some hybrids may have a mix of bonds and money market funds at any given time to reduce volatility. These are the most common fund type and they come in a wide range of categories that appeal to different investment strategies.

Aggressive growth funds

These have a goal of capital growth, so they aren't designed to produce regular income through dividends. Often the fund manager focuses on small but growing companies and may trade in options and futures. An aggressive-growth stock fund manager might also seek to buy the initial offerings of small companies, possibly selling them again very quickly for big profits. That's an aggressive investing style and carries substantial risk. If the fund's stock picks are hot, returns can be very high, but if they turn cold or the market drops, this sort of fund can be the hardest hit. This type of fund is for investors with long-term objectives. Short-term investors should be wary.

Growth funds

Considered to be less risky, these funds go for long-term growth but seek some dividend income, too. Growth fund managers look for more established and proven companies that still have some room to grow. They may have holdings in bonds and money markets too. Long-term and medium-term investors favor these funds.

Growth and income (value) funds

If you're seeking to provide steady returns while protecting your principal investment, this is the type of fund for you. Growth and income fund managers usually buy shares in companies that exhibit some growth potential and also pay a reasonable dividend to shareholders. These funds carry less risk, but the rewards are generally not as grand either. Conservative investors of all types prefer these funds.

Income funds

These funds are designed to generate income for shareholders with dividend yields. Income fund managers buy some shares in mature but profitable companies that have little prospect for growth but pay nice dividend yields. They also generally concentrate on bonds and other securities that yield some income. These funds are often favored by retired investors seeking regular income to meet living expenses. I wouldn't recommend them for anyone seeking to generate wealth to meet long-term goals.

International, global and worldwide funds

An international fund generally contains stocks in foreign companies. Global and worldwide funds may include stocks in companies both in the United States and abroad. Although in the late 1990s the stocks in many Asian countries took a huge hit, if you are investing for the long-term, it's still wise to have at least 10 percent or so of your portfolio in some sort of broad international fund. After all, the

United States has led the world in growth for decades, but there are emerging international markets that will surely experience growth in the coming years. If the U.S. economy slows, it wouldn't hurt to have your bets covered with shares of companies overseas.

Sector funds

These are growth funds that buy stocks in specific industries, such as the Internet, telecommunications, precious metals, real estate or utilities. I don't recommend them for the typical small investor because this type of fund goes against my usual warning about putting all of your investments in one basket. This type also typically carries unusually high fees. In some instances, however, it can make sense to put a small percentage of your portfolio in a sector fund if you work in or have an interest in a particular industry and believe your "insider" knowledge gives you an edge in monitoring the fund. Historically, these funds seem to fare well in periods of high inflation.

Index funds

Most stock and hybrid funds are overseen by an individual or team of investment professionals whose goal is to "beat the market" by getting returns on their holdings that exceed the return of market barometers like the S&P 500 and the Dow Jones Industrial Average (the Dow). A fund manager might have to buy and sell stocks regularly to do that. In an index fund, however, there is very little trading. It's a mutual fund that is run virtually on autopilot. In fact, many are run by computers that monitor specified market indexes.

An index fund based on the Dow, for example, would buy shares in the thirty stocks that make up the Dow. Its manager would then only buy or sell shares as needed to invest new money or to cash out investors. The advantage of an index fund is the very low expenses. After all, it doesn't cost much to run one. Over the long term, index funds have outperformed about 75 percent of other mutual funds, mostly because they charge low fees—after all, a computer is less expensive than a human manager.

Many stockbrokers don't like index funds, as a rule, because they don't earn commissions from them. They aren't much of a mental challenge either, but these funds are virtually guaranteed to do as well as the market, which is something many human-managed funds don't do. It is hard to go wrong with an index fund, particularly during times when two thirds of the managed funds are not beating the market. It's not a bad idea for the novice mutual fund investor to start by investing at least a small portion of their portfolio in an index fund, particularly one that isn't tax-deferred. They don't make many taxable distributions. Once you have purchased an index fund you can build the rest of your mutual fund portfolio around it.

Funds of funds (FOFS)

Like bell bottoms and Lava lamps, this once-popular-then-scorned form of mutual fund is making a big comeback. These funds buy shares of other mutual funds instead of individual stocks. There are now nearly one hundred of these unconventional funds offered by some of the biggest fund families. These professionally managed funds offer diversification galore, which means less volatility and less risk. *Mutual Fund* magazine notes that in the market downturns of 1987, 1990, and 1994, the average fund of funds lost 20 percent, 11 percent and 4 percent respectively, while the average domestic diversified stock fund lost 29 percent, 20 percent and 8 percent. The FOFs lost less than two thirds as much as the average stock fund.

Of course that lower volatility also means below-average performance during market upswings. It's also true that FOFs can be expensive. Some have expense ratios of more than 11 percent. Advocates of these funds say the high cost is worth it for the peace of mind that comes with professional management and diversification.

You should know that FOFs have a checkered past. In the early 1970s, the man who invented the concept was jailed for violating federal securities laws. But in the last few years, the SEC has encouraged the development of FOFs and they appear to be increasingly popular as a way to simplify the sometimes challenging process of building a portfolio.

Bond funds

In general, bond funds generate income while preserving principal as much as possible. They are considered a good investment for retired investors, or short-term investors seeking to minimize risk because they invest in medium- to long-term securities issued by corporations and governments.

Holding long-term bonds, which are bonds that mature in twenty years or so, opens the owner to the risk that interest rates may increase, dropping the value of the bond. There are short-term bond funds, however. These concentrate on bonds maturing in two to three years. An intermediate fund contains bonds due within seven to ten years.

Tax-free bond funds are an important subclass in this category. These feature bonds issued by municipalities. Income from these securities is not subject to U.S. federal income tax. These can be a good investment for people in high tax brackets.

AFRICAN AMERICAN MUTUAL FUND FAMILIES

I believe in the value of African Americans doing business with each other as one of the best ways to build wealth for future generations. That is why I want to note that there are a growing number of mutual fund families owned and operated by African Americans that you might want to consider when looking at mutual funds.

Black Enterprise magazine, in particular, does a good job of tracking the growing number of these funds. There are now at least sixteen of them, and each year more and more black fund families appear on the scene. Among those now tracked by *Black Enterprise* are Ariel mutual funds, Brown Capital Management Funds, Highland Growth, Lou Holland Growth, Kenwood Growth, Edgar Lomax Value Fund, MDL Broad Market Fixed Income and Large Cap Growth Equity Fund, Profit Value Fund and Victory Lakefront.

Some of these funds are too new to have ratings in Morningstar, although one, Ariel, consistently ranks in the four-star category. Ariel mutual funds, operated by John W. Rogers in Chicago, started in 1986 and is one of the pioneers in this field. It now has more than $2.4 billion in total assets under management—$600 million in its three mutual funds. The Ariel Appreciation fund gained 19.55 percent in 1998, putting it in the 15th percentile among mid-cap blend funds followed by Morningstar. The Ariel Growth rose 9.89 percent and was in the 47th percentile of the same group, and the Ariel Premier Bond gained 7.30 percent, ranking in the 57th percentile of intermediate bond funds.

Ariel shares my dedication to changing the attitudes of African Americans toward investing and mutual funds. John W. Rogers has worked hard at encouraging African Americans to invest in the stock market and he has done well while doing good.

In July 1998, Alden J. McDonald, Jr., president and chief executive of Liberty Bank and Trust in New Orleans—the nation's fifth-largest black-owned bank—started Liberty Freedom, a mutual fund investing in large-cap stocks and aimed at first-time fund investors. The bank joined with Jackson, Shanklin & Sonia, one of the South's largest minority-owned brokerage firms, to market the fund and hired Randall Eley, an African American money manager, to be the fund's advisor. "Many African-Americans will feel more comfortable in dealing with African-Americans or people they know and trust when it comes down to investing," McDonald told the *New York Times.*

The Liberty Freedom fund and many of the other black-run mutual funds are aggressively fighting for your business. Many of them maintain high profiles at gatherings of African American professionals around the country. Eugene Profit, who started Profit Value, a top-ranked large-cap fund based in Silver Spring, MD, two years ago, told the *New York Times* that he tries to attract investors primarily through seminars and booths at major conventions. But at the end of the day, you should judge these funds not by the color of their managers, but by their return on your investment. Profit's fund returned 31.67 percent, placing it in the first percentile of large value funds, according to Morningstar. His fund now has assets of more than $2.6 million under management.

I am not suggesting that you buy these funds simply because they are owned and usually operated by African Americans. But I do suggest you check them out, if they meet your criteria, you should consider investing in them as a way of building wealth for yourself and your loved ones, and for the generations to come. I think it's important that African Americans do business with each other whenever and wherever it is possible.

PROSPECTING A MUTUAL FUND PROSPECTUS

When you call, write or E-mail a fund company for additional information, they will send you a prospectus, much like those sent to shareholders in company stock. These legal documents, mandated and reviewed by the SEC, are not easy to read, although in recent years many fund companies have tried to use plain English rather than legalese. The information most useful to you is generally contained in the first several pages. It will tell you the fund's investment goals, costs and performance history. Most funds also issue annual reports—again, like those sent out by companies to their shareholders. The annual report is generally easier to read and contains additional information on the stocks held by the mutual fund, as well as comments from the fund's managers.

HOW TO BUY MUTUAL FUNDS

Originally, mutual funds were marketed only by fund companies, brokerages and insurance agents. If you bought from a broker or insurance agent, you paid a sales charge, or load. If you bought directly from the fund company, you paid no sales charge, so those funds became known as "no-loads." Today, some companies such as Alliance Capital, Franklin, Putnam and Templeton sell only through brokers, so they are known as *load fund families*. Others, such as Janus, T. Rowe Price, Scudder and Vanguard, sell directly to investors, so they are *no-load fund families*. Some fund families, such as Dreyfus and Fidelity, sell both no-load and load funds. All of them have websites on the Internet.

The boom in mutual funds and the rise of Internet investing has given birth to mutual fund networks such as the Mutual Fund Marketplace of Charles Schwab & Co. (www.schwab.com), Fidelity Investments' FundsNetwork (www.fid-inv.com), and Jack White (http://www.jackwhiteco.com). Each of these networks offers thousands of mutual funds to investors. The networks are helpful because they assist you in managing a group of funds from any number of fund families while also keeping track of paperwork from each of them. Additionally, they make it much easier for you to move your money from one fund to another, even if they are not from the same fund family.

How do they make their money if they sell no-load funds? Mutual fund networks are such a magnet for investors that the mutual fund companies pay an annual fee to the networks for bringing customers to them and eliminate the load fees for the investors. The networks don't collect commissions from investors; instead most charge an annual management fee.

You can also buy mutual funds these days through financial advisors who offer "wrap" accounts, in which the advisors buy mutual funds and other investment vehicles for you, based on your criteria, and then charge you a fee that is usually a percentage of the assets you have under their management. If the advisor chooses well, you both profit. If he doesn't, you both lose. If you don't have time or the expertise to manage your own investments, this can be a good deal, but only if the management fee is reasonable. Most charge from 1 to 1.5 percent. Anything above that may be of questionable value.

Again, choose your investment advisors as carefully as you would your family doctor, or at least your plumber. Check them out with friends and, before you sign on the dotted line, ask to see the advisor's *ADV*. That's a form that the advisor is required to fill out for the SEC. It lists credentials, level of education and experience. Make sure you get both parts of it. The second section describes the advisor's fee schedule. You will be giving your advisor the power to buy and sell investments with your money, but make certain that you do not give away the power to take money out of an account without your permission. That might prove too tempting for some.

You can purchase mutual funds in three basic ways:

1. Lump sum. If you happen to have a chunk of money already in hand, you can invest in a mutual fund and get a head start on your investment goals.
2. Voluntary investment. You may contribute to a mutual fund whenever you have extra money to invest, or even when you don't have "extra" but decide to bite the bullet and do it anyway.
3. Systematic investment. This is the best method because it is part of your long-term plan to build wealth toward your goals. Most mutual funds will allow you to set up a regular monthly plan for putting money into their funds.

MUTUAL FUNDS PAY IN THREE WAYS

While the money you put into a bank savings account has only one way of growing, through interest paid by the bank, your mutual fund shares can grow in three ways.

1. *Dividends paid on earnings of the fund.* These are very much like stock dividends, in fact, they *are* stock dividends, and also bond dividends, depending on the contents of your fund. You can take your dividends in cash if you need them for living expenses or you can have them distributed as additional shares in the fund. Note that when you receive dividend payments in either form, the share price of the fund drops to cover the payout. Remember also that the dividends paid out on funds held outside of tax-deferred retirement accounts are taxable as income unless the dividends come from a tax-free municipal bond fund. Even if you get the dividends in the form of more shares, Uncle Sam wants his cut.

2. *Capital gains distributions.* If a fund manager sells shares in the fund's portfolio, then any net profits from the sale have to be distributed to the fund's shareholders. These capital gains are taxable if your fund is not held in a tax-deferred account. Funds are required to make their distributions by December 31, and most wait until the deadline. If you are looking to buy into a mutual fund late in the year, make certain to find out when distributions are made. It's much better to wait until *after* they are made, otherwise you will be liable to pay taxes on capital gains for the year that you haven't benefited from; again, this is only if the fund is held in a taxed account. Your best bet is to ask the fund company for an estimate of its tax liability before buying shares near the end of the year. If the estimated distribution is less than 8 percent, don't worry about it. You'll probably make up the difference in the market by getting in earlier.

3. *Share appreciation.* If the value of your home increases or appreciates and you sell it for more than you paid for it, then you'll make a profit. The same holds true with mutual funds. If the value of your shares increase and you sell them, you will make money. Of course, to determine your real profit you have to figure in all of the fees and other expenses you've paid to the fund company, just as you'd figure in how much you've paid to landscape, decorate and maintain your house over the years.

THE EIGHT DEADLY SINS OF MUTUAL FUND INVESTORS

In this chapter I've shown you the good and the bad of mutual fund investing. Before we move on, you need to read about the *ugly* too. Here are the most common mistakes made by mutual fund investors.

Deadly Sin No. 1: *Picking a Winner—From Last Year's Race*

I'm not a gambling man, but I can't imagine going to Churchill Downs and putting my life savings down on a horse because he won a big race the year before. After all, a lot can happen in a year; a broken leg, a wild fling with a filly, too many late nights at the horse trough. The same holds true with mutual funds. Magazines aimed at investors are forever touting the hottest funds of the year, but you really don't want to bet on last year's horse unless you've been in the stall and checked it out from nose to tail.

Burton G. Malkiel, Princeton professor of economics and author of the classic investment book *A Random Walk Down Wall Street*, studied mutual fund performance for twenty-five years and concluded, "It is simply impossible for investors to guarantee themselves above-average returns by purchasing those funds with the best recent records."

Individual Investor magazine offered a dose of reality when it reported that "[a]mong the 45 diversified domestic stock mutual funds that made the top 10 performance list during the five-year period ended in 1993, only five staged a repeat showing. On average, only 35% of the top 10 funds in a given year managed to beat the S&P 500 the following year."

When making fund selections for your portfolio, try to base your picks on at least a five-year record of performance, and, in particular, avoid those funds with high expense ratios.

Deadly Sin No 2: *Always Choosing Loads Over No-Loads*

If you invest $10,000 in an 8 percent front-end load fund that returns 12 percent a year and hold on to it for ten years, your original investment, which has been reduced to $9,150, would grow to $28,418. That same $10,000 invested in a no-load version of the same fund would grow to $31,058, a difference of $2,640 in your wealth. Now think about what sort of income that additional $2,640 would mean as it compounds and grows. If you really feel you need a broker's help, go with the loaded funds; otherwise, invest a little of your time for a bigger return. Often, you can find a no-load fund that has the exact same holdings as a loaded fund in the same fund family.

Deadly Sin No. 3: *Trying to "Time" Your Investments*

Far too many novice investors hold back their money waiting for the market to drop so they can buy at a bargain rate. *Individual Investor* magazine reported that someone who invested $5,000 in the S&P 500 index on the day the market peaked every year for a twenty-year period ending in 1993 would still have earned a 13.7 percent compounded annual return so that $100,000 invested over that twenty years would have grown into a nest egg of $465,397!

The moral of the story? Get into the game as quickly as you can, and discipline yourself to make regular investments no matter what the market is doing. In other words, use the principle of *dollar cost averaging* to its full advantage. As I explained early in this book, this involves investing fixed amounts on a regular basis, whether the market is rising or falling. By doing this, you end up buying more shares when prices are lower than the average price per share. You also avoid the risk of investing large amounts of your money when the market is at the top. In the case of mutual funds, dollar cost averaging is particularly effective if you invest in no-loads rather than loaded funds.

Deadly Sin No. 4: *Not Paying Attention to a Fund's Turnover Ratio*

In some funds, particularly the higher-risk small-cap stock funds, a high turnover rate is expected. In most other cases, it's generally wise to look for lower turnover rates because the more trading a mutual fund manager does, the higher the costs are for you. High costs eat into your investment and reduce the benefits of compounding. Some of the wisest investment professionals, such as Warren Buffett, are known for carefully selecting stocks and then sticking with them for decades.

Deadly Sin No. 5: *Buying a Mutual Fund Simply Because it's the Biggest or Best-Known*

As some of the best-known mutual funds have gotten bigger and bigger, there has been a backlash among investment professionals, and for good reason. The simple truth is that as funds have grown into the billions and even tens of billions of dollars, they become nearly impossible to manage effectively. Critics rightfully claim that even the most successful fund managers tend to go on autopilot when their funds get that big. Rather than striving for greater performance, they are content to coast and live on their past glories. Many spend more money on marketing their monstrous funds than on researching stocks.

So, when you are evaluating mutual funds, keep in mind that you may well be better off investing in one that is still growing and trying to attract new investors with strong results, rather than putting your money into a mutual fund that is more of a money magnet than a wealth creator.

Deadly Sin No. 6: *Being a Dunce About Diversification*

Jason Zweig, a columnist for *money* magazine, recently caught one of the nation's most renowned financial planners sinning in this category. The planner picked a portfolio of three mutual funds for a *New York Times* story on investing. Each of the three funds was a fine choice, but as Zweig revealed, it made absolutely no sense to put them together in one portfolio because they contained so many of the same stocks. Eighty-nine percent of the stocks in the first fund and 94 percent of the stocks in the second fund were also in the third fund.

Diversification in your mutual fund portfolio is a wonderful thing.

Along with dollar cost averaging, it is one of the few time-proven investment strategies. But diversification doesn't mean you pick mutual funds with different names. It means that you pick funds that contain different stocks from different sectors of the economy. You should always know what stocks your mutual funds contain so that you don't end up buying funds whose holdings overlap too much. There is bound to be some overlapping from time to time, but to get the full value of diversification, your mutual funds should balance each other out. If one fund owns a lot of entertainment stocks, you should have another that owns oil-related stocks. If one owns stocks in the automobile industry, you might consider another fund with holdings in electric utilities.

Deadly Sin No. 7: *Thinking Short-Term*

If you have short-term goals, you should not be in mutual funds. If your dream is to build up a huge pile of cash quickly, you had better be a very savvy stock picker, or a regular at the local casino. Mutual funds are for long-term investors trying to build lasting wealth. That means you don't jump in and jump out of them like a puppy in a puddle. You should select your mutual funds with great care and stick with them. If, after three to five years, the fund is not beating the market, then you should consider looking for a better investment, but give it time—and keep in mind that only one quarter of all mutual funds beat the market over the long term. It's up to you to make sure your funds are winners.

Deadly Sin No. 8: *Neglecting Your Mutual Fund*

It's 20, 15, 10, 5 years until you reach your investment goals. Do you know where your money is? While it is a mistake to micromanage your mutual fund holdings by jumping in and out of funds, it is an even greater mistake to pay inadequate attention. Monitor your funds monthly if not weekly. If the market changes, take the time to make sure your fund holdings are still aligned with your goals. At least once a year, do a major checkup to see if the manager whose skill attracted you to the fund is still on board. Has his or her philosophy changed? Is it still in line with your philosophy and your goals? Has the market changed? Is it still possible to meet your goals or do you need to make adjustments?

Everybody in the investment biz is in it for the money. But you are the only one whose first priority is building wealth for yourself and those you love. Even if you buy funds with the best managers in the business, even if you hire an investment professional to advise you, the success or failure of your investment strategy falls on your shoulders

Here are a few resources on the Net that may also help.

- Bill Rini maintains the Mutual Funds FAQ (http:// www.moneypages.com/syndicate/faq/index.html)
- Brill Editorial Services offers Mutual Funds Interactive, an independent source of information about mutual funds (http:// www.fundsinteractive.com/)
- FundSpot offers mutual fund investors the best information available for free (http://www.fundspot com/)
- The Mutual Fund Investor's Center, run by the Mutual Fund Education Alliance, offers profiles, performance data, links, etc. (http:/; shwww mfea.com/educidx html)

Next, I'm going to show you how to invest wisely in stocks and mutual funds for specific goals like purchasing a home, funding a college education and providing for a secure retirement. We've taken care of the entree and the vegetables. Now you get dessert.

Section III   Setting and Achieving Your Investment Goals

> *Accumulating money is so easy, I'm surprised more people aren't rich. That's the way money works. The important thing is not how much money a person makes, it is what he does with it that matters.*

—A. G. Gaston (pioneering black entrepreneur)

Carla walked into my office on Madison Street in Chicago and, after talking with me a few minutes, broke into tears. I don't normally make my clients cry, but I guess I gave Carla something she hadn't had for a while: hope.

We'd never met before but she'd come to me on the recommendation of mutual friends who are deacons at her church. She'd told them that she'd received a bonus from her employer, Ameritech, and wanted to invest it wisely. Carla had never invested in the stock market and she was wary of it, but her real fears sprang from the fact that just a year before, she'd gone through a very tough experience both financially and emotionally. At that time she was working for another long-distance company. Carla, who is single, was doing well, but her employer wasn't. She had just purchased her first home, a town house, when she was laid off because of a company-wide downsizing. For months every firm she applied to was going through the same thing. She then tried to establish her own consulting business, but she couldn't get it built up fast enough to keep up with her mortgage payments. Reluctantly, she put her town house up for sale. She found a buyer, but the deal fell through when he refused to offer enough to cover her mortgage debt.

Poor Carla lost her home in a foreclosure proceeding brought by her mortgage lender. She is a self-reliant woman and takes a lot of pride in her independence, but that experience left her fearful that she would never again be able to own her own home. That was why she broke down and cried when I told her that I could help her set up an investment plan that would enable her to one day have her own place again. I told her it would take some time and a lot of discipline but it could be done, even though she would probably need a sizable down payment and a healthy amount saved because of the foreclosure on her financial record.

The reason I got into this business, aside from my own need to make a living, was to help people like Carla. She made my day, and I think I probably made hers too. I did some calculations with her financial numbers—income, assets, liabilities, etc.—and then showed her step by step how she could save enough for a down payment by investing in a mutual fund program. She agreed to start by putting $100 a month into an investment account. Within three months, she decided to increase that to $250 a month. The money is automatically deducted from her paycheck so that she isn't tempted to spend it elsewhere. She said that by the end of the year, she planned to increase the deduction.

I made a believer out of Carla, but I didn't make any false promises to her. I told her it would take time, maybe even five years, to save enough for a down payment after she had established an emergency fund of reserve cash to handle any unexpected expenses. Still, she left my office with tears in her eyes, with a plan and with hope for a better life.

Purchasing your own home is one of the most important financial moves you can make. It is also extremely good for the soul. There are things about home ownership that can drive you crazy, of course, but owning your own home is a wonderful investment financially and spiritually. When you are living in an apartment, if the roof has a leak your only choice is to wait for the landlord to decide to fix it. In your own home, the timetable of the repair is entirely up to you. If you want to paint your bedroom, knock out a wall or turn the spare bedroom into a greenhouse for your gardenias, you don't have to get permission from anyone.

A house is one of the few assets that can generally be expected to increase in value over time. The interest paid on your mortgage also offers one of the few remaining tax breaks. It's deductible, bringing the cost of owning even lower when compared to the cost of renting. In addition, you can also borrow against your equity (the difference between what you still owe and what the home is worth) in your home to make other purchases while deducting the interest on the loan from your taxes.

Last year, the home ownership rate for all Americans reached an all-time high of 65.7 percent. But great disparities exist between the rate of home owning between whites, blacks and Hispanics. Nearly 72 percent of whites own their own homes. Just 45 percent of blacks and Hispanics were homeowners, according to the 1998 study conducted by the polling firm of Hart-Riehle-Hartwig Research for the Fannie Mae Foundation, which works to provide affordable housing in underserved communities. It is funded solely by Fannie Mae, the federally chartered mortgage company.

The survey found that African Americans and Hispanics have become increasingly optimistic that racial discrimination was becoming less of a barrier in the purchase of a home. The survey of minority home-buying attitudes also found the percentage of blacks who said they are "at least somewhat confident" their income and credit record would qualify them for a mortgage has soared from 49 percent two years ago to 74 percent today, according to news accounts. Yet, nearly half of the African Americans surveyed and 36 percent of the Hispanics said being a minority presented special obstacles when it comes to buying a home.

After the Civil War, Abraham Lincoln promised to give free black men and women forty acres and a mule, as well as $50, but his successor, Andrew Johnson, refused to allow it. The only good thing that resulted was that Spike Lee came along more than a hundred years later and found a good name for his movie production company. Many of the early black entrepreneurs who managed to acquire some wealth were often restrained from buying their own property by racist policies in government and financial institutions. It is no secret that even in modern times many banks have refused to loan money to blacks, or to anyone buying a home in a predominately black neighborhood. As recently as 1991, the Federal Reserve Bank noted that blacks and Hispanics were turned down twice, and sometimes three times, as often as white home loan applicants.

So, if you want to make excuses and blame racism and white people for your inability to purchase a home, I suppose you have ample material to draw from. If you would rather go after your dream of owning a home, read on. Together, we can make it happen in spite of racism, in spite of any other obstacles that might stand in the way.

THE TIME TO START SAVING FOR A HOME IS YESTERDAY!

Carla may have had certain obstacles to overcome when she came to me looking for assistance in saving for a down payment, but she had two things in her favor—patience and discipline. She knew that it was going to take time, but she was willing to set a goal and develop a plan. Too often, inexperienced home buyers put the cart before the horse. They go house shopping, fall head over heels for their dream home and then try to figure out how to get it.

It's not that easy. A lot of groundwork has to be done before you can march into a bank or any other financial institution and ask for a mortgage loan, which is usually the biggest loan you will ever apply for. A key factor in any lender's decision on whether or not to risk giving you money is your track record as a saver. Generally, you have to show that you have been able to save money and live within your means. That's why they ask you to sign waivers allowing them to check your credit history and savings and checking accounts.

It's important, then, to have the down payment ready before you go house shopping and especially before you go in search of a loan. To do that, you need a plan, and I am *the man with the plan*. In this chapter, I will offer you some examples of savings plans for home purchases, but there are a few things you need to consider first.

ARE YOU READY TO BUY A HOME?

Let's be realistic here. It makes no sense to purchase a home if you are still in those restless years or if you are likely to be transferred or looking for a job out of the area any time within the next five years. That doesn't mean you shouldn't start an investment program with the goal of buying a home right now. The sooner you start saving the better. The closer you are to being prepared to settle down and live in one place for at least three years, the more you should be putting away.

When you buy a home, you really should plan on staying in it at least that long so that you can recover all the costs of buying a place of your own. Those costs include (you might want to sit down now) the mortgage application and appraisal fees, home inspection costs, moving expenses, the real estate agent's commission and title insurance. Generally, it's said that your home needs to appreciate by about 15 percent before you recover all those costs.

I am a big advocate of home ownership, but in certain cases renting makes more sense. I've got friends in New York City, for example, who've been able to find rent-controlled apartments in very good neighborhoods. Their rents are much lower than their house payments would be in the same area, and because of that they are able to save and invest and live quite nicely. I also have clients who are young and mobile, most of them single, who are probably better off renting until they decide to settle down in one part of the country for a while. There is nothing wrong with owning a home if you are single, though. It can be a great way to start building assets early in life. Renting also makes sense if you can't afford to buy a home in a good neighborhood where its value will increase, but only if you have enough discipline to take the money that would otherwise be tied up in a house and invest it wisely.

The decision whether to rent or buy can be complicated because there are many and varied costs involved. Monthly rent and renter's insurance as well as annual rent increases, the purchase price of a home, the down payment required, the home's appreciation rate, tax benefits, property taxes, loan costs, homeowners insurance and selling costs are but a few of the primary factors that have to be weighed. If you are plugged into the Internet, there are many resources for helping you make your decision. One of the best I've found can be reached from America Online's Personal Finance channel. Go to the "Real Estate" home page and then click on "Renting." There you will find an icon asking "Should You Rent or Own?" If you click on that, it will take you to a calculator to help you determine what is best for you.

To make a fair comparison you have to look at the monthly cost of renting an apartment and the monthly cost of owning a home where you will be equally if not more comfortable. This table will help you determine the costs of home ownership.

When comparing the costs of owning a home to those of renting, keep in mind that over the long term, your rent will probably increase while your mortgage rate will remain the same over the life of the mortgage. Your property taxes, homeowners insurance and maintenance costs will probably increase, but that will be offset by the increased equity you will have in your home. In most cases, the cost of renting increases more than the cost of owning over the long term.

HOW MUCH HOME CAN YOU AFFORD?

I have seen many people fall into the trap of buying a home that they really could not afford because some loan officer told them that it was within their price range. Often, your lender only looks at your monthly income, your debt and your credit history in qualifying you to buy a home. You have to take responsibility for asking the tough questions such as, "Can I afford to feed my family and pay the mortgage? Will the monthly mortgage payment be so high that I won't be able put money

---

The Relative Costs of Home Ownership Versus Renting

1. Write down your monthly mortgage payment ....$ _____
2. Add to it the amount you will pay each month
   for property taxes ....$ _____
3. Total up those two figures ....$ _____
4. Write down your income tax rate (15%, 28%,
   31%, 36%, 39.6%) ....$ _____
5. Subtract the tax benefits by multiplying
   line 3 by line 4 ....$ _____
6. Figure after-tax cost of mortgage and property
   taxes by subtracting line 5 from line 3 ....$ _____
7. Add the monthly cost of homeowner's insurance .....$ _____
8. Add monthly maintenance costs (1% of property
   cost divided by 12 months) ....$ _____
9. Add lines 6, 7 and 8 for total cost of
   home ownership ....$ _____
10. Compare that figure with the monthly cost of renting a similar
    place to get a rough estimate of the relative costs of home own-
    ership versus renting.

---

away for my children's educations or for retirement?" While it's true that most people have to stretch the budget a bit to purchase their first home, you don't want to stretch it to the point of snapping. Your family's peace of mind is more important than having an extra bedroom, a bigger yard or a family room the size of Rhode Island.

The first step in determining how much house you can afford is to look at how much you have to make a down payment. It's best to put 20 percent of the purchase price down, because that will generally persuade a bank that you don't need personal mortgage insurance, which could add $100 a month to your mortgage bill. Putting together a 20 percent down payment is difficult for most people, however. In a competitive market, you can often get a home loan by putting as little as 5 to 10 percent down. The average home in the urban United States is now about $120,000, so a 10 percent down payment would be $12,000. You also have to figure in closing costs, which could easily add another $1,000 to that.

If you can make a down payment of $12,000 on a $120,000 house, that leaves a mortgage of $108,000. Mortgage rates are very low today. A thirty-year loan can be secured at about 6.75 percent, which would leave a monthly mortgage payment of about $700 for a $108,000 mortgage. There are a great many home-buying services and mortgage calculators on-line these days. Here are just a few that can help you determine how much you can afford to pay and what your mortgage payments will be: HomeShark at www.homeshark.com.; Bank Rate Monitor at www.bankrate.com; HomePath, the site sponsored by Fannie Mae, at www.homepath.com; and Microsoft's HomeAdvisor is at www.homeadvisor.msn.com.

DO YOU HAVE THE MONEY FOR MONTHLY MORTGAGE PAYMENTS AND OTHER COSTS?

As a financial advisor, I sometimes have to play the devil's advocate. It's not a role I cherish. I'd rather tell you that everything will always be affordable, but that's not the way the world works. If you come to me with visions of that great brick bungalow in Brookfield dancing in your head, be prepared to receive a reality check. I can help you save for that dream, but first I want you to be aware of all the "hidden" costs that come with home ownership and a monthly mortgage.

If credit-card bills and rent payments have been a pain in your neck, a mortgage is an 800-pound gorilla on your back. As Carla learned, the mortgage lender is not an understanding friend. If you can't make the payments, they will put your belongings on the street and change the locks. So you need to be realistic. It's great to find a house that you love, but you can't let your heart rule your brain. I've known people whose families have been torn apart because of the pressure of making mortgage payments they could not afford.

Generally, a bank or other mortgage lender will not give you a loan if the monthly costs of the loan (payment plus property tax and homeowners insurance) and other monthly debt payments such as car loans, credit-card bills and so on add up to more than 28 percent of your gross monthly income. If you plan to make a 10 percent down payment, your credit card, car loan, student loans and other monthly debt payments plus principal, interest, taxes and insurance should not total more than 36 percent of your gross monthly income. Those who can put 20 percent or more down can sometimes get a better deal. Lower interest rates make it easier to get a home loan, but generally, you will not be approved for a loan if the cost of the house is more than three times your annual income.

When you go to a mortgage lender, oftentimes they will give you "instant approval" for a mortgage, but their calculations are based only on your current annual income and, generally, on your current debt load. Their loan approval doesn't guarantee that you still will be able to make payments if you get laid off, have unexpected medical costs or if you need to take out another car loan.

It is up to you to conduct your own reality check before you make an offer on that dream house with the garden out back. Here are a few points you should consider:

Will you be able to make your monthly mortgage payments and still:

- Save for other goals, such as retirement or college tuition?
- Travel or entertain as much as you have in the past?
- Keep up with other expenses, such as credit cards and car loans?
- Take care of emergency expenses that may crop up?

Have you considered all of the costs of home ownership such as:

- Electric, gas, phone and water bills?
- Garbage pickup?
- Property taxes?
- Remodeling and maintenance, including interior and exterior painting?
- Lawn care?
- Homeowners insurance?
- Drapes, blinds and furnishings?

WHEN DO YOU WANT TO PURCHASE A HOME?

The time factor is critical when designing an investment and savings plan for home ownership. Ideally, you would start planning for your first home five years before you wanted to make the purchase. Most people don't want to wait five years or more to buy a house. Young couples and singles are eager to get into the housing market and I can't blame them. The sooner you get in, the quicker you start building equity. But the more you have for a down payment, the better the home you can get. If you only have a few months to a year before you want to buy a house, I really can't advise you to invest in the stock market unless you have a lot of experience. I think the best thing is to guard your principal—the money you have saved so far—and work to add to it by cutting expenses and finding other sources of income, including some I will suggest. If you plan to buy a house soon, I'd advise putting the down payment in a safe bank account or a money market fund that pays at least some interest. If you don't plan on actually purchasing a home for three years or more, I'd suggest you find a good balanced mutual fund that offers relatively low risk with a mix of stocks and high-grade bonds. The goal is to allow your down payment savings to appreciate faster than the rate of inflation.

ARE YOU WILLING TO GO ON A BUDGET?

If there is one thing worth budgeting for, it's your first home. It's often the biggest and best investment people make. Here are ways to get started:

- Make a note of your monthly income, savings and spending. Get a handle on where your money is going and where you could cut corners. If your phone bill is more than $100 a month, cut it back to half that amount. Could you cut back on eating out? Rent movies instead of going to the theater? Do you have a lot of high-interest credit-card debt? Study where you can trim expenses and discipline yourself to do it.
- Write down your investment goals. Be realistic in setting them, and then make them real. Paste a photograph or drawing of your dream house on the refrigerator. Tell all your friends, relatives and coworkers that you are determined to buy a house within a certain amount of time.
- Open a savings or investment account specifically for a house down payment. Make regular weekly and monthly deposits. The size doesn't matter as much as the act of disciplining yourself as a saver.
- Make a chart of your progress toward your investment goal. Post it in a prominent place so that it serves as a constant reminder that you are a man or woman with a plan.

HOW CAN YOU RAISE MONEY FOR
THE DOWN PAYMENT?

Most lenders will not allow you to borrow the down payment even from a family member, so you are going to have to come up with it some other way. Here are some sources that I've identified or read about over the years:

1. If you have two vehicles and can get by with just one, sell the second and put that money toward a house down payment. A friend of mine did this after getting married. His wife and he both had cars, but neither had a lot of cash; so they sold her car, which was the nicest of the two, and put the $5,000 toward their first house down payment. Their first house in suburban Chicago cost $89,000. Two and a half years later they sold it for $110,000, paid off their mortgage and used the profit as a down payment on a $120,000 house. Three years later, they sold that for $135,000 and used the profit and other savings to build their dream home. So, I'd say the decision to sell one of their cars proved to be a pretty smart move, wouldn't you?

2. Ask parents, grandparents or other relatives to co-sign for the house with you. Your lender may allow you to borrow money from them if they agree to co-sign for the home loan. I only recommend this if all other methods fail, because if you are old enough to buy a home, you should be willing and capable of budgeting, working and saving for the down payment. Do you really want someone else to share ownership of your first home?

3. Go to church. Praying could help, but there are also loan programs sponsored by Fannie Mae, the federal mortgage insurer, that allow you to make only a 3 percent down payment if a nonprofit church or some other valid nonprofit group puts down another 2 percent. Ask your pastor if he or she is willing to participate in such a program in exchange for service or later repayment.

4. Check with your local Veterans Administration and Federal Housing Administration offices to see if you are eligible for their home loan programs that require little or nothing as a down payment.

5. Find a home seller willing to enter into a rent-to-own arrangement in which you rent the house until you have saved enough to purchase it. Often, the seller will count the rent you have paid as a down payment toward the home.

6. Find a home owner with an assumable loan. Some highly motivated sellers will carry back a second mortgage for an equal amount and allow you to buy the home without making a down payment. Don't sign anything, however, until you've let either a lawyer or a good real estate agent review the arrangement.

6. Work a second job until you have saved enough for the down payment. It's amazing how the thought of owning your own home can be a motivator. With a specific goal in mind, you'll find that working a second job seems less like drudgery and more like a real grown-up way to make one of the most important and self-satisfying purchases of your life.

7. If you have been with an employer for at least three or four years, you may be able to borrow against your retirement fund at a low rate of interest. I consider this another last-ditch move because I believe it's so important to let your retirement savings grow without being disturbed.

8. Look in the attic or the basement. The market for antiques and collectibles is very hot right now, particularly because of trading on the Internet. Go to the library and find a recently published guide on antiques and collectibles and then go to the attic or basement and

see what you find. Even some old baseball gloves in good condition are worth a few hundred dollars, as are many old toys, particularly if they are still in the original packaging.

9. Barter. For a house? Sure. Bartering is a prime currency in this country's underground economy. People trade services and skills all the time, so why not make the down payment on a home by trading your special skills for the front door key? If you are a skilled auto body worker or mechanic, a golf pro, dental hygienist, carpenter, landscaper, plumber, computer whiz or driveway paver, you have skills that could be bartered. It's worth a try.

10. Check you local listings for foreclosure properties. Some lenders and government agencies will gladly unload foreclosed homes with little or no down payment to buyers with good credit histories, particularly if you are willing to put some sweat equity into making the property more valuable.

As with most investment goals, the most critical step is the first one. Start putting money away. Purchasing your own home can give you a huge boost in self-esteem. It can also provide the foundation for your financial future, as well as the roof over your head. I can think of no better way to start investing in the dream, your dream and the American dream, than investing in your first home.

Investing for College

10

My wife, Delores, and I always encouraged our daughter Khalilah to get a college education. We've done such a good job, in fact, that it looks like she may be going through four years of college and then on to medical school. We're proud of her, though I have to admit her decision to *keep* going to college has forced us to revise our investment strategies. We began planning early, but we hadn't planned on her continuing education to be continuing quite so long.

We will find a way to help her, because like most African Americans of our generation, my wife and I are well aware of the value of a good education. I think it is safe to say that no blacks of my age group took their college classes for granted. We were witnesses to Little Rock, AK, and Oxford, MS, in the 1960s, when young African Americans had to fight their way through spitting and cursing white mobs to get to their classrooms. Their courage was inspiring, and we were made to realize that if racists were so determined to stop us from getting into the doors of high schools and colleges, then an education must be a very powerful weapon against discrimination. For us, a college degree was not just a step toward a meaningful career and a better life, it was another important victory for equal opportunity.

UNDERSTANDING THE VALUE AND THE COST OF A COLLEGE EDUCATION

The practical value of a college degree has grown enormously since my days on campus, of course. Recent studies show that having a degree can more than double the amount of money you'll earn over a lifetime. Census figures show that the average household income for a couple with college degrees ($80,000) is nearly twice that of a couple with only high-school diplomas ($41,000). The average for a working couple without high-school diplomas is even less ($25,000).

In a story examining the impact of racial preferences in college admissions, the *Washington Post* looked at what happened to black students who entered certain colleges in 1976. They found that 56 percent had earned advanced degrees and that the black male graduates were earning an average of $85,000 a year. The paper also reported that "in virtually every type of civic activity, from social service organizations to parent-teacher associations," the black students were likelier than their white classmates to be leaders.

There is no doubt that we need to do all we can to get our children and grandchildren college degrees. With increasing emphasis on advanced degrees in the workplace, our experience in dealing with our daughter's decision to stay in school illustrates a major point of this chapter. When planning an investment strategy to finance your child's college education, you have to plan ahead *and* you have to plan for the unexpected.

Tuition costs have risen faster than the rate of inflation over the last decade, and trends show that students are staying in school longer in pursuit of master's and PhD degrees. As we have discovered, there are many additional costs to be considered; everything from a car to clothing, living and travel expenses. My wife and I were caught by surprise at the costs of many of these peripheral things. When I was in school, we hurried home on spring break. But it seems like college kids these days prefer to go to Jamaica or some other exotic location. I'm not saying that's a bad thing, necessarily, but it does require you to dig deeper into the wallet. However, *another* major point of this chapter is that your priority should always be your retirement fund. Take care of that first, and then invest for your children's educations. Does that sound selfish? It's really not. The worst thing you could do to your children is go into your most vulnerable years without adequate funds to support yourself. You don't want to be a burden to them and their families in your golden years, do you? And keep in mind that if you need more money for their educations, you can usually borrow against your retirement fund.

We are fortunate in some ways because my daughter chose to attend Spelman College in Atlanta, GA, an all-black institution that is frequently cited for being one of the top regional liberal arts colleges in the country. *Black Enterprise* named it one of the best "bargains" among private colleges in the country. My wife and I are big champions of historically black colleges and universities for a number of cultural and personal reasons. My wife is a graduate of Fisk University in Nashville, TN, and I am on the board of Huston-Tillotson in Austin, TX, both of which are all black. These colleges and doctorate-level faculties offer the opportunity to obtain a strong academic foundation. Historically black colleges provide a nurturing, supportive environment in which African American men and women can develop higher levels of self-esteem and self-confidence. Black colleges are also appealing from a financial standpoint since most offer competitive programs at lower cost than other private colleges.

On average, private schools cost about $11,000 more per year than public schools. The College Board now puts the costs of a private university at more than $20,000 per year and a public school at more than $10,000. With those prices expected to rise well ahead of inflation, the time to start planning for college expenses was yesterday.

THE SOONER THE BETTER WHEN SAVING FOR COLLEGE

From our experience, and from those of many of my clients, I am well aware of the stress that comes with planning for and financing a college education. This financial goal is particularly problematic because most parents have to invest aggressively to build a big pot of money in time for enrollment day. Yet, it is such an important goal that most people feel they can't afford to risk losing any of their initial investment or principal. Balancing those interests is the most challenging aspect of planning for college financing.

That is why you'll want to take full advantage of your two financial friends—compound interest and time. Take Joe and Charlene, who figure they will need $50,000 to finance their child's education at a public college. Figuring a conservative annual rate of return of 7.75 percent, they would only have to invest $110.38 per month if they start putting money into a college fund as soon as their child is born. Thanks to the wonders of compound interest over the years, their contribution to the $50,000 will only have to be $23,843. But if Joe and Charlene wait until their child is eight years old, they will have to invest $282.79 each month to raise $50,000 and their final contribution will be much higher—$33,935.

If you have not started planning for your child's college education yet, you need to seriously begin considering how much time you have to save, how much money you can afford to put away each month and how much you will have to borrow down the road.

SETTING YOUR EDUCATION INVESTMENT GOALS

Step One: Calculate the projected cost of your child's education

The first step in your planning process is to calculate the estimated cost of your child's education. Use the chart to find your child's age and the estimated cost of a four-year college education at both public and private institutions. Enter the appropriate amount(s) in the college planning worksheet provided below. For example, if you have a six-year-old, you have twelve years to build the $157,602 that a private college will cost when he or she is ready to attend:

Investment Needs for College

Child's Age	Years Until College	Public College Cost	Private College Cost
Newborn	18	$97,203	$211,201
1	17	$92,575	$201,144
2	16	$88,166	$191,566
3	15	$83,968	$182,440
4	14	$79,969	$173,756
5	13	$76,161	$165,482
6	12	$72,535	$157,602
7	11	$69,081	$150,097
8	10	$65,792	$142,949
9	9	$62,658	$136,142
10	8	$59,674	$129,659
11	7	$56,833	$123,485
12	6	$54,126	$117,605
13	5	$51,549	$112,004
14	4	$49,094	$106,671
15	3	$46,756	$101,591
16	2	$44,530	$ 96,754
17	1	$42,409	$ 92,146

Assumes 5% annual increases. Figures are estimates only and are based on averages for tuition, room, board, books and personal expenses compiled by The College Board for the 1996–1997 academic year. (Chart courtesy of Putnam Investments)

Step 2: Decide how much you will need to invest to meet estimated expenses

If you've won the Powerball lottery, earned a huge bonus at work or inherited Auntie Rose's Microsoft stock, you are well ahead of the game in having a pot of money to begin investing immediately for your child's education. If you are like most people, however, you probably have to begin systematically investing a fixed amount each month. The chart below will help you determine how much you will need to invest for your child's education. (The chart does assume a hypothetical rate of return.) Enter the appropriate amount(s) in the college planning worksheet that follows.

Investment Needs for College

Child's Age	Years Until College	Required Monthly Investment		Lump Sum Needed	
		Public	Private	Public	Private
Infant	18	$202	$440	$23,140	$50,279
1	17	$214	$466	$23,868	$51,859
2	16	$228	$495	$24,618	$53,489
3	15	$243	$527	$25,392	$55,170
4	14	$260	$564	$26,190	$56,904
5	13	$279	$606	$27,013	$58,692
6	12	$302	$655	$27,862	$60,537
7	11	$328	$713	$28,737	$62,440
8	10	$360	$781	$29,640	$64,402
9	9	$398	$865	$30,572	$66,426
10	8	$446	$969	$31,533	$68,514

11	7	$507	$1,101	$32,524	$70,667
12	6	$588	$1,278	$33,546	$72,888
13	5	$702	$1,524	$34,600	$75,179
14	4	$871	$1,893	$35,688	$77,541
15	3	$1,153	$2,506	$36,809	$79,978
16	2	$1,717	$3,731	$37,966	$82,492
17	1	$3,406	$7,401	$39,159	$85,084

Assumes investment earnings of 8% per year, compounded monthly. The figures are not intended to be a projection of any investment results. Your investment returns will vary. No adjustment has been made for income taxes, the impact of which may be significant. (Chart courtesy of Putnam Investments)

Now for the final calculations. Plug in your answers from the previous charts into the worksheet offered below and calculate your totals. (You might want to be seated, with a supply of fresh oxygen nearby.)

College Planning Worksheet

Child's Name	Child's Age	Years Until College	Dollars Needed	Lump Sum to Invest Today	Amount You Should Invest Monthly
	.				
					Total Cost of College Education $
					Total Lump Sum $
					Total Monthly Investment $
					Total Annual Investment Needed $ Multiply monthly investment needed by 12 months

These charts are meant only to help you determine the amount needed to meet college expenses. If you find that the lump sum or monthly amounts you've calculated aren't realistic goals for your family, adjust your target investment. Please remember that regular investing does not guarantee a profit or protect against loss in a declining market. Investors should consider their ability to continue purchasing shares during periods of low price levels. (Table courtesy of Putnam Investments)

AVOIDING TAX CONSEQUENCES
ON COLLEGE INVESTMENTS

Keep in mind that there are ways to shelter at least some of your college investments from a full tax hit. You should talk with your lawyer or tax advisor to get complete information regarding your specific situation, but here are a few options to keep in mind. In recent years Congress has provided a wide array of tax deductions, tax credits and tax incentives to help middle-class Americans pay for college. But it's not always easy figuring out what will work for you and your family. We've learned over the years that government programs won't solve all of our problems, and sometimes they only make things worse.

THE HOPE SCHOLARSHIP AND
LIFETIME LEARNING TAX CREDITS

In 1997, Congress approved two new tax credits for post-secondary education—the Hope Scholarship tax credit and the Lifetime Learning tax credit. Now in effect, the Hope Scholarship allows a 100 percent credit on the first $1,000 paid in tuition and college fees (not including room, board or books) for college freshmen and sophomores only. It also gives a 50 percent credit on the next $1,000, for a total credit of $1,500. The amount a taxpayer may claim is reduced based on adjusted gross income. It is phased out for taxpayers with annual gross incomes exceeding $50,000 ($100,000 for married taxpayers filing jointly). Note that you can only use the credit for the first two years of school.

The Lifetime Learning Credit kicks in after the freshman and sophomore credits covered under the Hope Scholarship run out. There is no limit for the number of years you can use the Lifetime Learning credit, but it cannot be used for a student already receiving the Hope Scholarship. Under the Lifetime credit, which increases to $2,000 after the year 2002, you can deduct 20 percent of the first $5,000 you spend on tuition and related expenses, for a maximum of $1,000. You can only do this for one child per year, for a maximum of $1,000 per family per year. (If you have more than one child in college at any given time, you should qualify for martyrdom or sainthood, neither of which falls within my area of expertise.)

After 2002, the amount will increase to 20 percent of the first $10,000 of qualified expenses for a total of $2,000. The income limits for the Lifetime Learning credit are the same as those of the Hope Scholarship. However, unlike the Hope credit, the Lifetime credit is calculated on a per-family, rather than a per-student, basis. This means that the maximum available credit does not vary with the number of students in the family.

Another important note: You are not allowed to take these tax credits in any year that you withdraw money from an education IRA (see below).

Deductions for Student Loan Interest

As of 1998, there is a deduction for interest on education loans, but only for middle-income families. The write-off also has limits: $1,000 for 1998; $1,500 for 1999; $2,000 for 2000; and $2,500 for 2001 and later years. Only interest required to be paid during the first five years of the loan is deductible. The deduction is phased out for those with annual gross incomes of between $60,000 and $75,000 for joint filers and between $40,000 and $55,000 for singles. There's no write-off for married individuals who file separately.

You can take advantage of this tax break if you make more than the limit by borrowing money in your child's name even if you plan on paying it back yourself. As long as the child is not listed as a dependent on your tax return—and isn't making a huge annual income while in college—he or she can claim the deducation.

Education IRAs

These IRAs, known as EIRAs, allow you to contribute up to $500 annually for anyone under age 18. Contributions are nondeductible and eligibility is unaffected by any amounts contributed to regular IRAs. EIRA eligibility phases out for donors who are joint filers with annual gross incomes between $150,000 and $160,000 and singles with annual gross incomes between $95,000 and $110,000. If you pass the limit of eligibility, grandparents, godparents or friends who are eligible can make the $500 contribution for your child. Gains in education IRAs accumulate tax-free and can be withdrawn tax-free as well. Eligible college expenses include tuition, books, supplies and room and board. If your child decides to skip college, you can use the EIRA funds to pay college expenses for any family member. If you don't, you face income tax and a 10 percent penalty on all withdrawals. Please note that withdrawals from an EIRA will disqualify you for the Hope Scholarship and Lifetime Learning tax credits that year.

Penalty-Free IRA Withdrawals

You can make withdrawals from a regular IRA to pay higher education expenses without being hit with the 10 percent penalty that usually applies to withdrawals before age 59 ½. Remember, though, that these withdrawals are subject to federal income tax and the alternative minimum tax, if applicable. Roth IRAs allow penalty-free and tax-free withdrawals of any contributions—but not gains—as long as you have held the account for five years.

The Roth IRA may actually be a better vehicle for college savings than the EIRA if you are participating in a 401(k) or similar retirement program. Although the two IRAs have a lot in common, you can contribute $1,500 more each year to the Roth and there are no penalties if you don't use the money for college when you cash out. Using a Roth would also leave you eligible to use the Hope Scholarship and Lifetime Learning tax credits, but using an EIRA would make you ineligible for either in a given year.

Because IRA gains are taxed as income when you make a withdrawal, I caution that using an IRA account to pay for college may not be the best move. Taking out a student loan with deductible interest may be a better way to go. For example, let's say you are in the 28 percent tax bracket and each year you set aside $4,000—the maximum IRA contribution for married couples—for ten years and earn 9 percent a year. If you put the money in a taxable account and withdraw it after ten years, paying a 21 percent capital gains tax rate, you end up with $47,480. If the money is invested in a Roth IRA, you get $46,818; and in a regular deductible IRA your total after taxes is $35,618. The only way a regular IRA comes out ahead is if you take your annual tax savings each year ($1,120, or 28 percent of $4,000) and put it in a separate taxable account.

Instead, I'd advise you to set up an account in your child's name. If you give your child annual $4,000 gifts for ten years, her account would be worth $64,421, or $4,182 more than your taxable account. Keep in mind that you can't take the money back—so your child can use the money for any purpose, even a trip to the Virgin Islands, once he or she reaches legal adulthood.

Tax-exempt mutual funds

These funds feature municipal bonds that can help you earn high current income that's free from federal and, in some cases, state income tax. Please note that while most tax-exempt funds principally invest in obligations exempt from federal income taxes, a portion of a fund's income may be subject to the federal alternative minimum tax. Income also may be subject to state and local taxes. Capital gains, if any, are taxable for federal and, in most cases, state purposes.

Custodial accounts

One option is to set up a custodial account under the Uniform Gifts to Minors Act (also known as Uniform Transfers to Minors Act in some states). These accounts can reap tax savings over the years of your investment plan. Children under age 14 are allowed to receive $650 of unearned income (such as capital gains and dividends) on a tax-free basis. An additional $650 of unearned income is allowed to be taxed at the child's lower rate of 15 percent, and thereafter any additional unearned income over $1,300 is taxed at the parent's top marginal rate. After the child reaches age 14, all investment income above $650 is taxed at the child's rate.

Please note, however, that custodial accounts may actually be harmful down the road because they are considered as assets when admissions offices are measuring your ability to pay against your need for financial assistance. I'll explain more about this later, but in general, custodial accounts may be a good idea only for those who are certain that they will not qualify for any sort of financial aid because of a high family income.

Gifts

Any parent or grandparent can give up to $10,000 each year ($20,000 for a couple) to a child without incurring any gift taxes. A lump-sum gift could be the ideal beginning for a college planning program.

STATE-SPONSORED TAX SAVINGS PLANS

In 1996, the U.S. Congress ruled that assets in state-run college savings accounts could grow tax-free until a child reaches college age. Most states now have such plans in operation. Many require that you attend a public school within the state. The plans vary from state to state in how they work but all allow assets to grow tax-free. The tax advantages also improved when states decided to allow the funds to be used to cover room and board expenses as well as tuition and books. When you withdraw funds to pay for college expenses, the money is taxed at the child's income tax rate, which is generally much lower than the parents'. If you don't use the money to pay for a college education, you can be charged a penalty in addition to taxes. Also, keep in mind that most state college savings plans do not have the volatility of the stock market, but that also means that they have not offered a return matching that of the market or even a good intermediate or long-term bond fund in recent years.

There are four types of college savings plans:

Tuition Savings Plans

The best aspect of this plan is that your child can generally go to any school he or she chooses. But unlike plans that require attendance at a state school, this one does not guarantee tuition. It is up to you to make sure your investments grow enough to meet the cost when your student is ready to enroll. Be sure to investigate the investment plan in your state. Some plans are administered by mutual fund companies that invest your payments into equity and fixed-income funds, while other states simply put your money into safe but low-yield U.S. Treasuries. It is also in your best interest to learn exactly what the penalties are if your child should decide not to go to college. Some states will lay a heavy tax on your savings while others have a minimal fine.

Contract Plans

The plan requires that you select a state public college, university or junior college in advance and sign a contract to pay the current tuition rate. You can pay it all or make payments with interest compounded annually. In my opinion, this plan has some problems. How can you decide years ahead of time that your child will agree to go to a public school in that state? What if you've moved to another part of the country by that time? And what if tuition at the state school rises faster than your investment portfolio?

My advice is to think carefully about contract plans; there are better investment plans and it's probably not wise to limit your child's college choices.

Unit Plans

This type of plan allows the parents to prepay any amount of college tuition [without buying a contract for a set number of years] at a particular school. This low-risk plan is similar to buying a bond guaranteed to return the rate of tuition inflation. Distributions are taxed as income to the child. In these plans, a state sells "units" worth a percentage of the average tuition at one of its public schools. In most cases, though, the units can be transferred to other colleges around the country. Your return is whatever the rate of tuition inflation has been at the state school. Units can also be transferred to any family member. These plans vary widely from state to state.

The Massachusetts Plan

As in the unit plans, this one allows you to pay the current price of tuition and fees for entrance in the future, but in this plan, devised by the state of Massachusetts, distribution is tax-free. You get that tax benefit by buying state general-obligation bonds that return the rate of inflation plus the difference between the rate of inflation and the average annual tuition increase of participating colleges (up to 2 percent over the inflation rate). If tuition rises faster, the participating schools in the Massachusetts College Savings Program don't charge you. While most of the state's public and private colleges have signed on, Harvard and MIT were not participants at the time this book was being researched. It is open to out-of-state residents. If your child decides not to go to a college in the program, you can get back your principal plus the consumer price index, tax-free. Of course, you could earn more if you invested that same money in stock and bond funds with a greater return, but if you are extremely risk-averse, this may be a plan to consider.

Students are required to pay taxes on any scholarship funds that are not used specifically for tuition or fees. The IRS does not allow you to deduct interest paid on loans used to finance education, except if you finance it with a home-equity loan.

Step 3: Deciding how to invest

As I noted earlier, deciding how to invest for a college education is tricky because most people need to build up a big amount quickly, but they don't want to risk losing any of it. That is a tall order. The safest investments, like bank savings accounts, CDs and U.S. savings bonds are slow growers. The stocks with the most promise of rapid growth generally carry the highest risk.

Before you make your decision on how to invest, you should first decide what your comfort level is with risk. Only the most affluent people and serious gamblers are comfortable with high levels of risk. Most of my clients want a balance between risk and reward. Any willingness to see that balance tilted one way or the other should be weighted according to two factors: the age of your child and the amount of money you begin with.

A few things to consider based on your child's age:

• If your child is an infant or preschool age, you have more time to build a college fund. You'll probably want an investment with the potential for long-term capital growth, so you're willing to take on a bit more risk in hopes of higher rewards.

• If your child is in grade school, you most likely should consider investments that offer a balance of growth and income. Your risk levels are moderate in exchange for what will probably be a more moderate return.

• If your child is in high school, you will probably be most comfortable with an investment strategy that's low-risk and designed to preserve what you have saved so far while going after some gains.

DIVERSITY INVESTING

We hear a lot these days about "diversity in the workplace" and the benefits of having a workforce comprising people of all ages and races. Well, I am a big champion of diversity, but of a slightly different sort, in your investment strategy too.

As I tell all my clients, there are no guarantees in stocks or mutual funds. They are not Federal Deposit Insurance Corporation (FDIC)–insured bank products. Over the long run, the stock market has risen steadily, but there are also periods in which the market turns downward. Inflation, which is currently at all-time lows, can rear its ugly head and have a serious impact on investors' portfolios if their income investments are not keeping pace. The wise investor should understand that volatility and make investments accordingly.

The best defense against volatility in an investment strategy is diversification. This is particularly true when your goal is to fund your child's education. A mutual fund, which includes stock and bond holdings in dozens and even hundreds of different companies, is a diversified, professionally managed portfolio of securities. Investing in a mutual fund allows you to pool your shares with those of thousands of other investors who share similar investment objectives. When your money is spread out over a number of investments your return isn't dependent on any single stock or bond. The result is a far broader diversification than you could achieve on your own.

Mutual funds also offer liquidity, or quick access to your savings. You can move your money in and out of your mutual fund account whenever you like. When it comes time to pay college tuition, the money will be there. Once again, however, remember that mutual funds, like the stocks or bonds they contain, can go up or down in price depending on the market. When you cash in, they may be worth either more or less than their original cost to you.

DIVERSIFIED INVESTMENTS MINIMIZE RISK

I generally recommend a diversified mutual fund investment portfolio for parents trying to build up a college fund. Such a portfolio, or group of different funds, usually includes mutual funds with varying degrees of risk. These funds are drawn from categories that include:

- Income and tax-free funds, which generally offer lower risk but also lower potential for rewards;
- Growth and income funds (also known as "balanced funds"), which offer the potential of greater rewards with more risk; and
- Growth funds, which offer the greatest potential for earnings but also carry the highest levels of risk.

A diversified portfolio containing funds from each of these categories provides more opportunity while minimizing risk: When you buy a variety of funds ranging from aggressive to steady to low risk, you reduce volatility, which allows for more consistent earnings over time. A 1991 study reported in the *Financial Analysis Journal* found that 91.5 percent of a portfolio's performance is due to asset class selection and the timing of the purchase of assets. So having a good mix is important.

If your children are under eight years of age, for example, I would probably advise you to put 40 to 60 percent of your money in high-reward, high-risk growth mutual funds, which are primarily stock funds; 40 to 50 percent in growth and income funds, which include some bond funds; and no more than 10 percent in the income and tax-free funds, which carry the least amount of risk but also have the potential for the least amount of rewards.

If the children are older than eight, I would advise a somewhat less risk-tolerant strategy. I'd have 30 to 40 percent in growth funds; 40 to 50 percent in growth and income funds; and 20 to 30 percent in tax-free and income funds. For parents of children approaching or in their teens, I'd recommend a portfolio that offers more protection from market volatility: one with 20 to 30 percent of assets in growth funds; 30 to 40 percent in growth and income funds; and 30 to 50 percent in tax-free and income funds.

Those are basic guidelines, of course. Every client comes to me with a unique situation that I try to accommodate when devising an investment strategy. You should understand the guidelines but tailor your strategy to your own circumstances in order to get the highest return for an acceptable amount of risk.

A CASE STUDY IN INVESTMENT DIVERSITY

In 1996, two of my clients, Tom and Charlene, asked for my help in devising both their retirement strategies and a college savings plan for their young sons. I've known this couple for probably ten years. Tom and I are both members of the Alpha Phi Alpha fraternity and met at a social gathering for the fraternity's members in the Chicago area. Those gatherings, by the way, are great for socializing, and for business networking too.

Tom works in pharmaceutical sales and Charlene is a computer consultant. Both are in their midthirties. They are upwardly mobile, with a very nice income. As they moved up the income ladder, Tom began to feel that he was being too conservative with his savings. Then he and Charlene did a little research and found that the cost of a four-year college education would be in excess of $150,000 by the time their boys finish high school. They decided that they had better get some help.

They initially had an aggressive growth strategy in their mutual fund choices, but I cautioned them to be a bit more conservative in order to avoid volatility. I recommended investing in three mutual funds; a low-risk growth and income fund, an aggressive growth fund with moderate risk and a sector fund with high risk.

I won't give you the specific name of the funds because I don't want to endorse one family of funds over another in this book. But here are descriptions of each, their holdings and their attributes.

The Growth and Income Fund

This particular fund was rated three stars out of a possible five star rating by Morningstar, the mutual fund rating service. It has an average risk factor, an average rate of return by Morningstar's measures, and a forty-year record of solid performance. Its managers look for attractively priced stocks of large, established companies whose performance potential appears to be changing for the better. The managers target companies introducing new product lines or undertaking restructuring measures, cost reductions or new distribution channels. Stocks with above-average dividend yields boost the fund's income while providing a cushion against market downturns. As a balanced fund, it seeks capital growth by investing in common and preferred stocks, and also in U.S. government and corporate bonds, and convertible securities. It may invest up to 20 percent in foreign securities.

In the fall of 1998, this fund held stock in Xerox, Pharmacia & Upjohn, Texas Instruments, PNC Bank, Merck, American Home

Products, IBM, Goodyear Tire & Rubber, Owens-Illinois and Baxter International. (All information is quoted from Morningstar.)

The Aggressive Growth Fund

I selected this fund in part because it invests in technical stocks, which Charlene is interested in and knowledgeable about as a computer consultant. I think it is important to invest in areas in which you have some knowledge, or at least a general interest. Warren Buffett, who is widely regarded as the most savvy investor around, has long refused to invest in risk-laden technology stocks, even though they have been the most lucrative in recent years. His reasoning is that he knows very little about the field.

This particular fund has a three-star Morningstar rating and is considered to carry above-average risk and above-average returns. It generally includes securities of smaller and less-seasoned high-tech companies, which is why it can be volatile. Its managers may also purchase stock-index futures contracts and related options and trade for short-term profits. In the fall of 1998, its holdings included Cendant, Computer Associates International, Costco Companies, CBS, Telecom-TCI Ventures, Compuware, Clear Channel Communications, Parametric Technology and Fannie Mae.

The Sector Fund

I chose this fund, in part, because it invests in the stocks and other securities of companies in the health-science industry, which Tom is involved in. It is rated five stars by Morningstar's analysts, who consider it to be above-average in risk and high in return. In the fall of 1998, its holdings included the stocks of Warner-Lambert, Merck, Pfizer, Schering-Plough, American Home Products, Glaxo Wellcome, Bristol-Myers Squibb, SmithKline Beecham, Eli Lilly and Johnson & Johnson.

THE BIG PICTURE

Tom and Charlene, like most of us, have many things to take into account when planning for college. When we first began working together, they wanted to invest also for a new house and for their retirements. I wouldn't advise anyone to plan for any one of those important goals without taking into account the other.

Even though we began saving early on, my wife and I have had to adjust our goals over the years. Our college investment strategy has had to be revised not only by my daughter's decision to stay in school longer, which is very common these days, but also because we had not really planned for all of the extra costs of her college education. I advise parents to plan for more than four years of college financing. You also need to consider all of the additional costs aside from tuition, books and dormitory costs. Many students need cars, which require a lot of maintenance. A lot of them have expensive tastes in clothing. Most will need regular infusions of cash for social activities and travel to and from school. If they move off campus or into a fraternity or sorority, those costs can escalate quickly.

SAVE FOR YOUR RETIREMENT FIRST

Tom and Charlene are great examples for this chapter not so much because they now have a thoughtful college savings plan for their sons, but because they did something else that is very important *before* they started putting money away for their children's education. They took care of their own retirement savings first.

Both of them are putting the maximum or nearly the maximum amount in their respective retirement savings plans. They know that by the time their sons get into college, those retirement funds will be especially comforting as back-up resources in case of emergencies. I've seen far too many well-meaning people set up special savings accounts, investment programs or life insurance policies to provide for their children's educations and hurt themselves and their children in the process.

How does that happen? It has to do with the way colleges and universities determine a student's financial need. I advise every parent, no matter what their incomes, to apply for financial aid when their children decide on a school by completing the Free Application for Federal Student Aid (FAFSA). Your child can get these from high-school guidance counselors, the public library or from the financial aid office of the college or university. Some schools also require that you complete a more detailed Financial Aid Form (FAF). Check with your target schools to see which forms they prefer.

After you fill out the FAFSA form, you send it in to an independent agency that does evaluations to determine how much your family can afford to contribute toward your child's education. Their findings are sent to you in a Student Aid Report (SAR), which says how much you will need to contribute to your child's education, no matter what school is selected. The SAR is then sent to the schools that your child is applying to, which each proposes a funding program that can be a mix of your contribution, student loans, campus jobs, grants and scholarships. The school's funding package proposal can be negotiated, but generally your contribution is set in stone by the SAR.

It costs nothing to apply for financial aid through the school that your child decides to attend, and even if your family income is relatively high, your child may qualify for low-cost student loans, campus jobs or other forms of assistance that are not based solely on financial need. There are many federal grant programs, including the Pell Grants, that do not have to be repaid; and scholarships offered by businesses, foundations and other private organizations have increased 55.1 percent in recent years, according to the *Chronicle of Higher Education.*

For African Americans, the Minority On-line Information System

(MOLIS) provides a scholarship search web page at http://www.fie.com/molis/scholar.htm. Another helpful web page is Financial Aid for Minority Students at http://www.finaid.org/finaid/focus/minority.html.

Black Excel: The College Help Network is also an excellent source. It offers a comprehensive guide to historically black colleges and a list of more than 350 grants and scholarships for African American students. Their web address is http://cnct.com/home/ijblack/BlackExcel.shtml; E-mail can be sent to *ijblack@cnct.com*, or call (718) 527-8896. You can also write to Black Excel at 28 Vesey Street, Suite 2239, New York, NY 10007.

Loan debt can weigh down a college grad for years while eating into his or her income, so it is important that you investigate all avenues of financial aid—but be cautious. Scam artists have infiltrated this lucrative field too. While most private scholarships offered are on the up-and-up, scholarship expert Mark Kantrowitz of Carnegie Mellon University has published a list of things to watch out for when shopping for tuition help.

- *Application fees.* Kantrowitz says you should never have to pay money to get money. Even low fees of $5 or $10 should be a warning sign.
- *900-number services offering scholarship information.* Also not recommended. Kantrowitz says if they're charging you to dial, they're probably only looking to take your money, not give it to you.
- *Everyone is a winner.* Scholarships that are awarded to any who apply are highly suspect. Kantrowitz says "breathing" is not generally considered a talent worthy of a scholarship.
- *No phone number provided.* If a scholarship application form is sent to you without a phone number for the organization, be on the alert for a fly-by-night scam.
- *Requests for personal information.* Beware the organization that

asks for your bank account number, a credit card number or a Social Security number.

- *Phone notification.* Always ask for confirmation in writing that your scholarship has been awarded. If the organizations asks for money before giving confirmation, walk away, quickly.

CHASING SCHOLARSHIP MONEY WISELY

There are billions of dollars in financial aid given each year, and you should be aggressive in protecting yourself, as well as in going after your fair share. It may take a lot of effort, but it will pay dividends down the road when you graduate with minimal debt. You'd be surprised how many people come to me for help because they've been saddled with college loan debt and are unable to save for their first houses or for their own retirements. As always, your goal should be to borrow as little as possible.

I advise parents to talk with their child's guidance counselors about all financial aid programs, including scholarships, grants and loans, available in their community through civic organizations, clubs and also employers and professional organizations. Always be sure that you fully understand the terms of any loans, grants or scholarships. If you have trouble interpreting the legalese, ask your financial advisor, accountant or lawyer to examine the fine print. Any mistakes you make now could cost you a bundle over the long term.

In some cases, commercial lenders tack a guarantee charge of up to 4 percent on to their fees and deduct it from the amount of government loans that they administer. If that is the case, you can probably find a lower fee and better repayment terms elsewhere. *SmartMoney* magazine recommends the website run by financial aid expert Mark Kantrowitz as a great resource for parents searching for ways to finance their children's educations. America Online also offers a wide range of advice and many other resources on its Personal Finance page.

Many people get intimidated first of all by the high cost of higher education and secondly by the paperwork involved in applying for financial aid. It can be daunting, but the requirements for receiving some sort of financial aid are probably not as stringent as you might think.

The completed and submitted FAFSA and FAF forms are analyzed and graded according to the parents' income and assets, their age and need for retirement income, the number of dependents, number of family members in college and other financial circumstances. The standard financial needs analysis calculates the amount of money the parents and child each will contribute toward the total costs of the school and expenses.

The most important thing to remember when starting to plan an investment program for your child's education is that when a financial analysis is done of your family's income, they do not consider retirement savings as an asset if they are held in a tax-free or deferred tax account. But they do consider as assets any funds placed in a taxable savings account, including those set up in your child's name. As a result, having money set aside for educational expenses can actually hurt you when it comes to being considered for financial assistance. Therefore, it is far better to be fully invested in all available tax-free or deferred tax retirement plans than to have a large taxable account. One additional tip: It's wise not to sell any of your mutual funds, stocks or bonds in the year before your child will need the financial aid because any profits from those sales counts as additional income that could reduce your chances of being granted assistance.

Even if you don't qualify for financial assistance, it is far better to have the security of a well-funded retirement plan than a big nest egg for college expenses. You should take care of your retirement needs first because *your* financial security is the priority. I've said many times in this book that you should take full advantage of any 401(k) plan or similar retirement plan offered by your employer. Many company retirement plans allow you to borrow against at least a portion of the money in your account and, in most of these cases, you pay the interest *to yourself.* Now, that isn't a bad way to finance your child's college education.

A home equity loan is another attractive method because it allows you to borrow against the equity built up in your home (the difference between its current market value and the amount you still owe). A home equity loan generally features lower interest rates and the interest paid on the loan is tax-deductible.

IF THE KID IS PACKING FOR COLLEGE AND YOU HAVEN'T SAVED A DIME...

For those who are biting their nails because they have a high-schooler looking at college catalogues, but no funds set aside, don't begin pawning the china and silverware yet. There are options. The federal government sponsors a Parent-loan for Undergraduate Students (PLUS) program that allows parents with good credit to borrow up to the full cost of their child's tuition. The PLUS loans, which must be repaid, generally come with interest rates that are substantially lower than those charged by most private financial institutions.

Changes in the federal tax laws as of 1998 have made it even more tempting to take out a loan to pay for higher education costs. Now parents can deduct interest payments for the first sixty months of repayment on all private and government-backed student loans, including the PLUS loans. The size of the deduction was limited to $1,000 in 1998 but will rise to $2,500 by the year 2001. The deduction is not allowed for singles with incomes between $40,000 and $50,000 or joint-filers in the $60,000 to $75,000 income bracket. You can learn more about this deduction by calling 800-4-FEDAID.

For the panic-stricken, the worst thing you can do is to roll the dice and start making risky investments at the last minute. There is no sense putting your entire family's security at risk. Instead, look to purchase some moderate-risk mutual funds that generally outperform the market. You can research these by checking on-line at Morningstar's web page, or by asking for advice from an investment expert. Even if your child is already fourteen, you can put $5,000 in a fund with a 10 percent return (8.9 percent after taxes), pump in another $300 a month during his high-school tenure and build up a $24,253 down payment by the family scholar's first year in college. It won't cover much more than the first two years at a public school, but it *is* better than hocking the bedroom set.

MORE ON-LINE HELP

Consumer Reports recommends the following websites for those seeking a "crash course" in finding, funding and preparing for college.

- www.collegeboard.org offers financial aid calculators, including one that compares the amount of debt the student plans to assume with the amount of income he or she might expect to make in any given field. It also offers a College Scholarship Service/Financial Aid Profile that many schools use to award non-federal student aid.
- www.ed.gov is the U.S. Department of Education's site, where you'll find its Student Guide to Financial Aid as well as the Free Application for Federal Student Aid, the required form for anyone applying for college financial assistance.
- www.fastweb.com offers access to information on thousands of scholarships. You can conduct a search based on such criteria as your ethnic background, academic interests and extracurricular activities.
- www.finaid.org offers links to college financial aid offices, financial calculators and information on prepaid tuition plans.
- www.nelliemae.org is the website for the New England–based company, which makes and buys student loans. Along with general information on student aid, it offers calculators, including

one that helps you compare financial aid award packages of the schools that accept your child.

• www.salliemae.com has useful calculators that let you figure out your family's expected contribution to college costs and how much you need to invest to meet a particular savings goal. It also has a scholarship search program and a host of other information on financial aid.

11

Before I became a stockbroker and investment advisor, I worked for the U.S. Postal Service as assistant to the postmaster of Washington, DC, Martin Simms, another African American. The postal service has historically been a place where blacks could find stable, long-term careers, although it was difficult to break through the racial barriers to top management. I look fondly on those days with Martin Simms at the postal service. He had started there as a very young man and worked his way up over thirty years. I was among the one hundred people at his retirement party in 1976 when, in a fit of sentimentality, he announced that he was going to send each of us a Christmas card every year. That was our nation's bicentennial year, as you may recall, and a regular U.S. postage stamp was going for thirteen cents, so Martin was committing to spending $13 a year just for the stamps needed to wish his former coworkers a Merry Christmas.

I saw Martin again just recently. He is in good health and getting along, although his retirement has not been as smooth as he had hoped. We had an interesting discussion that highlights one of the major problems faced by people who do not plan carefully and thoughtfully for their retirements. Martin noted that since 1976, the cost of his Christmas card pledge—and just about every other of his living expenses—had grown considerably while his income had not.

With the price of a regular stamp now thirty-three cents, or nearly triple what it was in 1976, Martin is paying $32 these days just to mail his Christmas cards to his former coworkers. He can handle that, of course, but inflation has also hit the cost of greeting cards as well as everything from gasoline to baked beans. The problem is that penny by penny, dollar by dollar, it all adds up to a big headache for Martin and other retirees who did not take inflation into account. The sneakers that cost about $20 in 1976 now sell for nearly $100. The price of a gallon of milk has doubled; so has bus fare.

The one thing that has not gone up since Martin's retirement is his pension check. It's the same amount today as it was when he first left the postal service. He told me that he had not counted on inflation when he made his promise to us at his retirement party, nor had he planned on it when he estimated his living expenses for his retirement years. Because his pension has not kept pace with inflation, Martin has had to get a part-time job to meet his living expenses. After thirty years of work, he has had to go back to laboring for an hourly wage.

Martin is not alone. Far too many folks plan poorly for their retirement years, and many of them have to go back to work at least part-time to meet expenses. I understand that often people get so caught up in living day to day, paycheck to paycheck, that they feel they don't have the luxury of saving or planning for retirement. It's also true that in the past the vast majority of black men didn't make it to age 65. Hard lives and poor health took a heavy toll, and so their sons and daughters were never witness to the problems of living for many years without retirement funds. But that too is changing. We are all living longer and better these days for many reasons. We need to start planning better too. Elderly African Americans are three times as likely to live in poverty as elderly white Americans, according to the first National Summit on Retirement Savings.

Statistics like that make me angry, and even more determined to spread the gospel of investing for retirement. It has become second nature for me to ask people I care about if they are planning for their futures. Often, the response I get is "things will work out." African Americans are spiritual people who trust in a higher power, but remember that God helps those who help themselves. Neither God nor government should have to bear the burden of seeing us through our most vulnerable years on this planet. Have faith, but have a plan too.

It's frightening to think that a third of all Americans are not saving for retirement. Sixty-six percent of those who are not saving claim they have too many other financial responsibilities. Twenty-five percent said they don't save because they don't have a retirement savings plan at work. This is all according to the 1998 Retirement Confidence Survey organized by the Employee Benefit Research Institute, the American Savings Education Council and Matthew Greenwald & Associates.

RETIREMENT PLANNING MISTAKES CAN WIPE OUT THE FRUITS OF YOUR LIFELONG LABORS

Who is going to take care of all of these poor folks when they hit old age? Who is going to take care of you, if you don't have a thoughtful plan for your retirement? Did you know that if you are ten years from retirement right now and grossing more than $40,000 a year, you may need at least $1 million to support yourself through your retirement years? It's true. Inflation, taxes and a much longer life span for both men and women in this country are having a huge impact on retirement savings for many, many Americans such as my friend Martin Simms.

Since 1990, the inflation rate has remained below 5 percent, which is a great improvement over the much higher rates of the early 1980's, but there are no guarantees rates will remain low through your retirement years. Even if inflation remains relatively low, it can impact your savings and investment dollars. If you earn a 4 percent rate of return on your savings or investments and inflation grows by 5 percent, you lose money. For your savings to grow, you must get a rate of return higher than the current inflation rate. That makes inflation a critical factor in your financial success. It impacts your purchasing power, just as it drove up Martin's living expenses in relation to his pension.

In 1981, you needed an income of $44,000 to have the same purchasing power that an income of $25,000 provided just ten years earlier. By 1991, with 5 percent inflation, you needed $66,332. By the year 2001, at the same rate of inflation, you will need $108,048 to maintain the same lifestyle. *That* is why you need to plan for inflation in your retirement strategy.

Underestimating the impact of inflation and taxes on savings and investments and overly conservative investment practices are the biggest mistakes people make in their retirement planning, according to a survey of 3,000 financial planners by the College for Financial Planning in Denver. Eighty-two percent of the financial planners surveyed said their clients started saving too late while compounding their future problems by failing also to factor in the impact of inflation when projecting their retirement living costs. Eighty percent of clients were too conservative in their retirement investments and 67 percent failed to consider the impact of taxes on their retirement income, the planners reported. The survey also found that 44 percent of clients didn't begin to focus on retirement planning until age 50 or older.

That's not too wise considering that a typical sixty-two-year-old man can now expect to live to eighty-three and a sixty-two-year-old woman to ninety. How much you will need to live comfortably in your retirement years depends mostly on your health and your lifestyle, of course. Some medical experts project that it won't be unusual at all in the next century for both men and women to live to age 120 and beyond. If that's the case, you are going to need a lot more gold for your golden years, and maybe some silver and platinum too. Obviously, if you want to spend your retirement years living in a fancy condo overlooking your private country club, it's going to cost you more than if you remain in a house that's paid for and stick with horseshoes as your sport, or play the public golf courses.

I advise my clients that they will need at least 80 percent of their working incomes in retirement, and if you want to be really safe, figure 100 percent. Multiply that figure by your life expectancy and you'll have only a *starting point* in determining how much you will need. Here is a worksheet that will help you come up with more specific information.

Retirement Worksheet

1. How much annual income will you want in retirement (figure 70 percent of your current adjusted gross income just to maintain your current standard of living). $_____

2. Subtract the income you expect to receive annually from:

   * Social Security (if you make less than $25,000, enter $8,000; between $25,000–$40,000, enter $12,000; over $40,000, enter $14,500)   −$_____

   * Traditional pension, if any   −$_____

   * Part-time income   −$_____

   * Other income   −$_____

   Now, add all of the above for the amount you'll need to make up each year of your retirement.   =$_____

   To get an estimate of the lump sum you'll need to have on the day you retire, follow the next steps. The formula assumes you will have a constant real rate of return of 3 percent after inflation, that you'll live to age 87 and you'll begin to collect Social Security at age 65.

---

3. To determine the amount you will need to save, multiply the amount on the last line above by the factors below. $_____

   If you plan to retire at age 55, your factor is 21.0.

60	18.9
65	16.4
70	13.6

4. If you expect to retire before age 65, multiply your Social Security Benefit from line 2 by the factors below.   +$_____

   If you plan to retire at age 55 your factor is 8.8

60	4.7

5. Multiply your savings to date by the factor below (include money accumulated in a 401(k), IRA, or similar retirement plan).   −$_____

   If you want to retire in 10 years your factor is 1.3

15	1.6
20	1.8
25	2.1
30	2.4
35	2.8
40	3.3

   Total savings needed at retirement: =$_____

   Please note: this formula will show you how much to save each year in order to reach your goal. Compounding is factored in.

6. To determine the annual amount you will need to save, multiply the total amount by the factors provided.   +$_____

If you want to retire in 10 years your factor is 0.085

15	0.052
20	0.036
25	0.027
30	0.020
35	0.016
40	0.013

Chart based on a model from the American Savings Education Council, Suite 600, 2121 K Street NW, Washington, DC 20037-1896.

ENSURING YOUR RETIREMENT SECURITY IS UP TO YOU

According to the U.S. Department of Commerce, the average retirement income consists of 39 percent from personal savings and investments; 15 percent from pension; 23 percent from employment; 20 percent from Social Security; and 3 percent from other sources. You may not be able to count on Social Security for that sort of retirement support. In 1950, there were 7.3 workers paying into Social Security for every retiree. In 1995, there were only 4.8 workers per retiree. It is estimated that by the year 2030, when the tail end of the baby boomer generation hits retirement, there will be only 2.8 workers per retiree.

The Social Security system is faced with serious problems. Odds are that you will never collect a dime of all that money you've been putting in since your first job. I'm fifty years old and it's already being predicted that by the time I reach retirement age Social Security benefits will be reduced. They may even cut them off after five years of my retirement. You can check Social Security records of your earnings and get a statement of your estimated benefits by calling your local Social Security office or 800-772-1213. Ask for the "Request for Statement of Earnings" card or Form SSA-7004. If you think the record is wrong, you can contact your local office and use your tax records or pay stubs to support your claims.

Optimists believe that our elected leaders in Washington, DC, will come up with a solution. But you can't risk your welfare on the whims of politicians. I'd advise you to hope for the best and plan for the worst by investing carefully for your retirement years.

As anyone who has been laid off, downsized, right-sized or otherwise shown the door these days understands, there is not much security in company-funded pension plans either. Fewer than half of the companies in this country now have pension plans anymore. Increasingly, Americans move from job to job, company to company, and sometimes in and out of the same company during their careers, so there really is no relying on pension plans as a major source of retirement income for most Americans. The good news is that in the past, the average working person with limited funds was pretty much limited to a company pension plan. Fortunately, however, many other forms of retirement investing have developed in recent years.

DIAL 401(K), 403(B) OR 457, FOR A GOOD TIME IN RETIREMENT

In a sense, everyone who has a job has a tax problem. The harder you work to get ahead, the more taxes you pay. If you work two jobs and make twice the money, you pay even more taxes. But there are ways to minimize taxes, even for regular middle-class folks. There are tax shelters available to you too, and in this chapter we will be taking a look at those that allow you to invest for retirement.

While the number of company-funded pension plans has been dropping, many employers now offer tax-deferred retirement plans. I spend half my working hours urging people to "go the maximum" in these plans. The other half of my time is spent accepting thanks, cookies, cards and pats on the back from those who have followed my advice. Men and women who have never before dreamed of building a retirement nest egg now have substantial amounts of money socked away in their company retirement plans.

Louis Arnold, Jr., is one of those folks. As a foreman in an electrician's shop, Louis had tried to save in the only ways he knew, with a bank savings account and by buying U.S. Savings Bonds. Like a lot of folks, though, Louis couldn't keep his hands off that money. When something came up, he'd raid the savings account or cash the bonds. Louis was in his midforties when I began encouraging him to take advantage of his company's tax-deferred retirement savings plan. He was becoming concerned about his retirement savings even though he had a pretty good union pension. He told me he just didn't know much about stocks, bonds or mutual funds and he didn't know what direction to go.

Today, at sixty years of age and nearing retirement, Louis has the look of a very secure man. I visited him recently in his shop, and he had his radio tuned to a news channel, so he could listen to the stock market report—music to his ears.

"If something happens in retirement, I'm prepared for it," he told me. "I've been blessed." Louis will retire with a pension that pays him more than $40,000 a year, and he will have more than $200,000 in his tax-deferred retirement account as backup. He will also have the mortgages fully paid on both his house and a commercial building he's purchased. "Every hour I work, I'm putting money toward my retirement. It comes to about $8,000 a year that I never see, but it hasn't hurt my lifestyle a bit," he said.

Tax-deferred retirement plans are a wonderful way to save, but you need to understand how they work. Unlike traditional pension plans, which the employer managed, *you* have control of how the money in these plans is invested, but your options are generally limited by your company.

THE 401(K) PLAN

The most common of these plans is the 401(k), which allows employees to contribute a percentage of their salaries—usually about $10,000—to a retirement plan that generally consists of several mutual funds, money markets and company stocks. Nonprofit organizations and government employers offer 403(b) plans and 457 programs, which limit employee contributions to $8,000 a year. (The mind-numbing numerical names are derived from the section of the Tax Code that contains each program.)

These plans all allow you to deduct your contributions to them from your taxable income, reducing your annual tax bill. For example, if you contribute $3,000 of your $40,000 annual income to your 401(k) plan, you only pay taxes on $37,000 that year. Such plans also allow you to defer taxes on the earnings in your retirement account until money is withdrawn. Usually you would not withdraw from these accounts until your retirement years, when you're in a lower tax bracket. There is a penalty for early withdrawal prior to age 59½ (don't ask me why the half-year enters into it). The federal government imposes a 10 percent penalty for early withdrawal and the state penalty varies. There are ways to get around paying the penalty but you should consult a tax expert for the loopholes, which can be sewn up quickly.

All in all, the 401(k) and its related plans are great deals for American workers, so it's no surprise that millions and millions of people have taken advantage of them. Consider that if you had put just $100 a month in a 401(k) plan for the past twenty years and your company matched it at a rate of 50 percent, you would now have $184,000 awaiting you in retirement. (That is, if your investments in the account at least matched the S&P 500 index.) If you had put the same amount of money in a Roth IRA, you would have $147,287. A large-cap mutual funds portfolio would have yielded only $108,259.

If you aren't putting the maximum amount in your company's tax-deferred retirement plan, you should be. If you are self-employed and have not started your own plan, you should. In fact, you are being irresponsible if you don't put at least *some* money into your company's retirement plan each paycheck. It's a matter of taking responsibility for your future, and it's the best deal going.

In fact, in many tax-deferred retirement plans, the employer provides a "matching" contribution in which the company contributes a certain amount based on what you pay in, usually fifty cents to the dollar, up to a limit set by the employer (usually 6 percent of your income). That is free money! It doesn't get any better than that. Those matching contributions put additional dollars in your plan and help you build your retirement savings even faster. If your employer allows monthly contributions and you aren't investing the maximum allowed, you are throwing money away. I strongly urge you to "max out" your contribution even if it forces you to cut back elsewhere. There is no better way for the average working person to build wealth than investing fully in one of these plans. Check with your employer's benefits department to see what sort of plan is offered and how you can take full advantage of it. If your employer does not have such a plan, demand that they put one in place, or look for a company that does. You will thank me in your retirement years. Many people already have.

An additional benefit of the 401(k) plan is that nearly 90 percent of them now have loan provisions. You can borrow money from your own retirement plan and repay yourself without penalty. You pay market rate interest, but you pay it to yourself through an automatic payroll deduction. In most cases, you can borrow up to half of your vested account balance, with a limit of $50,000. Most allow five years for repayment at competitive interest rates. Some allow you to take even longer to repay if the loan is for a down payment on a primary residence. Most employers do not place restrictions on how you use your money; after all, it *is* your money. That's also why there are no credit checks. In fact, many of the plans are now automated so that you can get the cash in just a few days.

The loan provision on these plans can be a great benefit, but as your investment advisor, I'll tell you not to tap your retirement funds unless it is an emergency. The reason these plans are so wonderful is that they allow your money to grow tax-free until you need it the most—in retirement. You're better off letting it grow undisturbed. If, for some reason, you have trouble repaying *this* loan, you risk putting your own retirement in jeopardy. If you fail to pay it back, the plan treats it as an early withdrawal, with stiff penalties and taxes. I advise my clients that they should not even consider tapping their retirement funds for loans unless they plan on staying with the company administering it for the full term of the loan. Consider the 401(k) your nest egg that should be cracked only in dire emergencies. Some studies have shown that far too many people borrow from theirs for nonessentials like vacations and cars. I'd recommend a home-equity loan over a loan against your retirement plan in almost every case.

Hardship withdrawals are also permitted by many retirement funds for medical expenses, to avoid foreclosure or eviction, to make a down payment on a principal residence, cover college tuition costs or for funeral expenses for a family member. But these are even more damaging than loans. You have to pay income taxes on any withdrawals and a 10 percent federal penalty for early withdrawal. That could eat up as much as 50 percent of your hard-earned savings and cause serious damage in your retirement years. Some plans even cut off any further contributions once a hardship withdrawal has been made, which means your company no longer will make matching funds—a deadly blow to most retirement plans.

The 403(b) Plan

Like the 401(k), contributions to these plans are tax deductible. These are sometimes known as tax-sheltered annuities because insurance company investments can satisfy the requirements for the 403(b) plan. But retirement plan participants can also purchase no-load mutual funds for their 403(b) plans. Employees of nonprofit or government organizations are allowed to contribute up to 20 percent of their annual salary or $9,500, whichever is less. Employees with fifteen years or more on the job may be allowed to contribute more. You should check with your company's program administrator for the requirements at your employer. Unlike a 401(k), this plan can be offered for very little expense to the employer, so if yours doesn't have it, you should ask that it be included in the benefits package.

The 457 Plan

Someone once asked me if this was a retirement plan in which you carried a .457 magnum handgun into the bank and demanded a million dollars. No, it is not that sort of plan. It is similar to the 401(k) and 403(b) plans in offering you the freedom to contribute money from your paycheck before paying taxes on it. There are a couple of important differences, though. With the 457 plan, the money you contribute is not separate from your employer's finances. These plans also limit contributions to $8,000 a year, so most financial advisors recommend that their clients contribute to a 457 plan first before doing any other investment because the money grows tax-deferred and reduces their taxable income.

TAX-DEFERRED SEPS, KEOGHS AND SIMPLES

Self-employed people and small businesses that are not incorporated have their own version of the tax-deferred retirement funds. The most popular is the Simplified Employee Pension Plan, or SEP. These are known as "Super IRAs" because they have all the advantages of an IRA and more. This plan allows small business employees and the self-employed to contribute up to 15 percent of their adjusted gross income. SEP contributions count as a business expense for the owner, thus lowering his base income for tax purposes.

Earnings kept in the plan are allowed to grow and compound without being taxed until they are withdrawn. There are two special benefits that put the "super" in SEPs. First, they can be established at the time you actually file your taxes—even if you take extensions—instead of on January 1, as with most other plans. This means you can delay your payment into your SEP as late as October of the following year as long as you get the proper extensions from the IRS. Second, there are none of the complicated administration requirements carried by other plans for small businesses or the self-employed, such as Keogh Plans, which have strict guidelines.

A Keogh plan also allows you to make tax-deductible contributions, as much as 25 percent of your net income to a limit of $30,000 per year. Earnings are tax-deferred. There are many versions of the Keogh plan; and in some cases, you have to contribute to it each year even if you haven't made a profit. If you have employees you have to contribute the same percentage of income for them as you've put in for yourself. I wouldn't advise anyone to set up a Keogh plan without professional assistance.

SEPS, on the other hand, are very simple to set up and are a great way to save for retirement, particularly for one who works a regular job with a company that has a 401(k) or similar plan, but also has a business on the side. These moonlighters can make tax-deferred contributions to both their company plan and a SEP for additional tax relief and, more importantly, for even more retirement savings.

The SIMPLE plan is a relatively new option. These "Savings Incentives Match Plans for Employees" are offered for smaller companies with fewer than one hundred employees and no other retirement plan. The maximum an employee can put in is usually $6,000 a year. As its name implies, it is less complicated for companies to put in place. SIMPLEs do have a heavier penalty for early withdrawal, 25 percent as opposed to a 10 percent federal penalty on 401(k) plans.

A warning here: Some employers, usually small businesses, try to skimp on retirement plans by letting insurance company salespeople sell "private pension plans" to their employees. Be very wary of these plans, which essentially are nothing more than cash-value life insurance policies that combine insurance with savings accounts. If you don't need life insurance—and you probably don't if you have no small children—the coverage is a waste of money. Your employer doesn't have to contribute to these plans, so they're tempting for small-business owners. Your money will compound tax-free *but* you get no up-front tax deduction like that offered with SEPs and Keogh plans.

IRAs

In the early 1980s, the U.S. Congress made it possible for every wage earner under the age of 70½ to contribute tax-deferred income to an IRA. Thanks to the Taxpayer Relief Act of 1997, IRAs have been made even more attractive. They aren't as beneficial as some of the retirement plans now being offered by employers because you are allowed only to deduct $2,000 per year from your taxable income for an IRA. Many see this as unfair, particularly for those who don't work for companies with retirement savings plans that allow you to put more money away. It would seem more fair to allow those who don't have any other retirement option to put more into an IRA, and maybe someday that will be permissible. (Please note: Congress is forever messing with the rules governing IRAs, so always check with your accountant or financial advisor before investing in them, or withdrawing from them.) But for now, if your employer doesn't have a retirement plan or if you have maxed out your contributions to the company plan, an IRA is one of your few decent options. IRAs save money in two very important ways:

1. Short-term tax savings are boosted because an IRA allows you and your spouse to invest $2,000 each (once you've met certain requirements) off the top of your gross income, which reduces your taxable income. If you are in the 28 percent federal and 7 percent state tax brackets, you could save $700 in just one year by starting an IRA.

2. Earnings on your IRA are tax-deferred until you reach retirement age, which means you will very likely be in a lower tax bracket because your income will drop upon retirement.

IRAs are "self-directed," which means that you choose how the money in them is invested, whether in stocks, CDs, bonds or mutual funds. You can make one lump-sum annual payment, pay in small amounts during the year or make no contribution at all. You have until April 15 to make your contribution for the previous year; but I advise my clients and my readers to make a lump-sum contribution each January if possible because that allows your money to grow even more quickly.

Currently there are three types of IRAs: the traditional IRA, the spousal IRA and the Roth IRA.

The Traditional and Spousal IRAs
All have the same basic guidelines. If your employer doesn't offer a pension or a tax-deferred retirement savings plan, and if you meet certain income limits, you can contribute up to $2,000 in pre-tax

income into a deductible IRA each year. Singles with an adjusted gross income of $30,000 and married couples with adjusted gross incomes up to $50,000 are eligible in 1998. Those limits will go up gradually until 2007, when employed married couples filing jointly will be eligible to make the fully deductible IRA contribution at incomes up to $80,000 and partially deductible contributions to an IRA at incomes up to $100,000.

Spouses without a paid job are now allowed to deduct $2,000 from their taxable income each year and put it in an IRA even if the other spouse or partner is covered by a company retirement plan, provided the couple's adjusted gross income does not exceed $150,000.

You cannot withdraw money before age 59½ from an IRA without paying a 10 percent penalty on the amount withdrawn—except for two specific purposes. You won't be penalized if you are a first-time home buyer using the money to purchase your principal residence. First-time home buyers can withdraw from their own IRAs or from those of their children, grandchildren or other relatives of either spouse. There is a lifetime limit of $10,000. The only other penalty-free IRA withdrawals are for legitimate higher education expenses at bona fide schools.

If you are single, the amount you can contribute phases out between $95,000 and $111,000 in adjustable gross income. If you are married and file taxes jointly, the contribution phases out between $150,000 and $160,000.

The Roth IRA

It's like a traditional IRA with a twist: It's "backloaded," meaning that you are not allowed to take a tax deduction for the money you put into it, *but* (and this is the good news) when you take money out, you don't have to pay any taxes on the amount withdrawn. In addition, you can take out your initial deposit anytime without taxes or penalties, *but* (and this is the bad news) you have to leave the income or interest it earns in the account for at least five years before you can withdraw it without taxes or penalties, and you have to be at least age 59½.

One other bit of good news is that you can withdraw up to $10,000 from a Roth IRA without penalty for a first home purchase. Also, the entire holdings can be withdrawn if the owner of the Roth IRA has died or become disabled.

The drawbacks of the IRA are the penalties for early withdrawal and a rule that you must begin withdrawing by age 70½ or face a tax penalty. You'll also be penalized for contributing more than the maximum allowed each year.

Even with those drawbacks, it would probably be wise to consider converting any existing IRAs to a Roth. Anyone with an adjusted gross income of less than $100,000 a year can shift existing IRA funds to a Roth, which means all future growth of that retirement IRA fund grows tax-free. It makes good sense, especially for younger investors. Consult a tax professional before making the conversion, however, because some state governments have not yet decided how they will tax earnings from a Roth IRA.

To give you an idea of how different IRAs compare, here are some case studies that show how which IRA you choose can make a difference, and how the Roth IRA favors young investors in particular. The examples, calculated by *Consumer Reports*, assume each couple invests $4,000 annually and earns an 8 percent return until they retire at age 65. Upon retirement, they draw down their accounts in equal increments over twenty years, earning a 7 percent return on the balance remaining in their accounts. Their combined federal and state tax rate is 31.6 percent.

Case Study #1: A thirty-year-old married couple

Total Savings Upon Retirement at Age 65
Deductible IRA: *$887,277*
Nondeductible IRA: *$744,409*
Roth IRA: *$744,409*
Taxable Savings/Investment: *$420,469*

Cumulative Withdrawals After Taxes in Retirement Through Age 85
Deductible IRA: *$1,098,214*
Nondeductible IRA: *$924,606*
Roth IRA: *$1,313,400*
Taxable Savings/Investment: *$632,432*

Case Study #2: fifty-five-year-old married couple

Total Savings Upon Retirement at Age 65

Deductible IRA: *$79,724*
Nondeductible IRA: *$62,582*
Roth IRA: *$62,582*
Taxable Savings/Investment *$54,248*

Cumulative Withdrawals After Taxes in Retirement Though Age 85

Deductible IRA: *$101,309*
Nondeductible IRA: *$88,165*
Roth IRA: *$110,417*
Taxable Savings/Investment: *$81,596*

TREAD CAUTIOUSLY WHEN CONSIDERING AN ANNUITY

Variable annuities are insurance policies wrapped around an invest-ment portfolio, usually one containing mutual funds. They are a vehicle for long-term retirement savings, not a place for short-term savings or investment. The attractive aspects of a variable annuity are the fact that it grows tax-deferred, like an IRA; and when you retire, it pays out a regular income, based on how well the underlying investment performed, for as long as you live. Because they are tax-deferred investments, however, variable annuities are not something you'd put in a tax-deferred retire-ment account. If you did that, you'd be paying twice for tax protection.

Annuities are complex. They often carry an intricate mix of fees, charges and stiff penalties for early withdrawal. They usually have a sales load, high expenses and a charge for mortality insurance. Annuities have become increasingly popular in recent years, in no little part because brokers earn big commissions on them. The general consensus among investment advisors is that a well-managed mutual fund is a better in-vestment because of lower fees, and simple term life insurance is a cheaper and better form of life insurance.

As far as I'm concerned, the only reason to consider a variable annuity is if you've maxed out your 401(k) contribution, invested in an IRA and still have savings you want to shelter from taxes. Or perhaps you're intim-idated by the thought of managing your own retirement account. In that case, you might consider a low-cost variable annuity from a big mutual fund provider. Or you could consider an *immediate annuity*, which works like your own pension fund. Immediate annuities are sold by insurance companies and directly from annuity companies.

The most beneficial aspects of annuities are that your earnings on your investment grow tax-free until withdrawal and that there's no limit on how much you can contribute, but these are mostly perks for high-income savers. The insurance part of the package is a "death benefit" that guarantees your heirs will get your full principal. However, as I noted, the negative aspects of investing in annuities outweigh the positives: Their complex set of fees, penalties and charges may wipe out the value of any tax advantage.

If you do decide to purchase a variable annuity or an immediate annuity, I'd advise you to choose one with a combination of high-quality mutual funds and low fees. I would also advise you not to get involved with annuities unless you have exhausted all other tax-deferred savings methods and also not without the assistance of a financial planner. You should purchase an annuity only if you plan on leaving the money in it for at least fifteen years because it takes that long for the benefits of tax-deferred compounding to overcome the high annuity fees—if then.

INVESTING WISELY IN YOUR TAX-DEFERRED RETIREMENT PLANS

For most of my clients, their 401(k) or similar retirement plans are their first encounter with the stock market, mutual funds, bonds and investing outside of a bank savings account or CD. It can be intimidating because there is *so* much information out there and so many options. The worst thing that can happen is for you to work hard and save for years only to make the mistake of investing your savings unwisely. To put everything into low-yield CD or money market funds is a mistake. It is also dangerous to put all of your savings in high-risk stocks or mutual funds. Do you remember the investing principle of asset allocation that I described in Chapter Four? It's the "don't put all of your eggs in one basket" principle. The secret is to strike a balance that you're comfortable with, one that suits your particular circumstances.

Most company retirement plans (the 401(k), 403(b) and 457 programs) will allow you to invest your assets in a wide selection of mutual funds, stock funds, bond funds, money market funds and, often, stock in your own company. Unless you are wired into Dionne Warwick's Psychic Hotline, it can be difficult for the inexperienced investor to decide what combination of funds to select. I know of one corporate employee who made his selections based on what his smartest coworkers were picking. I guess that beats closing your eyes and pointing. It also beats playing it too safe, particularly if you are a long way from retiring.

As I advised in the chapters dealing with saving for a home and saving for college, how you allocate your assets in your retirement plan should be based on your savings goals and your age. Most working-class folks need to make investments that grow their savings for them so that they can have security in their retirement years. That means taking on some risk because the high-fliers can also take a plunge. For younger investors, that isn't so much of a big deal because over time stocks have historically gone up, even after periods of decline. For those closer to retirement, it is wise to take only moderate risks so that you never endanger the money you'll need to live on.

Here are some general guidelines based on the factors of age and risk tolerance.

For your twenties to thirties

Goal: Maximum Growth
Risk Tolerance: High
Allocations
    40%–60% Growth Funds (stocks with high growth potential)
    40%–50% Growth & Income Funds (a combination of stocks and bonds)
    0%–10 % Income Funds (interest-paying bonds, dividend-paying stocks)
OR

    0%–10 % Tax-Free Funds (municipal bonds)

For your midthirties to late forties

Goal: Growth and Some Income
Risk Tolerance: High to Moderate
Allocations
    30%–40% Growth
    30%–50% Growth & Income
    20%–30% Income OR Tax Free

For your late forties to late fifties

Goal: Growth and Income
Rick Tolerance: Moderate
Allocations
    20%–30% Growth
    30%–40% Growth & Income
    30%–50% Income OR Tax-Free

For your sixties and beyond

Goal: Income and Protection From Inflation
Risk Tolerance: Moderate to Low
Allocations
    10%–20% Growth
    20%–30% Growth & Income
    50%–70% Income OR Tax-Free

SET YOUR PRIORITIES, ALLOCATE YOUR ASSETS

Most company retirement plans offer mutual funds that fit into all of the categories listed. If yours doesn't offer at least one mutual fund in each category, you should talk with your company's benefits office and urge them to provide a balance of funds. If you aren't sure what category a fund falls into, ask your benefits advisor or look the fund up on-line at Morningstar.com. You can also call the 800 number provided by the fund company in its literature, which your benefits office should have available.

OTHER OPTIONS IN YOUR RETIREMENT FUND

Guaranteed Income Contracts

Many retirement plans offer a guaranteed income contract (GIC) option, which could be considered a safe haven of sorts. GICs are offered by insurance companies that invest your money in bonds and stocks. The insurance companies take their profit from any income generated by the investment, minus the interest rate they pay you. In other words, they pay you to play with your money. You benefit because you get a guaranteed rate of return for a fixed period. There is no guessing. GICs have been popular in pension funds, but in recent years with the long bull run on stocks, they have lost favor. One concern is that if the insurance company that offered your GIC goes bankrupt—and it has been known to happen, though rarely— you lose everything. It has happened to some pension plans in the past. Some GICs, however, are backed by securities such as Treasury notes, which give fund managers more control over where the money is invested. The problem I have with GICs is that they don't offer much in the way of long-term growth. It's my feeling, one shared by many other investment advisors, that you would be better off invest- ing in a mixture of bond and stock funds that have a higher yield. Why should the insurance company make money on your retirement savings? Why shouldn't *you* be making that money?

Company Stock

Many companies allow their employees to invest in company stock within their 401(k) programs and other retirement plans. It is particularly popular to encourage this when a company fears being bought out. The more stock in employee hands, the less likelihood of a hostile takeover. I've known people to do incredibly well with their company stock holdings, but I certainly wouldn't encourage you to put any more than 25 percent of your assets in your company stock unless it's a very hot commodity. I'd say 25 percent is a good move particularly if your employer allows employees to buy stock at a discount, which is fairly common. Otherwise, I wouldn't let too much ride on the company you work for. Look at it this way: If your company is doing well, you reap the benefits in higher pay (hopefully) and a more secure future (also hopefully). If it's doing poorly, you could be looking at unemployment. Do you really need to tie your retirement plan's welfare to your company, too? Probably not. If your employer *only* offers you the company stock option in your retirement plan, you should ask why. A good retirement plan includes a range of options so that each employee can find a comfortable balance. After all, who wants a bunch of nervous Nellie employees worrying all day about their retirement savings? It only makes sense for both the employer and employee to feel good about the company retirement savings plans.

Section IV   Smart Money Moves

> *Politics doesn't control the world, money does. And we ought not to be upset about that. We ought to begin to understand how money works and why money works. If you want to bring about feeding the hungry, clothing the naked, healing the sick—it's going to be done in the free market system. You need capital.*

—Andrew Young

Stock Market Strategies

12

I joined Mt. Moriah Masonic Lodge #32, Prince Hall Affiliation, in Evanston, IL, years ago because my family has a long tradition of involvement in the Masons. I've always enjoyed this organization for its social activities and community service opportunities. It has also turned out to be a great networking resource. I've helped quite a few of my Masonic brothers and sisters build wealth by investing.

At our lodge, I'm often quizzed on the stock market by Brothers John Deere, Leonard Kendrick and Arthur White. They generally ask only a few questions about their investments when times are good but when the stock market takes a downturn my Masonic brothers stay very close to me. In fact, I don't need to track the stock market anymore, I can tell how it's doing simply by listening to the types of questions they ask when we get together.

So far, I have provided you with the basic information you need to understand the stock market and how to select stocks, bonds and mutual funds that serve your goals. It is also important to understand when to buy and sell in the stock market.

I cannot predict the future, but it appears that after a bull run of nearly seven years, the market is entering a more volatile period, which always makes investors nervous. In 1995, there were three days when the Dow moved up or down 100 points or more. In 1996, there were six of these high-volatility days of 100-point swings. In 1997, there were fifty-two days on the wild roller-coaster ride up 100 points and down 100 points. Most economists are predicting that this volatility will continue for a while, so it might be helpful for you to have a basic grasp of investing strategies for both bull and bear markets.

Historically, those who have waited out the downturns and bought good stocks at discounted prices have been rewarded. I've seen individual investors torture themselves over the question of when to sell stocks in their portfolios. Knowing when to sell is just as important as knowing when to buy and what to buy. There are no surefire rules for when to sell but there are some general guidelines. Most of all, you should set goals that match your needs, buy a diverse mix of stocks or mutual funds that fit your risk tolerance and other specifications by dollar cost averaging and hang on for the ride.

This book is designed for long-term investors, so the basic strategy of investing in good stocks, bonds, and mutual funds and holding on to them still applies. The long-term outlook for the market is still positive. If you buy quality stocks and mutual funds and stick with them over the long haul, you'll build more wealth than with almost any other investment, even if you buy stocks at the market peaks.

Trying to "time" your buying and selling is rarely a good idea, particularly for those who are not professionals. I've found that those investors who miss major market turns and then try to play catch-up often get burned. It may seem like a good idea to try and buy stocks only when they are about to rise and to try and sell just before they fall, but it's a tricky and treacherous strategy to try and outguess the market. Most people would rather be investors than gamblers.

In times of high volatility, I field a great many phone calls from clients who are concerned, and sometimes panicked, that the market is going to strip them of their savings. My Masonic brother, Arthur White, is particularly avid in his interrogations. You see, Arthur is a very conservative man. He is so conservative that he waited until his seventieth birthday to get married for the second time. (It may have been that he was waiting for the price of wedding cakes to drop.) I was invited to his wedding and

I asked the newlyweds, as I often do, if they were investing for future goals such as the college education of their children. Arthur cut me short by noting that his children and stepchildren were all out of school, and his grandchildren were just finishing college.

Arthur's investment goals are a bit different from the typical newly-wed's, but he keeps a close eye on the stock market. Arthur grew up humbly in Suffolk, VA, the Peanut Capital of the World. He remembers seeing George Washington Carver in a parade as a boy, and he also recalls "having to ride in the back of the bus and the front of the train." Brother White is a thoughtful man who was really ahead of his time when he started purchasing stocks in the 1950s. He'd saved up $1,500 or so from his paychecks as a supervisor at a manufacturing plant. He took about half of it to a neighborhood brokerage above a Walgreens store in Evanston and bought shares of Avon.

He held on to those shares for nearly forty years, even though the stock didn't do much for him. I used to call him now and then and tell him that he'd made a dollar a year. Finally, he followed my advice, cashed out and bought a growth and income mutual fund that has done well, averaging about 18 percent gains in the last five years. Naturally, he wants to make sure those gains are not depleted. When the market takes a downturn as it did in the summer of 1998, Arthur grills me about the safety of his investments. Sometimes, I have to calm him down to keep him from cashing out and putting his money in low-return bank accounts.

If he had sold his mutual fund shares during that steep downturn, he would have missed out on an even steeper upturn that followed a few weeks later. I told him—and I want to make the point with you in this chapter—that the serious long-term investor learns to ride out such down-turns, and even to capitalize on them by buying good stocks that have been taken down with the market.

During the downturn in the fall of 1998, one of my clients decided to sell his 100 shares of Sun Microsystems. In fairness, he needed some cash to pay taxes so he sold the shares while they were valued at $44 each.

By November, those same shares were valued at $74 each. You can bet that client wishes he'd found another way to raise the necessary cash.

He wasn't alone. Across the country, individual investors went weak with fear that the stock market was facing its first bear market in twenty-five years due to global economic problems that would push the United States into a recession. The Investment Company Institute, a mutual fund trade group, reports that in August of 1998, investors yanked $11.2 billion from stock funds. It was the first one-month period in ten years in which more money was taken out of mutual funds than went in. In short, investors panicked in spite of being cautioned repeatedly about riding it out and hanging on to their existing asset allocations.

The sad news was that most of those investors who withdrew their money from stock funds simply threw it into low-yield money markets instead of seizing the opportunity to buy quality stocks on the cheap. The Investment Company Institute reports that in August of 1998, $50.94 billion flowed into money market funds. Now, a lot of that money flowed right back into stocks and mutual funds as soon as the market turned higher, but many, many investors missed the opportunity to add to their holdings at bargain-basement rates.

In far too many cases, investors ended up with portfolios that are less diversified. The *Wall Street Journal* reported that scores of 401(k) investors chose to buy even more of their own companies' stocks, which really isn't a good idea, particularly since so many people already have too much invested there. (Remember the warning about keeping too many eggs in one basket?)

It seems that investors have developed a couple of bad habits.

Bad Habit No. 1: In good times, they believe the market will keep going up so they keep buying stocks even when they know they are overpriced.

Bad Habit No. 2: When the market takes a downturn, they assume the worst and begin selling and stashing their money in low-yield accounts instead of using the opportunity to buy quality stocks at Kmart prices. *(Attention stock shoppers, there's a Blue Light Special on Microsoft shares in Aisle No. 3!)*

Often, I remind Brother White and other clients and friends that the only constant in the stock market is that it is always changing. It's up one day and down the next. Impatient investors can always find scores of reasons not to invest, but investment opportunities often arise during the rough times. To delay an investment decision "until things settle down" may cost you potential growth in income. Here are eight investment strategies for building wealth:

RULES TO LIVE AND INVEST BY

No. 1: *Don't panic*

When the stock market takes a dive, or your particular stock swoons, repeat to yourself over and over, "I'm in this for the long haul . . . I'm in this for the long haul." If you aren't in it for the long haul, or your deadline is fast approaching, then you need to lessen your risk by moving money out of stocks and mutual funds and into lower-risk investments.

Remember the old tried-and-true saying "The first thing to do is to do no harm"? The worst mistake you can make is to panic and then watch as the inevitable rebound comes and your long-lost stock soars to new heights. Unless you are ready to get out of the game, don't jump at the first sign of a bear market. Ask yourself if the stock still meets your goals and if it still fits well in the mix of your portfolio. If it does, hang on. If it doesn't, sell.

No. 2: *The 10 percent rules*

C. Beth Cotner is a highly regarded mutual fund manager at Putnam Investors fund, where I do a lot of business. She follows a 10 percent rule that says if a stock holding goes up 10 percent or at more than twice the market rate within ten days, she sells 10 percent to lock in some profit. Sometimes, when the stock drops, she buys some more.

I have my own 10 percent rule. I advise my clients that if a stock falls 10 percent from their purchase price, then they should review some key factors and make sure that the stock still meets their requirements. I don't advise them to automatically sell because there can be a lot of factors involved. You especially don't want to sell a blue-chip stock that's likely to stage a comeback, or sell a stock being dragged under by cyclical problems.

Many investors believe in setting high and low target prices for their stocks and selling when either target is hit. I prefer to review my position by asking some basic questions that go to the core of my investment strategy. I've presented information on most of those factors in previous chapters but here are key questions you should ask before deciding whether to sell or hold any stock or mutual fund. Some are a bit technical, but if you're working with an investment advisor or stockbroker, he or she should be able to answer any of these questions.

- Have the investment's fundamentals changed?
- Has the outlook for the entire economy changed since you bought the stock? What impact will that have on your investment?
- Has the investment performed in line with expectations, and if not, why?
- What is the technical outlook for the stock or stocks? What are the support and resistance levels?
- Has the investment reached your target price objective?
- Given the current outlook for the investment, has the risk/reward profile changed from the time of the purchase? How?
- Check the most recent news releases for the stock or stocks in

the mutual fund. Are they trying to explain what has happened or are they making excuses?
- Are there any better places that you could invest your money at this time?
- Based on all you know at this point, would you buy this stock or mutual fund right now?

No. 3: *If the water rises to eye level, abandon ship*

Investing for the long term does not mean that you have to be the last rat on a sinking ship. If you learn that the company whose stock you own is in deep trouble—if it has lost its focus or its market to a bigger competitor—then it may be time to bid the stock good-bye. Often, emotions get in the way of good sense. Some investors just don't want to admit that they made a bad pick. Others hang on hoping the stock will return to a break-even price. That is often a costly mistake. "Waiting to break even is often a sucker's game," reports *Individual Investor* magazine. "Consider that a share that has lost 75% would have to rise 300% to break even, or that shares that have plummeted 90% would need to increase 900% to get even."

No amount of wishing and hoping and praying is going to save the stock of a company that has lost its market. If you see in the annual report that the company is taking a one-time charge for restructuring, that could suggest that things aren't going well at the home office—which should put you on alert and send you looking for more information. Other signs of problems in a stock:

- The rest of the stocks in its sector are rising but it falls or stands pat.
- The company buys a business that appears to be outside its niche market.
- The company sells off an entire division.

- Top management leaves in a hurry.
- The company issues press releases detailing what is supposedly positive news, and the stock goes nowhere.

No. 4: *Keep buying solid stocks and/or mutual funds*

If stocks that you like remain fundamentally sound and if your strategy is still long term, then keep buying even as stock prices climb; if they decline, buy more.

If you had purchased an index mutual fund just after the Dow's 512-point plummet in the fall of 1998, you would have come out smelling like a rose by the end of the year. The reason dollar cost averaging makes so much sense is that no one knows when a bear market will hit bottom or when a bull market will hit the top; so if you keep purchasing stocks month to month, statistics show you will come out ahead. Keep in mind that in recent years, the Federal Reserve Board (the fed) has come to the rescue in times of crises in the stock market. When the Fed cuts interest rates, the money supply increases and investors start buying stocks again. I wouldn't dare to say that this will happen in *every* financial crisis, but that's been the pattern in recent years.

No. 5: *In bear markets, buy defensive stocks*

In declining markets, it can pay to have shares in businesses that people need in good times *and* in bad. Meat and potatoes, aspirin and toothpaste fill the bill. So do the businesses that sell them. With an aging population, drug companies and drugstore companies are increasingly attractive. Utility stocks often are good defensive investments, too, because everyone still needs electricity, water and natural gas. Don't forget, however, that it is still important to base your decision on the fundamentals by checking out each company's product line, business strategy, competition, growth prospects and value in the market. Don't forget that more and more American companies are impacted by global events, so make sure that those you buy have the strength, and the cash reserves, to handle recessions in other countries.

No. 6: *Monitor your asset allocations*

After a boom in the market, your asset allocations may be thrown out of kilter. When the market turns bearish, you might take time to fine-tune your holdings. Minimize those stocks with reduced earnings expectations. Look for those stocks that you believe will outperform the market over the long term. It may be that your portfolio has become overbalanced with stocks. You may need to look at bonds as a fixed income investment.

No. 7: *Instead of dumping stocks, adjust your expectations*

The great bull market that began in 1982 may not be over, but the old bull is slowing down. The 15 to 20 percent annual gains have created unprecedented wealth and if you were fortunate enough to claim some of it, count your blessings. But you can't count on such huge gains forever. Most forecasters are predicting a return to single-digit annual gains, which are just fine. The historical rate of gain is 7 percent for stocks adjusted for inflation. That's not a bad return compared to nearly all other forms of investment. Many believe that while corporate earnings may slow down, new technologies across a wide array of industries will keep the economy rolling along. It's also expected that the best American companies will be able to grow their businesses among emerging nations.

No. 8: *Be tax smart*

In most cases, it doesn't make sense to trade stocks or mutual funds in a taxable account, particularly if you are in the 28 percent and up tax bracket. Your trading gains are subject to taxes that can take a serious cut. If you are trading in a taxable account, you should make sure to take enough short-term losses to compensate for any realized short-term gains that would be taxed at your top federal rate up to 39.6 percent. It is also advisable to use net short-term losses to cover long-term profits dollar for dollar, although that's not as rewarding since net long-term gains are taxed at 20 percent or less. If your realized losses already exceed your capital gains, you can use the excess to shelter up to $3,000 ($1,500 for married taxpayers filing separate returns) in salary, interest or dividends.

A FINANCIAL PLANNING CHECKLIST

No investment strategy should be made in a vacuum. You have to consider all of the unique aspects of your financial situation. The following checklist is based on one created by the American Association of Individual Investors, a primary resource for anyone seeking to build wealth.

- Have you determined your short- and long-term financial goals? Do you review them regularly and update them if things have changed?
- Are you saving and investing enough to fund those short- and long-term goals?
- Are you making wise use of tax-deferred savings plans such as IRAs, 401(k)s, SEPs and Keoghs? Are you contributing the maximum? Do you make investment choices that suit your time frame, goals and risk tolerance?
- Are you getting the most out of your employee benefits program? Do you understand all aspects of it? Do you have a strategy for exercising your stock options and using any deferred compensation plans?
- Are you saving and investing for the education of your children? Do you understand that money held in an account in the child's name may count against any future attempts to get scholarships or financial aid? Do you know that tax laws are becoming in-

creasingly more lenient in allowing parents to use tax-deferred retirement savings to pay college expenses without penalties for early withdrawal?

- Do you have an emergency fund? I recommend that you have three to six months' take-home pay stashed in a money market account that can be easily accessed. Do not touch it except for dire emergencies. This isn't a Christmas stocking or vacation fund.

- Do you regularly check your asset allocation? Bull market runs and downturns can throw off the balance of your investment portfolio, leaving you with more or less in one category or another than you may want.

- Do you have adequate insurance? Will your family be protected if you die? Do you have enough disability insurance to meet expenses if you or your spouse is unable to work? Have you investigated an umbrella policy?

- What about a will? Do you have one? Is it up to date? Does your family know where to find it? Do they know who your attorney is?

- How's your credit? Are you paying attention to the rates you're paying for your home mortgage, car loans and credit cards? Are they the lowest available? Does it make sense to refinance or pay off car loans or credit cards? What about a home-equity loan?

- Have there been any changes in the last year in your family situation? Births, deaths, divorces, marriages—all can have an impact on your financial plans and goals. Make it a point to review your family situation at the end of each year so that you can make adjustments.

Does this sound like too much work? Well, if you find someone who built lasting wealth without ever breaking a sweat, please let me know. I'd like to shake that person's hand, and borrow a few hundred thousand.

Sure, it's work to set goals, select investments and track them over years and years. But it can also be fun. In the next chapter, I'll introduce you to perhaps the most enjoyable way to practice and profit from all the information I've provided you in this book. Investing in the dream does not have to be a lonely pursuit. In fact, thousands and thousands of African Americans have discovered the joys of forming investment clubs— and they've profited in many ways from their experiences.

Quentin Sampson's granddaddy lost all the savings he'd stashed in a "safe" bank account in the great bank crash of 1929. Because of that experience, he made it a point to instruct his grandson that banks were not to be trusted. Nor was the stock market a place for blacks to put their money, according to Quentin's postal clerk father, who encouraged his son to save but to stay away from the rich man's game of stocks, bonds and mutual funds.

As a result of their advice, Quentin Sampson grew up to be a saver but not a wealth builder. After taking a few college courses, he went to work for People's Gas & Light Company in Chicago and stayed there for thirty-five years. He did quite well for himself because of his natural ability with numbers and technical skills. In fact, Quentin became a computer wiz before most people had computers and over the years established himself as the company's computer troubleshooter. "Anytime someone's screen locked up, they called me," he said with a laugh.

People's Gas & Light offered its employees a stock purchase discount that Quentin found hard to resist in spite of his father's warnings about the stock market. He enrolled in his company program, and when he saw how well those stocks performed, he began dabbling in other stocks. His strategy in those early days left something to be desired, he now admits. Initially, he purchased shares based solely on reports he'd heard on television news programs or read about in magazines. His goal was to "make a lot of money all at once."

As you might expect, that philosophy failed miserably. Quentin had just about decided that his father was right about the stock market when he learned of an investment club formed by some of his coworkers. "My wife told me that she would leave me if I went broke, so that inspired me, too," he said. "Like a lot of black folks, I grew up thinking that you had to be rich to be in the stock market, but an investment club is a great way to learn how to participate without being rich. It's all about education, education, education because people are afraid of the stock market if they don't understand it."

Quentin learned and he prospered. He became a big fan of Warren Buffett and monitored the growth of his Berkshire Hathaway fund for many years. When Quentin first learned of this legendary fund, a single share was valued at $16,000—far beyond his reach at the time. But after investing wisely and building his wealth for nearly ten years, Quentin purchased one share of Berkshire Hathaway in 1994. He did it by selling other investments to raise the $23,000 purchase price, but it was well worth it. At the beginning of 1999, that single share was worth $70,000— and it had actually dropped from a value of $80,000 at one point in 1998.

Quentin says he is far from being rich, but eleven years after his retirement he has twice as much money saved than he had on the day he left People's Gas & Light. Through wise money management, he has built a very comfortable retirement. At age 68, Quentin is an avid investor. He often travels around the country to stockholders meetings held by the companies he's invested in. He's also taken several ocean cruises and purchased a rental property in Florida with his stock earnings.

At the time of his retirement, Quentin was making $45,000 a year. He was not a wealthy man, but from what he has learned by participating in investment clubs, he has built lasting wealth. "In retirement I'm not only maintaining my lifestyle, I'm exceeding it," he said. "Now, I don't live extravagantly—I drive a Taurus, not a Lexus—but I'll have enough for my kids to fight over one day."

Quentin calls himself a late bloomer as an investor but I think of him more as a gardener. Everywhere he goes, investment clubs seem to rise out of the ground and blossom. The number of investment clubs established by African Americans is growing by leaps and bounds, according to my observations, which were confirmed in a recent report in *USA Today.*

"When I got involved with the NAIC, I think you could count the blacks involved on one hand. Now I've visited with at least three black groups in South Florida and they've all started clubs," said Mary Ellen Pryor of the Beanstalk Investment Club of Miami in the newspaper's account. Another NAIC member, W. O. Smith of Atlanta, said that as many as 40 percent of those attending the group's functions are African American. He told *USA Today* that more and more blacks are joining investment clubs because "[t]hey want to own their share of America too."

Quentin Sampson is another reason for the explosion in black investment clubs. In retirement, he has become a full-time advocate for investment clubs as a way for regular folks to build wealth. He is a national director of the National Association of Investors Associations and a director of the Chicago council of the nonprofit NAIC. He is also the founder of several investment clubs, including the Harvey (IL) Model Investors Club, and another club whose membership consists solely of his own relatives.

"From my observations and the things I've read, it is clear that very few blacks realize the potential for building wealth in the stock market. Joining an investment club is a way to educate yourself so that you can learn to invest in your own name and build wealth," he said. "I didn't hear much about the stock market growing up, so I didn't get into it until late in life. My kids and grandkids won't have that excuse because I am always talking to them about investing wisely."

In the previous chapter, I gave you basic strategies for investing in the stock market. I can't guarantee that you will become wealthy by following those strategies, but I will guarantee that if you join a well-organized investment club, you will increase your understanding of the stock market and your investment skills dramatically. And you'll probably make some new friends and have a little fun too.

Investment clubs bring together like-minded people for a common purpose. When the members work well together, investment clubs can be highly enjoyable and financially rewarding. But you should always keep in mind that the primary reason for joining an investment club is to learn how to select stocks and how to invest wisely so that you can build wealth in your own accounts.

JOIN THE CLUB, BUT FOR THE RIGHT REASONS

I've known of investment club members who have lost sight of that goal. Some came to see their clubs purely as a social organization. Some tend to put their own interests above the good of the club. That's why you have to be careful when joining or forming an investment club. If you just want to have a good time, find a dance club or some other social group. If you aren't willing to work at educating yourself and sharing information, then don't waste your time or the time of others who are serious about learning how to build lasting wealth.

Quentin acknowledges that unless the members of an investment club are dedicated, it can quickly fall apart. "I wish our family investment club was more like a regular one but often family clubs don't work that way. We don't meet regularly enough and a lot of times, everyone just leaves the decisions up to me. We end up conducting our business on the telephone a lot," he noted.

Throughout this book I've emphasized that African Americans have a lot of catching up to do when it comes to building lasting wealth. I've given you a great deal of information to help you move forward. Once you have completed this book, I think a wise next step would be for you to form an investment club or join one with other blacks who are serious about increasing their knowledge and their wealth. I am not alone in believing that investment clubs are a great way for African Americans to do that.

Investment clubs are the African American community's best hope for achieving economic equality, according to Duane Davis, a stockbroker and certified financial planner who co-founded the Coalition of Black Investors, based in Winston-Salem, NC. COBI, as it is known, is a national coalition that promotes financial literacy by addressing simple and complex issues ranging from savings plans, economic and investment education and the formation of investment clubs to raising capital for new businesses. It also serves as a link to connect black investors with investment clubs. It bills itself as the place for black investors to communicate with each other on issues of mutual interest.

COBI, which is headed by Davis's wife, Carol, an attorney and the founder of Sisters Making Sense investment club, has established a set of goals that I strongly endorse. Those goals are as follows:

- To promote investment groups and financial literacy among African Americans;
- To formalize a forum for sharing financial ideas, successes, failures and opportunities;
- To coordinate information regarding the public companies held by individual clubs and private investors with the purpose of having an impact on their corporate agendas, hiring practices and minority vendor participation via the African American voting block;
- To help African Americans create wealth through investments in public and private enterprises, and to facilitate the intergenerational transfer of that wealth;
- To promote the positive effects of pooling individual and collective resources; and
- To promote and facilitate meetings, seminars, travel discounts and association discounts for members.

Investment clubs are a great way for African Americans to get in on the game, according to Duane Davis. Through clubs, blacks can invest more money in greater numbers and at a faster rate. Investment clubs provide a forum for us to gain financial savvy. Members learn and earn together, sharing knowledge, resources and risk. With increased buying power, clubs cash in on our ability to work collectively for the common good.

COBI will link black investors and investment clubs to each other and with black entrepreneurs seeking to raise capital. For more information on this organization, you can visit their website at www.cobinvest.co, or you can contact them at Coalition of Black Investors, P.O. Box 30553, Winston-Salem, NC 27130-0553. The telephone number is (336) 922-6240.

INVESTMENT CLUBS ARE POWERFUL INSTRUMENTS FOR POSITIVE CHANGE

The economic and educational potential of investment clubs is unlimited. Fraternities, sororities, churches, professional associations and extended families should consider forming their own investment clubs as a way of increasing investment knowledge and building wealth. Two investment clubs that really stand out in my mind are the Dividend Divas and Dons Investment Club in Baltimore, MD, and the St. George's Junior Investment Club of Washington, DC.

The Dividend Divas and Dons Investment Club was created by participants in the Healthy Start program in Baltimore. This federal program provides educational programming to young parents and expectant mothers in regions with high infant mortality rates. Members of the program in Baltimore established an investment club as a way to teach participants about personal finance and the stock market. NAIC members from around the country have provided their expertise, and an investment club in a neighboring community donated ten shares of Baltimore Gas and Electric to help get the new club started in the spring of 1997.

Members of the Dividend Divas and Dons contribute only $5 a month to the club's investment fund, but the amount of money put in is not nearly as important as what the members take away. One members opened her first checking account after learning how to do it through the club. Others have discovered that the stock market is open to anyone and everyone willing to learn how to use it. "Even though I get a social services check, I have learned that I can still save something," said Victoria Ellis, a twenty-six-year-old mother of five, in an article about the club in *Better Investing* magazine. "It's teaching my twelve-year-old son, too. We read the [business pages] together every day."

As the current generation of African Americans becomes increasingly involved in the stock market, it is our duty to educate our children and grandchildren. That's the goal of the St. George's Junior Investment Club (SGJIC) formed by the congregation of St. George's Episcopal Church in Washington, DC. This investment club is composed entirely of young African Americans between the ages of eleven and eighteen. There are fourteen current members of the club and eleven alumni who have graduated from high school and moved on to college but still contribute their monthly dues.

This successful youth investment club was started in January 1996 by Grafton J. Daniels, an eighty-six-year-old retiree who joined his first investment club in 1962 and since then has helped launch more than a dozen clubs in the DC area. The SGJIC was begun with an initial investment of just $750, but after only two years of learning and analyzing and investing, the club held stocks with a market value of $9,200. They did it by saving their small allowances and earnings instead of spending the money on candy and movies, and already they have seen the benefits of building wealth for the long term.

The SGJIC is one of dozens of investment clubs for young people.

The NAIC reports that nearly 10 percent of its members are under the age of thirty. Since young people between the ages of twelve and nineteen have more disposable income than previous generations of teens, it makes sense to teach them wealth-building methods at that age. Jeffrey Fox, a securities analyst and director of investment education at the NAIC who also edits *Investing for Life*—a study course for young investors—notes that while teenage investors tend to be aggressive, they have time on their side. With at least fifty years until retirement, even their bad stocks have plenty of time to grow in value.

FORMING YOUR OWN INVESTMENT CLUB

As a devoted Johnny Appleseed of investment clubs, Quentin Sampson is constantly urging African Americans to form their own clubs in which members contribute as little as $25 as month, pooling both their money and their research, in order to build a portfolio of stocks while increasing their understanding of how the stock market works. "There are 13,000 companies traded in the U.S., and picking those company stocks that are right for your portfolio can be a challenge. When you join an investment club that follows NAIC principles, you learn how to eliminate three fourths of the stocks offered and hone in on those that fit your investment philosophy," he said.

The NAIC was formed in 1951 by four Michigan investment clubs. Its goal was to create a nationwide educational network through investment clubs. By the end of 1998, there were more than 37,500 investment clubs in the United States alone—up from 10,000 in 1993. The average investment club is 8.5 years old and has fourteen members who each contribute $58 a month and enjoy annual returns of 12.4 percent on their investments, according to the NAIC. The organization sells its official guide to starting and running an investment club to both members and nonmembers. I recommend the guide, which costs just $10 in softcover for those who join the organization.

Investment clubs can affiliate with the NAIC for $35, plus $14 per member. Individual memberships to the NAIC are $39 a year. You can join on-line at the organization's website at www.better-investing.org. Membership in the NAIC includes a subscription to the organization's *Better Investing* magazine, access to a number of helpful stock selection and investment planning guides and invitations to regional and national meetings and seminars.

GETTING ORGANIZED

The first step to forming an investment club is to recruit a few friends who are seriously interested in learning about investing in the stock market. If you belong to any kind of service organization, like the Masons or Lions or Kiwanis, you can build your investment club with fellow members. Even a poker or bridge club or the church choir might serve as the basis of your membership. Quentin Sampson notes that once word gets out, you'll probably have no trouble getting a dozen or more people together. Most clubs have between twelve and twenty members. You don't want to have many more than twenty because it can be difficult keeping so many people organized. It's also a good idea to invite people with a wide variety of knowledge and skills to join your investment club. Along with looking for members who get along well with each other and can work together, it doesn't hurt to find people with backgrounds in accounting, law, and a variety of businesses.

Diversity of interests and experience is fine, but you should all agree in advance on your club's investment philosophy. You don't want your club to be torn apart because some members are far more risk-tolerant than others, or because some are in for quick gains while others are investing for the long term. Roughly half of all investment clubs disband after the first eighteen months because of conflicts between members over trading philosophies, usually involving those who want to stay with stocks for the long term and those who want to make regular trades according to market shifts. Quentin advises that the clubs that have stayed together the longest and enjoyed the most financial success are those that have invested with long-term goals.

Everyone seeking to join your club should understand that there is work involved, particularly for the person who serves as club treasurer and has the responsibility of keeping the books. The NAIC recommends that all club members learn how to audit the accounting books for the club and that other members frequently review those books as a security measure. There have been reports of investment club scams in recent years, including one in Colorado in which fifty club members were bilked of $950,000 by a club treasurer who had deposited their money in his personal account instead of in stocks. It is also recommended that investment clubs elect or appoint a new treasurer every two years.

The club treasurer is not the only member who has homework. Each member will be asked to make regular presentations on individual stocks to the group. That will involve studying and analyzing stocks and their companies. The NAIC provides guidelines for doing this and there are many resources available (including *ValueLine* and scores of Internet sites), but it can take up considerable amounts of time, so membership should be seen as a commitment to helping educate fellow members.

The NAIC also provides guidelines on how to elect club officers, assign duties and handle the considerable amount of accounting required to make and track investments as a group. It advises that you make a point to follow these basic rules in setting up your investment club:

1. *Establish a regular meeting time and place.* Investment club members meet in libraries, community buildings, schools and churches. It's probably best not to meet in anyone's home just because it places a burden on the host, but if you have members eager to host meetings, then go right ahead. Just keep the television and stereo turned off. And keep the alcoholic beverages in the cooler until the meeting is

over. Drinking and investing don't mix any better than drinking and driving.

2. *Require every member to contribute the same amount in dues each month.* Many clubs have monthly payments of $20 or less, while some are considerably higher. Set a rate that is comfortable for everyone and stick with it for at least the first year. By that time members may want to agree on a lower, or a higher, rate.

3. *Have clear bylaws on how members can cash out if they resign from the club.* This is a must. You don't want to have lawyers involved when a member seeks to resign and withdraw his or her share of the club's investments, so whether you use NAIC guidelines or formulate your own, make certain that every member signs them. It will save you considerable anxiety, and money, down the road.

4. *Allow for members who may become temporarily inactive due to the demands of business or family.* Generally, this will allow for members to remain in the club even if they can't attend meetings, as long as they continue to pay the monthly dues.

5. *Don't be afraid to bring in experts.* Many clubs form relationships with local stock brokerages who provide advice and do the club's trading. Of course, with the explosion in on-line brokerages, a full-service broker may not be needed for the entire life of the club; but many find it helpful in the early stages of development to have access to a professional. Your club should be careful, however, not to rely so much on the broker's help that you don't develop your own investing and stock analysis skills. After all, that's what an investment club is all about.

6. *Don't forget to have fun.* The most successful and long-lasting investment clubs are those whose members enjoy each other's company.

Always remember that the investment club's primary purpose is education. If a member is constantly pushing for better returns, or for constant trades, you might remind that individual that he or she has the option of opening a personal account. Building wealth should be your *personal* goal, for sure, but building knowledge and expertise in investing should be the primary goal of your investment club.

THE FOUR PRINCIPLES OF INVESTMENT CLUBS

There are four basic principles that investment clubs should follow in order to be successful over the long term, according to the NAIC. They will sound familiar to you because I have been stressing these same principles for individual investors throughout this book. These principles provide a good review for both the individual and club investor. Quentin Sampson and I agree, also, that it is very important to take care of first things first. *Before* you begin to invest either on your own or through a club, you should have these two matters taken care of:

1. An emergency fund set aside with three to six months' salary, and
2. All credit-card debt paid off or on a payment plan that will eliminate it within one year.

The best investment you can make is to be prepared for unexpected bills and to get control over high-interest debt. It may work well for you to begin investing small amounts at first until you get these two priorities taken care of, then you can begin contributing more and following the Four Principles of Investment Clubs.

1st Principle: *Invest regularly*

By setting aside a regular amount to put in each month, you take a lot of the volatility out of the market. Rather than worrying about its inevitable ups and downs, your club should remain committed to investing over the long term to take advantage of the market's historical tendency to provide an average annual compound rate of return of about 10 percent.

2nd Principle: *Reinvest all dividends*

Again, this principle is designed to maximize your club's profits by taking full advantage of the miracle of compound interest while also reducing any potential tax exposure from capital gains. Do you need a reminder of how compound interest can benefit you and your club? Remember that Native American who sold Manhattan Island for $24 in 1626? Don't be too quick to assume that he was taken advantage of. Maybe, just maybe, he knew a bit about compound interest. Had he invested that $24 at 6 percent interest compounded twice a year, his ancestors now would have more than $50 billion, which would allow them to buy back most of Manhattan with all of the improvements—or all of the mess, depending on your point of view, of course.

3rd Principle: *Invest in growth companies*

The NAIC is a firm believer in common-sense investing. Their process for selecting stocks is designed to hone in on businesses and companies whose sales and earnings are advancing more rapidly than gross domestic product, and whose records suggest they will be far more valuable five years in the future. Of course, the NAIC is not alone in believing in the value of growth stocks. "An extraordinary long-run earnings growth rate is the single most important element contributing to the success of most stock investments," wrote Burton G. Malkiel, the respected author of *A Random Walk Down Wall Street.*

One of the more interesting things you will find at the NAIC website is a listing of the 200 stocks most commonly held by its affiliated investment clubs. Since these clubs follow the NAIC investment guidelines, nearly all are considered growth stocks, or at least they were at the time they were purchased. The top ten stocks owned in 1997 were Motorola;

Pepsi-Cola; Merck; McDonald's; Intel; AFLAC (a medical insurance company); Coca-Cola; Lucent; RPM, Inc. (a maker of waterproof coatings); and AT&T. Now, from a 1999 perspective, some of those stocks don't look all that much like growth stocks, but remember, investment clubs and wise investors buy stocks for the long term—and you should do the same.

4th Principle: *Diversify your investments to reduce risk*

Quentin Sampson likes to quote "The Investor's Rule of 5," which states that out of every five stocks you purchase, one will exceed your expectations, three will meet your expectation and one will make you wish you'd never heard of it. Even if you follow a carefully constructed philosophy for selecting stocks, you always are going to have some winners and losers in your portfolio. There are just too many factors beyond your control. Coca-Cola lost a widely respected CEO and was hit by the financial crisis in Asia and South America in the late 1990s, causing many analysts to downgrade one of the most widely held stocks. If Coca-Cola was all that you owned, you got burned, at least in the short term. You can control the diversity of your portfolio, however, so there would be no excuse for that. If your individual or club portfolio holds a diverse mix of stocks from a variety of sectors it should maintain respectable returns over the long term. Don't ever forget this old investing proverb: "The investor who's wise, diversifies."

PROSPERITY IS YOUR BIRTHRIGHT!

I recommend investment clubs to African Americans particularly because we are a communal people. Sharing information and learning together suits us. There can be no greater reason to join forces, to leverage our resources, knowledge and energies, than to build lasting wealth. There is no better time to begin doing that than now.

In 1998, stock market investors in the United States were taken on a wild ride. The market nosedive in the fall of that year tested the resolve of millions of investors. It was a period of global instability both economically and socially. The Asian and Russian markets were in turmoil and scandal rocked our own government. Many investors took their money out of stocks and stock funds. And then they watched in amazement as this nation once again displayed the strength of its economic foundations. In spite of the global and inner turmoil, the U.S. financial markets staged an incredible resurgence that left many investors scrambling to get back in the game. Those that remained on the sidelines lost out. Those that either stayed in or reacted quickly to the revived market were rewarded: Their wealth increased. Time and time again, this scenario has played out. Time and time again, the American economy has rewarded those who have invested and hung on during volatile periods.

Invest in the dream! Do it thoughtfully. Establish an emergency fund first. Reduce your debt. Set investment goals. Determine your tolerance. Buy within your comfort zone. Diversify and dollar cost average to reduce your risk. But do not fail to invest. Do not miss out on the opportunity to build lasting wealth.

In recent years and months, investment firms in this country have awakened to the vast potential of the African American financial market. They are holding seminars and dinner parties to court you and your money. They recognize the power of your money. You must do the same. If you do nothing, you will reap nothing. But if you begin to plant the seeds now, you will benefit for the rest of your life.

Always remember that the dream of economic and financial freedom is attainable. It is yours to claim whether you make $20,000 a year or $120,000 a year. You can build wealth by investing wisely. Begin now.

Good luck.

Jesse B. Brown

Index

About the Author

Jesse B. Brown has helped hundreds of African Americans invest wisely. Recently profiled in *The Wall Street Journal*, he is a prominent personal investment advisor and stockbroker specializing in the financial needs of middle-class African Americans. He lives and works in Chicago, where he is a community leader. For more information, his website is *www.investinthedream.com* and he can be reached via e-mail at *Krystal@Enteract.com*.